OL' MAN ON A MOUNTAIN
A memoir
Stuart Omans

ISBN: 978-1-62660-032-4

Book interior design by Michael Campbell, MCWriting.com
Cover design and photos by Anna Truby

For more about Stu Omans, please visit stuomans.blogspot.com
or write to olmanonamountain@gmail.com

Ol' Man
on a
Mountain

a memoir

Stuart Omans

For Jan...

My wife, friend, and co-adventurer for fifty-one years. And the kindest person I know.

CONTENTS

AUTHOR'S NOTE

This story is not a work of fiction; it is a fleshed-out memoir, containing episodes and incidents that my wife and I experienced when we moved to the mountains of North Carolina. Although the stories are fundamentally true, we have decided to rename the participants and locations to protect the privacy of the people who became our friends and neighbors. In some cases we have combined characteristics and attributes in the interest of better storytelling, but the narrative is essentially just as it happened and just as we lived it.

How many slams in an old screen door? Depends how loud you shut it.
How many slices in a bread? Depends how thin you cut it.
How much good inside a day? Depends how good you live 'em.
How much love inside a friend? Depends how much you give 'em.

— SHEL SILVERSTEIN

Friendship is born at the moment when one person says to another:
"What! You too? I thought I was the only one."

— C.S.LEWIS

Everyone is kneaded of the same dough,
but not baked in the same oven.

— YIDDISH SAYING

PROLOGUE

AT OUR WEEKLY POKER GAME the other night one of our regulars, a specialist in getting my goat, became piqued at something I said and stuck me with an old label. I think we were arguing about the need for fair immigration laws. With vermillion face and stentorian voice, he interrupted the flow of betting with "You Liberals all sing the same boring song."

"Liberal" is still a useful pejorative? I may be a little peculiar and am still proud to be thought of as liberal, but boring? In reply, I simply raised his bet, got myself a can of diet decaf coke, took a helping of low-fat chips, and thanked him not to label, stamp, and slip me into one of his convenient little envelopes. I felt better.

He won the hand anyhow. He usually does. He's a darned good poker player.

But it occurs to me now that his stingy scorn has a direct connection with the story you're about to read... a story about opening. As the world gets more accessible and communication nearly instantaneous, it strikes me as nuts that so many of our old prejudices seem to be sustained and increasing, the urge to label and spit out names grows stronger, and our ability to open ourselves to others gets narrower. It's weird, isn't it?

I guess that's why I hope you'll open our book and enjoy it as an expanding, intersecting tale of two Jews surprised; two Baptists comparably surprised; a coming together of two families apparently as different as hog jowls and haftorats, as bagels and beehives, but essentially so alike, meeting at a wonderful place in time that I have called Maple Run, North Carolina.

One family's story is of immigrants travelling from Russia and Poland to Chicago, speaking Yiddish and leaning liberal, socialist, and union; new Americans who lived in flats above their bakery shop ovens or behind their struggling tailor shops in ninety-nine percent Jewish neighborhoods until they could expand their businesses and relocate and relocate and relocate until they arrived at manicured suburbs, also Jewish. A chain of bakeries and a trend-setting chain of men's boutiques were the results of their work, with grandchildren finding their way to law and academic degrees at Harvard, Chicago, and, in my case, Northwestern universities.

And the second family, conservative Baptists who were descended from eighteenth-century immigrants, who settled on 100 acres of fifth-generation family-owned Appalachian land and began their married life in a primitive farmhouse surrounded by woods and fields of tobacco and corn, cattle, varmints, and beehives, and whose grandchildren were staying near the land but who also headed off to the university.

This book tells the ongoing story of our mutual meeting and of how it changed and enlarged both our families' lives in unanticipated ways. Should the intersection of our two clans and their labels have been predictable as anything other than a recipe for slapstick? Dark comedy? Social disaster? Northern urban Jews and Southern country Baptists liking and, yes, loving each other? My poker buddy would have been amused to take the sure bet against such a meeting.

I hope you'll think our experience has been something a bit more complex than the labels and envelopes with which we arrived and, therefore, more honestly human than those would ever allow. What I hope you'll find in this tale is a story about growing, good will, and deep affection.

Have I exaggerated in the telling? A little. My bubbe (grandma) would say, "groys gedilla"—big deal, or so what? Nobody dies from a little stretching. And they might even have a little more fun along the way. She insisted that we needed to see events in our lives as a little ridiculous and always complicated.

Bubbe Choma laughed at labels because she'd lived them first hand, going through a variety of pogroms, her family so despised because they were Jews that she eventually lost most of them in Mr. Hitler's attempt to cleanse his world of a large portion of the "dog people," the remnant fleeing Russia to the United States without a nickel or an English word, who built a family and a bakery business in their adopted land, and used as her anchor "Lach a bissel kinderlach" (laugh a little, my children) whenever life ran sour. She always followed this by "Tsa nischt so geferlach": It's not so bad. "It," I came to understand, was anything not life threatening. "Ken alla mol sein erger." (It can always be worse.)

Bubbe remembered an event that happened to her in Russia when she was eleven years old that she repeated for us not only as a memory but as a teaching metaphor that I recognize informed our perceptions and I hope continues to inform our lives.

She and her younger sister were hiding under their house during one of the raids by Cossacks, who would ride into the shtetl (village), burn down a few houses, and rape whatever Jewish females they could find. Age did not matter. This time, as the Cossacks were about to leave, one of them came over and looked under the house. He saw the children, crawled in, and reached for the nine-year-old. My Bubbe had stolen an old pistol and had it with her. She aimed it at him. In Russian, she calmly told him that if he came any closer, she would blow off his head. He might manage to get her sister, but he would die. He believed her, crawled back out, said not a word, got on his horse, and rode away. The pistol had no bullets.

When she told us the story, the point she stressed was not how horrible the episode was or how frightened she was, but how comic was the confused and frightened look on his face as he saw a little girl with so big a gun. "A zhlob (oaf) in a fancy uniform is still a zhlob," became one of her and our favorite sayings. She'd top it off with, "a balegolah (wagon driver) ist alla mol a balegolah." And then she'd shake her head and laugh. A guy with a bozo mentality is always a guy with a bozo mentality, no matter his fancy uniform, his fancy title, or where he's from. And a mensch is still a mensch and so rare no matter where you find him.

Ol' Man on a Mountain

IT'S A
DIFFERENT BIBLE

IT WAS JUNE 2004. JAN AND I had just rolled ourselves out of our car after a twelve-hour drive following a visit with our friends, Steve and Gretchen, at their mountain home in Maple Run, North Carolina. We'd been repeating this drive each summer for about twenty years as a way of escaping the Florida heat and humidity. Theirs was an ideal location for escape, situated as it was above a whitewater river that acts as Mother Nature's perfect air conditioner. During the years we had been going up to the mountains we either stayed in a child-friendly lodge willing to tolerate our active, pugilistic, trickster sons or, more often, stayed with our friends in their remarkable, albeit idiosyncratic and teetering, house. When our sons were little (the first two are eighteen months apart), indulgent lodges were hard to find. And once they got to be preteens and were better armed with a precocious little brother, it became even harder.

Each summer we looked forward to the drive up, anticipating two weeks of swimming and hiking, eating out on the balcony, or picnicking on giant boulders in the middle of the river. The two weeks always passed too quickly. Then would come the reluctant farewells. Without the anticipation, the twelve-hour ride seemed like sixteen, and from Georgia on, even stopping briefly for gas reminded us of how stifling the rest of the summer would be back in Florida. And once we were back home in Florida and closed the door, all we wanted to do was switch on the a/c and sleep. Steve and Gretchen knew to give us a few days to decompress before calling.

How odd it was then to receive a call from Steve not five hours after we'd arrived home. Even more peculiar was the way he began our conversation: No "hello" or questions about the trip home. No requests that we call their children. Just an excited, "You need to get in the car and come right back up here."

"And I think you need to avoid those strange weed-puffing neighbors this early in the day," I said. "Have you gone completely nuts? We're exhausted."

"Stu, no kidding, I think we may have found your property."

"Okay, I get it. Now what's the punch line?"

"There is no punch line. "

"We just got home. We're grumps. A return trip now will mean divorce."

Steve is a six-foot-six, blue-eyed, blond-haired, brawny, kindhearted Viking who wears Hawaiian shirts his wife finds at resale shops and ripped, paint-stained blue jeans that he's preserved from his graduate-school days. I don't think he owns a suit, and if he does it's a Salvation Army special. I've rarely seen him without work boots. He is cautious about only a few things, usually the wrong things. For example, he is never worried about climbing towering trees without safety lines or burning gigantic piles of brush in close proximity to forests. But he is extraordinarily cautious about large expenditures for land—indeed, even about small ones. So, as tired as I was, I was listening now.

"Tell me something about the property."

"Not a chance. You need to see it. All I'll say is that coming back from Tennessee late this afternoon, Gretchen and I saw a handmade sign on Highway 321 just north of our place. The sign must just have gone up. It's about a mile from us on the other side of the road. And it has a very good private asphalt driveway that goes up the mountain right to a substantial looking house."

Having hand built a few gravel roads and knowing the cost in sweat and money of even these minimal roads, my friend can get nearly orgasmic about thick, solid asphalt. And since he's been doing it all his life, the man knows construction.

"It's amazing." Steve said. "The place feels exactly like what you two have always said you wanted. And the price…"

I could almost hear him licking his chops and trying to catch his breath.

"...the price—seems fantastically low. If you don't go for this, we'll know you're not serious about getting a piece of mountain real estate."

"Can it wait a week? Until we're over jet lag?"

He hesitated. "Probably, but I wouldn't wait much longer. This place is, well, it's gorgeous. That's all I'm gonna say. It's going to sell, and soon."

Steve and Gretchen had purchased their property in 1979 from an old-time North Carolina family who saw no earthly use for the land. Located on the crest of a gorge, only a couple hundred feet back from a two-lane state highway and sloping down at about a sixty-degree angle through heavy woods, thistle, and briars to a wild river, the place was deemed by Steve's neighbors as just about worthless: "Too steep for farming, too many rocks, no good for building, and too darn close to the road. Good for nothing."

Steve and Gretchen are teachers, but most of all they are artists, people of monumental creative energies who longed for a cool summer place in the mountains to escape frantic Orlando and their demanding jobs. By 1979, as Chair of the tiny university's Fine Arts Department, against all odds Steve had managed to assemble an international faculty. When the administration, citing expense but really fearing the emergence of too darned much art, refused to give him additional space for a sculpture studio headed up by Johann, a mad Icelander who'd attracted flocks of devoted students in an astonishingly short time, Steve simply found space on the wide open campus, secretly bought geodesic domes out of his stingy budget, and put them together himself—complete with concrete floors, insulation, and window air-conditioning units. He accomplished this under the cover of one weekend when administrators were home training their horses, with the aid of only an army of students and Johann who earlier in his life had been his country's lightweight boxing champion. At fifty, Johann was still a two-fisted dynamo. What a twosome! When the university's administration returned, bright and rested on Monday morning, there stood two gleaming white geodesic domes where the previous Friday afternoon there had been a quarter-acre sandlot. There wasn't much they could do besides be shocked.

I mean, we're talking energy! With our two friends, any monumental project, the more improbable the better, became intriguing and, therefore, possible. They'd almost bought a smaller more conventional piece of land in Maple Run, North Carolina, but at the last moment the sellers changed their minds and raised the price, thus making the property unaffordable. On their return to Orlando, Gretchen felt so disappointed she went into some sort of land-deprived depression (that energy could also cause intense sadness), and as a result they returned to the mountains, saw the aforementioned dramatically useless piece of property, fell in lust with its possibility, and bought it with the help of a small loan from Steve's dad. Again, the only practical virtue of this new property was its price—it was *incredibly* cheap.

Wilfred, the seller, was honest about his estimate of its use: "Reason it's so cheap is it ain't good for nothing except to look at… but if you're fixing to buy it, we sure are ready to sell." Down at the general store, they all laughed for a long time about the crazy Florida people, the Floridiots, who snapped up Wilfred's land "like a bass on a hopper."

Working like pioneers during every school vacation—winter and summer—Steve and his family cleared the land, designed and cleared enough paths so they could walk down to the river, and then camping out, using bottled drinking water and bathing in the river, they raised a house on top of an enormous boulder where no habitable human structure should have been possible. "Ain't never seen nothing like it!" was the new local tune. "That boy is plumb crazy. Him and his family's on the job from first light to last, and that's the Lord's honest truth; gotta give 'em credit."

And so, we could visit most summers, swim in their river, dive under their waterfalls, picnic, and return home after looking for our own little piece of Eden, albeit with no success, because whatever we found and liked we could not afford, and whatever we could afford we hated. About all we ever saw that was affordable was tilted at an even steeper grade and was more remote than Steve and Gretchen's or, if relatively level, was located within easy walking distance of a dilapidated trailer inhabited by suspicious looking, empty-eyed people. We'd heard of meth labs up here and thought these folks might have been sent from Central Casting for a remake of *Deliverance*. But this newest development intrigued us both.

Thus it was that three days after Steve's phone call, we rolled ourselves back into the car and made the trek back to the mountains again, with me grumbling that this better be greater than great and Jan, as usual, bubbling over in excited anticipation.

Steve wasted no time when we arrived, hustled us out the door, showed us the sign and left us to drive up.

He'd not exaggerated. The property was gorgeous. Everywhere we looked there were flowers—lilies, roses, gladiolas, Rose of Sharon, in reds, pinks and whites—all surrounded by meadows bursting with wild flowers. The front steps of the house made for an odd contrast, constructed as they were from shards of bathroom tile embedded in cement. But from them we could see six distinct mountain ranges. And it looked as if this would be the view from at least three other sides.

We walked under a rose arbor in full bloom, knocked on the front door, and were greeted by a gaunt but very handsome man who appeared to be about sixty or so. He was dressed in spotlessly clean pressed overalls and newish cowboy boots and was holding what looked like a large shot glass. The shot glass on a Sunday didn't make sense to me, particularly since this was deep Baptist territory and a dry county. Behind him, sitting in an overstuffed floral lounger was a heavyset woman who seemed considerably older than he was. One of her legs, wrapped in an elastic bandage, appeared to be terribly swollen and was propped on a hassock; a cane rested at her side. From her hips to her neck, she was locked into what looked like a hard plastic shell. It had to be awfully uncomfortable even if had been fitted correctly, and from the way she sat there readjusting herself for even the few moments we stood in the doorway, it wasn't.

The woman was smiling one of those smiles you see pasted on people who are intent on demonstrating to the world that they are happy. Though her face looked puffy from medicine, she was still a pretty woman with a set of deep dimples. Hers seemed way too cheerful a greeting for strangers interrupting her Sunday. On the other hand, maybe this was part of Southern culture, courtesy, and hospitality, no matter what happened to be your personal circumstances?

We apologized for barging in, for coming up on Sunday, and explained that we had seen their sale sign and were seriously interested in seeing local property. He seemed hesitant to admit us, but she shouted, "Let them folks in"—with an authority contradicted by her disability. "You folks come on in here. And, Monroe, you shut the door. Now you two sit right down," she said and pointed to the living room couch. We sat. So commanding a voice from this lady was one of multiple surprises that day.

We explained how we'd arrived just today and had seen their sign, and she, in turn, immediately told us their reasons for selling. They'd decided after thinking about it a long time and after praying for guidance for the right path. They'd received that guidance and were moving to Atlanta for several reasons, the main one being the illness that now incapacitated her. She could no longer walk without a cane, tend her gardens, or even cook much anymore. Progressively, she found it hard even to move without help, and the prospects of recovery from the illness—it turned out she had the worst form of lupus, arthritis, and advanced diabetes—were not good. Her doctors were all in Atlanta. So were their two oldest sons and grandchildren. Their youngest son, who was somewhat disabled, still lived with them and he would move too.

As much as they hated leaving their land, she saw no alternative at this point in their lives. She explained, now in a quiet voice and without the greeting smile, that they'd planned to travel, to see the world in their senior years after so long a life of hard work, but now that clearly was not going to happen. She further explained that she reconciled herself to the illness by understanding that the Lord had most likely chosen her rather than someone else because of her strength and deep faith. She could handle it better than someone else.

Her husband had said nothing after letting us in, but now, listening to her, he raised an index finger over his head. An admonition? A signal? I'd seen in movies that a sign of connection with God was a raised finger. This was the first time I'd been in the room with someone doing it, if this was indeed such a sign. Maybe this was an affirmation of his own faith? She looked at him, stopped talking, and stared straight ahead. Truthfully, their situation frightened me. So did her explanation of faith as part explanation for her illness. I was also a little unnerved by their accents which I could barely decipher. From the looks on both their faces, they were having as great a difficulty with our Chicagoese.

Neither Jan nor I knew what to say, faced as we were with such sadness; we were almost embarrassed at our interest in buying their home. So we expressed our hopes for her recovery and repeated several times that whether or not we bought the property, we wished them a smooth transition. He nodded, and dribbled something brown from his mouth into the oversized shot glass.

I wondered if he was sick too. I'd never seen anybody do something like this.

We asked as politely as we could if we might walk the property. He, in turn, asked us directly if we were really interested, but before we could reassure him, she told him to stop wasting time, to put that glass up, stop the spittin', and take us around. He obeyed. She might be ill, but this dimpled lady retained command.

Out we went. What we saw literally took our breath away.

Steve was right. An amazing variety of trees bordered the house. Then they thickened into woods. Beautifully, no, meticulously tended lawns sloped down in front of and up behind the house. Along the driveway, Monroe pointed out five apple trees already loaded with fruit and punctuating the front lawn. He showed us plum, peach, and seven additional varieties of apple trees. A few had been there since his father lived on the property. "I planted nearly every one of them trees myself. Dug some of them out of orchards; some I brung up from seedlings. It ain't that hard if you know what you're doin'." There were three very large trees next to the house that I did not recognize.

"Oh, them are black walnut. Won't see the nuts until late summer. Things are as hard as rocks, but good eating. Got to ride over 'em with your car or four wheeler to get 'em open. Got to wear gloves too. Some kind of dye in them. Get it on your hands and it's the darnedest stuff ever to get off. Women used to use it in the old times when they made cloth."

He led us behind the house to the back lawn where he pointed to a tree at least twenty-five feet tall and explained that it was a sweet cherry. Behind it, interspersed throughout the lawn were more varieties of apple and peach trees. "Planted all of them too, and them blueberries. Took a long time until we were picking." On the side of the property just beyond some old-time slatted fencing there was an expansive meadow where a horse grazed.

Above the house we saw two strands of barbed wire, a mountain gate strung between 4 by 4s over a parallel series of concrete pipes set into the ground, a kind of dangerous-looking obstacle course that we learned later was a cattle grate, leading to a little road passing behind and to the side of the property.

Our reluctant guide put aside the wire with his bare hands, after it became embarrassingly obvious that neither Jan nor I were nimble enough to navigate under the bottom strand or over the top as he did, without ripping our pants and generous parcels of our skin to shreds. We tiptoed over the pipes, holding onto each other for balance, feeling accomplished when neither of us fell through and broke an ankle.

The road wound up the mountain, past a second building, an old barn, an older looking and even more picturesque dilapidated chicken coop capped by a rusted tin roof that was once red. A few hundred yards up the path we were blocked by a small herd of cattle, complete with suckling calves, and further up between looming ancient boulders and over freshwater springs, some burbling as they disappeared under these boulders, was still another far-reaching meadow covered with tiny wild strawberries and what seemed to us thousands of white mountain daisies.

Monroe picked a few berries, popped a couple into his mouth, and offered us some. Sweeter than any we could buy in the store, he assured us, "at them outrageous prices." He was right. They were wonderful.

As we went, he pointed out deer tracks and deep indentations gouged through fallen leaves into the trampled clay, which he explained (after quizzing us about their origins and having us fail the test) were "rubs" put there by bucks marking territory and advertising their male prowess for prospective lady deer who were abundant here.

I was enchanted; Jan amazed and more than a little scared. Imagine! Horned bulls within touching distance—and cows and even little baby cows sharing our path. Native, free produce. Gorgeous fruits. Wild deer. Mating rituals. Everywhere we looked up here were signs of raw, natural beauty and fecundity, barely touched by humans. Here was Wordsworth luxuriating among the meadows and his Gothic ruins, not embodied as crumbling churches but in the form of rusty old chicken coops.

At the top of a rise amidst a circle of granite boulders about a half mile above the house we came on a large pond. This, Monroe explained, was his catfish pond—"goes with the property"—spring fed and stocked.

"You eat the fish right out of here?"

"Always have."

"Come on."

"But you need t' come up here an' feed 'em once a week or so. To keep 'em nice an' fat."

He repeated. "Pond goes with the property. Why I've pulled fish out of here three foot long. Why, one time my boy, Jacky Lee, and my nephew, Noah, pulled in a fish so big, it took the two of them t' yank it in. Needed to go back down to the house and get a garbage can t' haul it down the mountain. Talk about good eatin'."

By the time Jan and I were led back down an alternate path, we were as ready to be yanked, skinned, and if necessary fried as those succulent leviathan catfish.

Just let me sign that contract!

Jan, though, had a couple of problems with the house. The first was that it looked too good—too fresh. Too modern. This was not a virtue in her mind. She had been picturing an old rundown farmhouse, a fixer-upper, or, if we got really lucky, a chinked, aged, bullet-scarred log cabin. She was dreaming of a structure more like the abandoned chicken coop than this tidy well-built home.

The original version of the house had been built by Monroe and his identical twin brother as a cozy, tight, four rooms: kitchen, living and dining room, good sized bathroom, a single bedroom, and large storage pantry. The fireplace for the original heating was fitted with a 1,000-pound steel insert that blew hot air into the living room via an electric fan. It was efficient enough to heat the house in five minutes. Later, when they had more money in 1996, they added a second story with three bedrooms, two more baths, including a Jacuzzi, many closets, a double garage, central heat and air, and even a small balcony off the main bedroom. It was all rock solid, literally, since much of the understructure and facing were made of rock hauled down from the mountain.

Our hosts listened to Jan's reservations with the closest thing to wide-opened mouths I'd ever seen except in my brother-in-law's dental office and told her what they'd learned as "young 'uns." They'd lived in those old-timey places, wind whistling through the walls, floors with big cracks and holes—and farmhouses, spring houses, and particularly outhouses were real overrated; so were drafty, bad fireplaces as your only heat, especially in the middle of a blowing mountain winter.

"Once," he began—it was the first time Monroe smiled—"after a real bad storm, I had to tunnel a couple hundred feet through the snow that was way up over our roof, just t' make it to the springhouse and then smash through a three-inch layer ice to get us some water. By the time I made it back t' the house, the water was froze solid in the bucket, so mama said t' go back and fetch some more. This time I was carryin' a pine torch and some matches so once I got the water I could keep it thawed. Well, I heard a scrunchin' that scared me most half to death; thought it was some animal tryin' to dig down for food—until I met my cousin from over the hill tunneling right smack into me. We was both half froze and covered with snow, looked like a couple of abominable snowmen, and both shocked as all get-along to see each other. But not as shocked as mama when I walked in and told her I done brought us home a guest for dinner. She just about split her sides with laughing. Them were hard but fun days."

Now he was laughing. That laugh-in-recollection was a response we were to see often as local people loosened to tell us stories from childhoods so removed from ours in radiator-warmed Chicago. There, if we got cold our mothers would tell us to sit on the metal radiator covers. We'd challenge ourselves to sit there, staring out the window at the snow until we were sufficiently warmed up—or broiled.

Later, after we'd bought the property, we heard more wonderful stories of mountain winters: sledding double on saved scraps of old linoleum down mountains of snow: no steering and no stopping until you reached the bottom, wherever or whatever that might be, as easily a snow covered tree stump or blanketed rock as a cushioned, flat bottom.

"Good times, but cold! Law! Real heat and good water lines and indoor plumbing connected to a dependable septic tank make living a whole lot nicer."

I don't think Jan was yet convinced, but it is hard to argue with someone who's shivering just remembering those old-time winters.

"Let me tell you, Jan, you'll be happy to have them features, just you watch and see."

We both had questions about a few of those very features. "Be sure to ask about the water," our friend, Bernard, had warned. "And get straight, verifiable answers," commanded his formidable wife, Gloria, who pound for pound was easily a match for Monroe's wife, Eunice.

They knew what they were talking about. Ten years previously Gloria and Bernard had bought twenty acres of mountain property four hours away, later finding that during the first hot summer their spring had dried to a trickle, rendering their gorgeous house nearly unlivable. In a panic, they hired geological experts to locate another, more dependable spring, but to no avail—after running up a thousand dollars' worth of the expert's time. Then they hired a different expert to drill a well. Seven-hundred feet and thousands of dollars later, he produced a deep, dark, dry hole, lined with only apologies.

Desperate, thirsty, perspiration soaked, and shower deprived, they resorted to a local divining man, an old-timer, who moved mysteriously through their woods, pointing a pronged stick in this direction and that until, when it suddenly jerked downward, he pronounced, "Well, here she is!"

Our sweaty friend Bernard was understandably a little skeptical. Gloria told us that she was so angry at Bernard's even hiring the old charlatan that she refused to leave her bedroom while they walked the property.

Bernard was ready to believe anything. "You're sure?" The divining man nodded.

"Positive? We've already spent a small fortune."

"She's here."

"You don't know my wife."

"Plenty of good, cold, water right here," the fella did a little one-two dance, "right under my feet." So the old-timer's brother-in-law, who owned a one-man well-drilling company, was called out, drilled the hole, and hit water at three-hundred feet. The divining man was there to watch. So was the intrepid Gloria.

"Told you so, didn't I?" he triumphed as he presented a hand-scrawled bill for five-hundred dollars along with another paper-scrap bill from his brother-in-law.

So, forewarned, we asked The Water Question. And we got The Water Answer.

"Well, family's been living on this land in one way or t'other over a hundred and fifty years," Monroe explained, "and the water's always come from the same deep springs. Never in a body's memory did it come up short. Fact is, we got more water on this property than a body will ever need. Plenty of water and that's a fact. You heard it. Got a reservoir up above that fills four-hundred gallon. Take you up if you want to see it. Only about three-quarter mile. I wouldn't lie about such an important thing as water. Wouldn't lie noways."

"Anyways," corrected Eunice as he shot her a look that was not Sunday appropriate, "simply because we are a good Christian family and that would be just plain wrong." From her chair, Eunice commanded, "Monroe run and get Jan an' Stu"—by this time we were all on a first name basis—"a glass." Which he did. And it was as cold and sweet tasting as she assured us it would always be.

"Delicious," I said.

"Delicious," Jan agreed.

"Dee-li-cious," echoed Eunice.

"And that's the way it is all the time," she smiled, "all the time."

Monroe went on to explain that the reservoir collected the fresh spring water that then came down the mountain via gravity through an underground hosepipe that he and his brother had installed. It ended at the house. Simple, efficient—and cheap as can be. There was no water bill such as the one we paid at home each month.

The septic tank just behind the house was relatively new and, unlike sewers that backed up in the city, was pretty much trouble free. It collected all the sewage. It needed to be emptied once every five years or so. "Probably less for you because you'll only be up here about half the year." The other water from the sinks and laundry ran through a separate drain right down into the woods where it emptied.

Simple and foolproof—and cheap.

Monroe's earlier reference to religion provided Jan the moment to go on with the question she and I had agreed would be key, the deal-maker or the deal-breaker on any purchase.

"You know," Jan began, as she sat across from her new friend Eunice, "we love your place, we are truly sorry you have to leave, and we feel, too, that if we did buy, it would be our solemn duty to take care of it as you have obviously so lovingly done. We feel like we would be more the care-takers, your stewards, than owners. After only a little while here somehow I feel like we were meant to meet at this moment in all our lives and that we were supposed to be here with you." My wife really does believe that the universe conspires for good if you send it the right signals. I admit I'm less sanguine.

Both Monroe and Eunice seemed on the brink of tears, so moved were they by my wife's understanding.

"I even feel as if some way we are already like a family."

Eunice lifted herself out of the chair and with great difficulty, using her cane, hobbled across to the room and hugged Jan. It seemed an extraor-dinary effort. "I don't know why, but I'm feelin' just about the same way. Feel like you're kin already." She lowered herself delicately onto the sofa beside Jan.

"So, forgive me if what I'm about to say appears out of place, or insensi-tive, but we are just a little worried. We do not want to come where we might feel unwelcome in the community or nervous because of people's responses."

Monroe and Eunice, especially Eunice, were now focused on Jan's every word, at least the ones they could make out and, I think, anxious about what might be coming. I think they were wondering what this Yankee–Or-lando woman with the empathetic feelings and the enigmatic accent was about to reveal. Jan was worried? About what?

Eunice was now worried, too. Were we hesitating because we were Flo-ridians? Or maybe we were developers? She knew we were from the North via Florida. Were we perhaps Democrats? Some sort of fugitives? What could it be? I could see them willing her to get to the point.

"When we came in I saw you had a beautiful Bible on the living room table. We keep one in our house too. It was my parents'."

They looked at each other; they looked at Jan. At each other; at Jan. What was it she needed to reveal?

"It's a different Bible."

"Well, what in the world has that got to do with anything, honey?"

"It's the Hebrew Bible. We're Jewish."

There. It was out. I swear you could have heard the proverbial pin, or was that a razor-sharp pitchfork, drop. I was getting ready to do my best imitation of an inchworm and sidle my way toward the door.

As we already had come to know was family protocol, Eunice was the first respondent.

She hugged Jan again. "Well bless your hearts! What's the matter with that?" Eunice took Jan's hand and, so help me, kissed it. Jan took Eunice's. I, on the third hand, was still sidling while trying to link Eunice's two sentences with the kiss.

Monroe's response was even more fervent. "The Israelites are God's Chosen People! I truly do believe that." His was not a statement. It was a declaration. "Why, look at me, the hair's standing up on my neck." Then nodding their heads in unison, they spoke what could have been a re-hearsed blessing. "We are honored to have you here in our home. May the Lord be praised!"

We were speechless. This was obviously not the response we'd expected. Jan was reassured. I was reassured, too—somewhat. I honestly believed they felt honored. I believed, however, that their fervor might be seasoned by the fact that they were on the cusp of selling a house. Why am I for-ever the skeptic? And what about the rest of the community? Monroe's twin brother, for example? Would he be as receptive? The anticipation of burning crosses or shotgun blasts in the middle of the night had faded a tad from my childhood conditioning, but their shadows lingered. If these people said we were as welcome as could be, which they did, well, couldn't we take them at their word?

"And I'll tell you what else," Monroe added. "If you're worried about taking care of all this land"—until he mentioned it, I hadn't been—"you don't need to be. My brother's son ..."

"Yes, Noah, that lovely boy." Here came Eunice's dimpled smile again. "He'll be a-tooling up here on his little four-wheeler, introducing hisself before you know it. Be up here before his Daddy. Did I mention that Monroe and Lorne was identical twins? Lorne's the shy one. Introvert."

"Well, I wouldn't say that," Monroe demurred.

"Well, nothing! I would and do. You know that he is. Secretive. Shy as can be. Shy as that telephone post out there. You're the one with all the personality."

He shrugged his shoulders.

Too much property? Noah? Introvert? Unrevealed family conflicts? We brushed it all away. None of it mattered. We were in love—with the views; the rusting, roofless chicken coop; the suckling calves; the limitless pure, free, sparkling water rushing down the mountain; the freer strawberries; the abundance of fruit trees; the catfish; the pristine septic tank. For good-ness sake, we loved the whole place, despite its being comfortable and despite its sporting what Jan described as the most unusual decorating job she'd ever seen—blue and purple walls spackled with black.

Cosmetic. Merely cosmetic.

After a little of my clever bargaining, we agreed to buy the property at ten-thousand dollars below his asking price. Was I a genius or what? When I told Monroe we wanted to call in a building inspector just to be sure that the structure was as solid as it looked, his amiable attitude altered. Adopted family or no. God's Chosen or no.

"At that price, I don't want no inspectors 'round here. No sir, don't like 'em. Never did. Just sucking off the government."

"But…"

"Ain't. No. Buts."

Given the circumstances and heartfelt pledges we'd all just made, the sisterly hugs between the ladies, the kiss, their near tears, and my shrewd negotiating, I was satisfied.

No inspectors.

We men shook on it. The women remained in tableaux, holding hands. Monroe said he would notify the other three prospective customers who were scheduled to arrive that very afternoon, one of whom he mentioned was a new preacher who was coming to the area.

"He'll be real unhappy," he told Eunice, "but a deal is a deal." Then in nearly the same breath he spoke to me. "I'll need a retainin' check, today."

I wrote the retainer to be escrowed with the local law firm he suggested, and Jan and I were almost the official new owners of a homestead that they told us had not been out of the family for one-hundred-and-fifty years. All four of us embraced again, in a sort of fervent ménage-à-quatre huddle, overflowing with mutual goodwill.

"You know," Eunice said as we were about to leave and tell Steve and Gretchen the news, "if you're staying until Friday, our church is having a barbecue supper. If you're interested, we'd sure love you to come. Give you a chance to meet some of the folks in the community."

We told them we hadn't planned on staying another four days, but with an invitation like theirs we would be there. We would be honored.

Back at Steve's, "You bought it? Just like that?"

Steve was impressed I think, or maybe he was just stunned.

"Just like that."

So, the Jews were moving in, and the resident Christians were heading for Atlanta. Oh, and we were due at church on Friday night. Just like that.

Homeplace and pool room.

HE HOLDS GOD
BY THE BEARD

IT TURNED OUT THAT THE CHURCH barbecue was a fundraiser for breast
cancer. It also turned out that almost every weekend presented one
fundraiser or another, usually sponsored by one of the many small churches
in an attempt to do their part battling a major illness. The practice almost
makes me want to be a member of organized religion, until I think about
it for a few seconds. I have actually tried from time to time earlier in my
life to join up, but the insistence of always being right is too much for me
to handle, as is the usual need for bigger and bigger edifices. I think my
bubbe's (grandma's) skepticism about religion had something to do with
my own. Strangely, so did my beloved paternal grandfather's orthodoxy.

In my grandparents' old synagogue on the west side of Chicago, it was
tradition in our family for me to sit with my grandfather through all of
the High Holiday services that took place from early morning to sun-
down. Just sitting next to Grandpa made the tedious prayers tolerable.
During that season it was traditional for the leader of the congregation,
its President, to make a plea for donations during the services when congregants were feeling most repentant and anxious about their relationship
with God.

My grandfather was a poor guy, but despite his lack of money he was
generous, and so one year when the President asked for donations, Grandpa immediately responded by offering ten dollars. The President stopped
the proceedings, "Omansky," he said, "I asked for donations." My grandpa
blushed. Even a little kid could feel his embarrassment. That was it for me
from then on. If this was religion, you could count me out.

Anyhow, our entire $5.00-a-person donation this night at the church barbecue would go to the cause, since most of the food was to be donated by a congregant who owned a restaurant down the mountain, and nobody helping to run the event would even consider taking a penny.

We learned at the general store that our appearance already was an anticipated event. Almost everyone we met in the course of purchasing a few groceries knew that we were buying the Simmons place and that we might be coming to the church supper on Friday.

We were celebrities.

It took five minutes to get there from Steve and Gretchen's. Though we were fifteen minutes early, the parking lot was already nearly full: mostly vintage pickups, a few newish ones, and many older-model sedans. Standard equipment seemed to be a rifle in the rear window of the pickups. And more than a few had small Confederate flags pasted to rear bumpers. Seeing so many of those flags got me back to that, "Oh no, what have we done?" feeling again.

The central meeting room had a good crowd, about forty people sitting at long tables organized in rows down the middle of the room and covered with white butcher paper. People were talking quietly. Other families were strolling in and greeting one another, but the greetings seemed strangely subdued.

Along the back wall was a line of longer tables, at that moment being covered with trays of food so plentiful you could barely see the paper. On one table, ladies were putting down platter after piled-high platter of shredded barbecued pork and fried chicken. There were bowls of coleslaw, beans, macaroni salads, and three types of potato salad. None of it looked like restaurant fare.

On another table was an astonishing variety of desserts: strawberry shortcakes in varying heights, blueberry cobbler, seven varieties of layer cakes, thickly frosted chocolate brownies, and one fruit and-whipped-cream dessert that looked suspiciously like the Appalachian version of English trifle.

Like the main feast, all the desserts had to be homemade.

Diabetes, here called "Sugar" (as in "I got the Sugar"), is common in these parts, and if these desserts were any indication of the typical conclusion to meals, it was no wonder why. I think I now also had the answer to a question I'd always had when visiting here. If people here worked so damned hard—and they did—why were so many of them fat? Now I knew: sugar, of course—wonderful, spectacular culinary inventions made with sugar!

Brilliant me.

Despite the array, not a soul was making a move toward the banquet. Neither were we. I understood our reluctance better than theirs. We weren't feeling exactly like lost lambs, but the unexpected whispering around us and all those bumper stickers weren't making us feel like guests at Cousin Ralph's Bar Mitzvah either. We were, after all, the outsiders, so we were trying to maintain respectful protocol, wondering if perhaps the quiet delay was because there was a religious ceremony or special prayers that were about to occur. Maybe we needed to say something to the whispering congregants?

Our awkwardness as outlanders wasn't helped by posters recently taped up on the walls that told us that tonight was a double occasion: the cancer fundraiser and prom night. Prom night is not only a family time here but a church time too, as maybe it remains elsewhere in small-town America. It's when the boys and girls, all dressed up, come by to visit the congregation and show themselves off. Tonight, it turned out, was the night they'd be "oohed" and "aahed," kissed and praised: the girls told by the senior men that if they had been only thirty years younger, the other boys wouldn't have a chance; the boys told they were just so handsome they could twist a good churchgoing woman's head plumb in the wrong direction. It was all good natured, a ritual probably extending back to at least when the parents of today's prom goers were on their way to their own adulthoods. Whatever, there was no doubt that we were in the middle of a lovely, comfortable time warp.

The girls appeared one by one, like Alice in Wonderland flowers, regaled in stiff pastel formals with ill-fitting bodices or crinoline skirts that puffed out and came to just below their knees. Each had an orchid corsage pinned at the waist. Most of their escorts wore burr haircuts and were dressed in white formal jackets, with carnation boutonnieres and satin-striped black pants, all beaming and sporting innocent young faces. Clearly there was an excitement at being so dressed up and movie-star famous for a little while, here in the midst of elders they'd known all their lives.

The scene felt reminiscent, yet only cosmetically reminiscent, of the late '50s when we were attending proms. These kids were dressed in getups like the ones we wore back then. Was that kid wearing my rental tux?

But in the late '50s in Chicago my crowd, after picking up our dates, headed to the Chez Parez after eating expensive lobster dinners at the much-too-expensive outdoor dance pavilion of the Edgewater Beach Hotel. Most of us were lower-middle-class Jewish kids pretending to be sophisticated— i.e., rich—and determined during the next years to hit the good professions—doctors, lawyers, accountants, even (in a bad scenario) psychologists. These duds were a dress rehearsal for our futures.

The kids coming in and out tonight were heading for the school gym. And they were heading there after high praise in their church and a little good-natured old-time kidding.

"Don't you do nothing I wouldn't do."

But there was more than kidding. Eunice was there, and she, it turned out, partly because of her affliction and partly because she was a long-time unofficial leader in the church, commanded the central voice among the female elders. The girls gravitated toward her not for jokes but for blessings.

"May the Lord keep you safe," she'd say, laying hands on the girls' bare shoulders and looking their accompanying escorts right in the eye. The message was clear. Safe! Eunice knew about the dangers of prom night. Unlike me, she wasn't seeing innocence on those freshly shaved faces. Perpetrators of indiscretions would answer to her.

Soon the prom goers were gone, and the adults and little ones, many in mothers' arms, were left to the dinner. Still, no one had moved a step toward the food and no one had approached us, the newcomers, either. In place of movement, there was plenty of avoided eye contact. We were all together in the same room, at the same fundraising party, but Jan and I were sitting alone at a table isolated from everybody else by a barrier of, at least, three folding chairs and a cultural plinth.

I wasn't as worried about the social separation—it and the bumper stickers sort of confirmed my nagging reservations and the warnings of our sons—as I was that the food, particularly the chicken, was getting cold, and possibly that Jan was growing irritated at my drooling. We were in some sort of Appalachian standoff. Even the infants seemed on sound lockdown.

Then the doors flew open and into the room rushed a little power pack of a man. Sporting a boyish crew cut, much like that of the prom boys, and stylishly suited, he looked around, made eye contact, and bounced right across the room, heading straight for Jan, sticking out his hand, introducing himself as Thomas Gilligger, the Pastor, and apologizing for being so late, a result of needing to visit a sick deacon.

His trip across that room impressed me as a remarkable act of jet-like evangelical social diplomacy as well as priority radar. He actually managed to greet every member of the church he passed without stopping, without appearing discourteous, and still get to his target—us, the new faces—in record time.

He winked at us as he looked around the hall, whispering that the congregation must seem to us a little shy and that their reluctance must not be taken as unfriendly. His emphasis was on the "musts." This was a guy who obviously was used to telling people the right way of behaving, the right way of thinking, and having them comply. I wondered if he somehow was related to one of my opinionated poker-playing chums back in Orlando.

A similar instruction from a rabbi would be more like, "You could come out, maybe?" or "Could you try to be at synagogue on time Friday night so as not to disturb the service?" if it ever happened at all. Most rabbis are too diplomatic or trained in self-preservation to commit such an error. But if the faux pas were somehow in an unlikely scenario to occur, it would elicit a congregant's response heated enough to ignite a modern Talmudic debate. "He's telling me how to behave? He holds God by the beard? And what am I, a plate of chopped liver? He knows my schedule?" If he survived, the impulsive Reb (rabbi) would never presume so far again, ever. We can be a tough audience.

But Pastor Gilligger was perfectly comfortable with his directives. "It's our courtesy, you see. They're all waiting for you to partake of the food first. Once that happens, dinner can begin." He motioned for us to rise and led us off to the tables and as soon as Jan took her plate, everybody else began following her lead, talking audibly, introducing themselves now between the baked beans and coleslaw.

Did this guy know his flock, or what?

We filled our plates, were handed enormous glasses of sweetened iced tea, and dropped in our donations to accompanying smiles and nods of approval from the church ladies in charge, who also pointed out the best spot for us to sit down: smack in the middle of the hall.

Before I'd downed my first mouthful, a new table neighbor was perched at my ear.

"Hi, I'm Charlie, Charlie Redville, and this is my wife, Josephine. You're the folks at Monroe and Eunice's place. Glad you're here. You just could not be more welcome. No, sir, not more welcome if you was a rich relative. Go right on and eat. Y'all look hungry. Don't let old Charlie stop you. Been livin' here all my life. Never went nowheres else. Never wanted to go nowheres else. Don't believe I ever will want to. You're gonna love it up there at Monroe's. Best views on the mountain. What do you think of our mountains?"

Was this avalanche before my first swallow one of the same people who a few moments before had sat sphinx silent? I swallowed. "Well, Charlie, to be truthful, we're sort of overwhelmed. Can hardly imagine ever going back to Florida right now."

"Yep, you got that right. We got a saying up hereabouts. 'There's only two kinds of people in the world: them that lives here and them that wants to.'" He laughed at his joke. "Come to think of it, we got lots of sayings. Here's one: 'It's hard to kiss them lips at night when they've been a chewin' on your...'" Josephine was not pleased and he stopped. "Tell you the end somewheres else when I know y'all better." He grinned.

"It's the truth too. Like I said, been here my entire life but don't make much of a living—not much work for a man like me. Hurt my back about ten year ago, real, real bad. Plumbin'. I was a plumber. So now I'm on workin' compensation. Most of all the money goes to my medicine. Not much left for livin' and that's the Lord's truth."

In less than thirty seconds we'd gotten a big, personal chunk of this stranger's life and what sounded like the beginning of a slightly off-color local proverb, right in the middle of the church meeting room, too. Charlie was my kind of guy!

Josephine, faded blonde, blue-eyed, in a plain flowered housedress like the ones my modest mother used to wear to cover up her beautiful figure but would never have thought of wearing anywhere outside our apartment, sat quietly as Charlie now spun on. Jan told me later that night that she was waiting for a pause in Charlie's monologue to see if Josephine could talk. When he paused for a second to take a breath, Jan seized her opportunity.

"Have you been here your whole life too?"

"Oh, yes," Josephine answered just above a whisper. "All my life on the mountain. Haven't been anywheres else. Once, to Charlotte."

Charlie blew on past her as if her few sentences were simply an opportunity, a verbal comma, that gave him the chance to breathe, refuel, refire his motor, and roll on.

"Josephine and me's been married, let's see, fifty years come this December, just before they finished buildin' Berry Creek School. She was fourteen; I was sixteen—prettiest girl in the class, an' of course best-lookin' feller." Another grin. "Had three girls by the time we were out of our teens. Three girls. All live here, too. So do all the grands. Fourteen. Sarah's a waitress down at Daneville Drugs. Violet's a nurse's aide at Shady Rest, where Monroe's brother, Will works—met Will yet? Real nice feller, you'll like Will—and Cora, well, our Cora's a schoolteacher. Teaches mathematics. Smart, just like her Daddy. Always was the smartest; just like her Daddy," he repeated just in case we'd missed it the first time. He grinned from ear to ear. A couple of his teeth were missing.

Josephine lifted an eyebrow, barely enough, maybe an eighteenth of an inch, so that it was discernible, and smiled a quiet, tired, pink smile; a tolerant smile that seemed far older than even fifty married years. Did Charlie's banter get on her nerves? It didn't seem to. It didn't on mine. He seemed a good-natured, astoundingly open man.

"You folks gonna live here all year long? Retired?" Charlie was firing more direct questions in these last few minutes than we'd been asked in the entire last week on the mountain.

"Well, we're trying to figure that one out. I was a schoolteacher (I was careful to avoid "professor," since I'd already got the sense that locals had some discomfort about people who thought themselves "big") until last July when I turned 63. Jan's an artist, a good one: a ceramicist, she works with clay." I couldn't avoid just a little brag. "And we still have a little bakery business back home that we've had for twenty-five years. She started it when our own three boys were growing up. We needed more income."

"I surely know about needin' more money, especially now what with the price of fuel and gasoline. Why the price of kerosene is just about enough to drive y' crazy… Well now y'all are some combination—a teacher, a baker, artist, hear that Phine, if that ain't fascinating?"

"Y'all still bake?"

"Some, but we've a dependable young man who's our manager."

"Me? I never would trust nobody to do anything. Need to do it my own self, with my own two hands. Since I can't do plumbing any more, I build musical instruments. For years now, in my workshop. Fiddles an' dulcimers. Best and most beautiful on the mountain." He took an unusually long pause, it turns out, a modest pause, for Charlie. "… I hope."

"Taught my own self. Started out with old pine an' oak pieces from my daddy's woodpile. Split 'em an' polished 'em. Lord! When I think of all the good firewood I wasted!" He laughed. "Now, of course, I walk the mountains for hickory, spruce. Lumber mills, too. Siding off of old barns. People don't realize what's in them old barns. Fine woods are getting harder and harder to come by, but if you're patient and y' know what you're looking for, you'll come by them. I'm wonderin', would you like to see some of my work? I brought three of 'em along tonight to show Dolger."

Would any sane person refuse such an offer?

Charlie pointed to a large man three tables away, three-hundred-and-fifty pounds if he was a solid ounce, and dressed in the local uniform—bib overalls, flannel shirt, John Deere baseball cap—presiding over a plate overburdened with chicken bones.

"You folks need to meet Dolger! Best bluegrass fiddle player around an' that's sayin' somethin' because we got aplenty. Got a bunch of poor ones too. Fact is, he's one of the onliest people I'll let play my fiddles."

Charlie was up and moving. "Hey, boy, ease up on that eating cause if you don't, you'll get even fatter than you are and your missus can't find overalls t' fit you now. Come on over here and meet Jan an' Stu, folks bought Monroe and Eunice's place. And she's a potter too, and I hear tell a right good one. You and that brother of your'n best watch your step. There's a new game in town, and she's sure prettier than either of you."

Dolger was from an old family of potters, it seemed, and had evidently heard most of this routine before because he barely turned from the over-sized barbecue sandwich newly deposited on his plate by a beautiful young woman. Two bites and his sandwich was a part of local history. He shoved himself away from the table, climbed over the next two—it was easier than trying to get by other people sitting in the row—and stuck out his hand.

"Pleased t' meet you. You got t' forgive Charlie. His mama dropped him on his head when he was just a young 'un, set his jaw a-going, and he ain't been able to stop moving it since. It can get a might irritating now an' again."

Charlie was loving it. "Well now, if'n you're about ready t' take a break from snackin' (he pronounced it 'snakin') maybe you'll play a little music for us. I long t' hear a master play this here fiddle of mine."

Charlie opened a polished wooden case made from a dark golden wood, inlaid and bordered by alternate tiny squares of light and dark tones. From the case he lifted a beautiful violin, handing it to Dolger, who slowly turned it over and over. In his big hands it looked like a child's toy.

"Charlie, my friend, you just never stop amazing."

Then he plucked each string. "Don't need a tuning neither."

"When was the last time I handed you an untuned instrument?"

Dolger nodded, this time without joking. "Never. That's the Lord's honest truth. Never. T'aint in you."

Heads began turning toward him as Dolger began to play. It was a blue-grass tune, one I know I'd never heard before but somehow felt to be familiar. And in his hands and on that fiddle it was beautiful, full throated, captivating. It sounded as if Dolger was playing several instruments at once. I wasn't the only person mesmerized in that hall. Virtually all the eating and talking had stopped but not out of shyness this time. It was more as if the quiet grew out of a kind of communal reverence.

The scene and feeling in that moment rekindled an almost forgotten moment from my childhood. The players were different, but the audience silence was the same.

When I was a kid, Eliot Goldstein came to study each afternoon in our three-room, street-front local library, our neighborhood hangout. Eliot was a few years older than my crowd and worked part-time in his father's fruit store. But he was also in his first year of medical school at the University of Chicago, and when he came into the library, often a little disheveled and dirty after a couple hours of stacking apples or washing celery, or putting together and delivering big orders, all of us, kids and adults alike, were enjoined by the whispering librarians to "Shush. Eliot's studying," and the reading room got vacuum quiet. Even the older high school boys, primarily there to pick up girls, either took their affairs outside or shut up. We all understood that a magically important effort was happening here.

Back in the church, notes were flying and dancing from Charlie's strings, deftly worked by the master player. As the tempo increased, people got less quiet and then began spontaneously clapping and stomping in time to the reeling sounds. And so did we. You couldn't not respond to this local virtuoso, so lively were his rhythms, so bright the tunes.

I looked to Jan to see if she was as taken with the music and transformed atmosphere as I. But instead of watching Dolger like everyone else, she was looking across the table at Josephine, who was, in turn, watching her Charlie. She, too, was taken into the music, no longer a tired middle-aged woman but a fifteen-year-old girl, bedecked in purple, a sprig of mountain violets in her shiny blond hair, the very best dancer at her high school prom. I thought I saw in her at that moment the child she had been, before the three children, before what must have been long years of scrimping and just getting along after her husband got hurt, before the needy, good-natured braggadocio of her immensely talented husband. I thought I saw the pretty girl with dreams of a sweet life. Now, in this moment she looked happy and young again as each person in that room was glorying in the music Dolger was making on the instrument created by her own Charlie.

"Shush. Eliot's studying."

Our new mountain community was beginning to teach us. We were among talented, resilient people whose outward looks would fool you if you listened with only half an ear and watched with only one eye. You could easily mistake bumper stickers for reality.

"Heck of a fiddle," said Dolger lovingly, handing it back to Charlie.

"Glad you admire it," replied our new friend.

"Sure you won't reconsider sellin' it to me. I'll give you double whatever you're asking."

"Can't do it. Man can't sell what he doesn't own, now can he?"

Oh, by the way, that night no one ever mentioned that we were Jewish, except the preacher when we gave him, a polite 'no' just after he asked us if we'd like to join the church.

"Jewish? Well bless my soul! Isn't that a wonder! You know you're welcome here anytime, any time at all. Well. Bless my soul."

It was then that he invited us to attend an upcoming river baptism. It would be especially unique since eight people were to accept the Lord and one of them was to be Big Dolger, himself.

"Being Jewish I don't reckon you've ever been to a real old-time river baptism." He didn't know how right he was, river or non-river. "Truth is, we only do one a year now. It's about goin' out of style. I truly hope you'll come."

We said we'd be there.

Ol' Man on a Mountain

WE TOO GATHER
AT THE RIVER

SUNDAY MORNING JUST BEFORE SUNRISE, JAN and I arrived at creek side. From the crowd of cars along the road it looked as if many of the congregation were already there. In these mountains, even in late summer, early mornings can be chilly; here beside the creek it was bone-chilling cold. But none of the gathered seemed to notice. This was a joyous occasion: Dolger was getting baptized. It was, of course, solemn as well, since as I understood it (Jan had gone religion searching again on the Internet) the river ceremony was particularly sacred. It marked a person's rebirth in God's crystalline tides. And that alone would go a long way to keeping any believer warm.

We'd come dressed for the weather: clean jeans, long sleeve shirts, and a wool cap for each of us. Unlike us, everyone else was dressed for church. The men wore white shirts and ties or suits. The women were in dresses. Some had on colorful hats tied with ribbons, the kind I had associated with old-time Easter parades.

We'd already met or seen most of the congregants at the barbecue. A couple of the men we'd not seen, but we assumed from their size and features that they had to be Dolger brothers. A few other people looked as out of place as we. They wore jeans and leather jackets and had a roughness about them as they stood a little removed, talking only to each other.

Charlie was there with his grands and, of course, a fiddle. As soon as he recognized us, he waved us down through the group, opening a space so we could stand right at the water's edge.

"Y'all look like you're ready for the North Pole. You Florida people just kill me! What'ya have flowing in them veins? Wait until November! Till February. Can't even start to think what you'll be wearing then. Wha…"

At a gesture from Reverend Gilliger, Charlie pulled up short, closed his mouth for probably the first time that morning, and started to play, accompanied, as if on celestial cue, by the sharp whistling "it's here" of cardinals, the cooing of mourning doves, and the swirling of the water over the rocks. Then at another gesture from the reverend, all of the gathered lifted their voices in song.

"Shall we gather at the river?" sang half of the congregants, to be answered by the second half, "yes, we will gather at the river." "Lifted in song" is the right expression. Even the small kids tilted their faces upward and sang, stretching their necks and their words, "the beautiful, be-a-u-ti-ful ri-i-ver." At first, Jan and I were lip-synching, faking it, mostly a beat or two after the congregation. We both knew the melody, but neither of us had heard all the words before. It's a hymn that catches you. By the time we'd all gone through several times, we were just about on beat. The scruffy men's club was trying as hard as we were. They were still behind. "…that flows by the Throne of God."

As the congregants sang, they also joined hands. Someone took mine, I took Jan's, and the pinafored little girl on Jan's other side reached up and took hers. Holding hands with all those strangers felt peculiarly natural and generous and spontaneous, and I could sense in that moment a tiny bit of how comforting it must be to have faith and be so integrated with like-hearted friends. For that moment the river was to the spiritually converted the Face of God. To us, too.

"The beautiful, be-a-u-tiful ri-i-ver… yes, we will gather at the river…" As the voices grew stronger and more fervent, Reverend Gilliger walked straight down into the creek, suit, shoes and all. (Now this, I thought, my temporary reverie broken, is carrying devotion too far. His shoes are ruined!) One by one, he called the candidates to come into the water and join him there. A young mother or a father would lead a beaming, nervous, beautifully dressed child, delivering him or her to the Reverend, who would place one hand behind the child's head and the other in the small of the back and submerge the child, once, twice, to emerge the third time sputtering to the sound of applause.

There was a simple theatricality about it that felt genuine, if that makes sense. The older participants, mostly teenagers, came next. They were no less enthusiastic, but their enthusiasm revealed itself in tears of relieved anticipation or joy.

As the hour wore on a different feeling overtook the crowd. It was an antic restlessness, as if we were all coming to a great dramatic moment. And so we were: the baptism of Dolger. Nobody could believe this was actually happening.

Dolger, it turned out, had been a hellion in his past life: a two-fisted drinker and a womanizer. His 120-mph motorcycle rides through the mountains still raised eyebrows and awestruck memories: "It's a wonder that boy's alive. By all rights he should be shoving up daisies." Nobody used the word "debauched," but it sure sounded like if they had, he'd be it.

Dolger carried a myth about him. He'd been a natural-born musician, a prodigy, playing with local adult bands when he was just a child in places where a good boy should never have been. His parents had tried to curtail him, without success. The more adventure, the more danger, the better he liked it. Once he'd sneaked out on a Sunday night to play at a local disreputable dance hall. It mysteriously burned to the ground the following Sunday.

From a long line of country potters, Dolger had turned out to be the best of them all. Even during his escapades, he'd been able to take the small family pottery and turn it into a thriving business. He was a big personality and a born promoter. Each fall he threw a three-day pig roast, inviting everyone he knew from all over North Carolina and Tennessee.

Until age forty-nine Dolger had never walked down the path of religion, only sporadically attending church in this close-knit community where regular attendance at revivals was expected. And those few times were only to pacify his aging mother. Around here not attending church raised eyebrows. His behavior marked him as a fallen man.

Then one day, love strolled through the front door of his pottery studio in the likeness of a twenty-five-year-old auburn haired, green-eyed, white-skinned, velvet-voiced mountain beauty. She'd come in to buy Christmas presents. The story goes that she walked through the showroom, and as she picked up one pot and another, she began to sing, unselfconsciously, not the music he was most used to but, of all things, "Deck the Halls," and Dolger, the mountain roué, the giant, motorcycle-riding, party-giving fiddler, fell head over size-14 heels in love. He went gaga! I wondered, seeing him now gazing at his bride, whether those perfect lips shaping "Fa-la-la-la-la" might have had anything to do with his being smitten.

Anyhow, so the story goes, he went over to her and started a-talkin' and kept a-talkin' and a-talkin' until she agreed to let him call on her. Although she knew his reputation, six months later she accepted his proposal of marriage, delivered on bended knee, at the foot of a six-foot-tall clay heart he'd been fashioning day and night to the exclusion of all other projects in his pottery. No one who knew him could believe it. And no one who knew her would believe that she'd been wooed and had actually succumbed. Her parents objected. Her sisters cried. Her preacher warned. The rumor was that she'd gone "plumb crazy." But then again, how could a gal refuse so monumental, so heartfelt a pledge, from a handsome man who'd dodged almost any real commitment his entire life?

Yes, she accepted, but with one caveat. And it was a doozy. Christie, as her given name suggested, had been born into a devout family. She'd formally accepted her savior at age eleven. Although she knew she loved Dolger and fully believed in him and his promises to become a new man and change his ways, she needed him to be formally baptized into the church. She wanted to have his children and raise them in the church.

And Dolger agreed. No one could believe that either. So, here he was, on a beautiful icy morning, dressed in a suit and tie, shod in patent-leather shoes, and, so help me, a panama hat. Christie stood by him, holding part of his hand in hers, with him looking like a giant kid on the first scary day of school.

The reverend beckoned for Dolger to come forward, and Christie walked him to the edge of the creek. They touched lips, a shy religiously appropriate kiss, a mere buss which I thought must be nowhere related to his former legendary self I'd heard described, and then and there he, too, marched, suit, shoes, and hat into the cold water to stand beside his preacher.

And now occurred the awaited moment. But there was a problem. Whereas in the previous baptisms the water depth had been fine, here it came to just a little over Dolger's shins. There was no way, short of a biblical miracle, that he could be submerged at this depth. So, the two men, balancing on each other, walked unsteadily from slippery rock to slippery rock a little further down the creek where it was deeper but where the current was stronger, too. This was better. The reverend was up to his waist; Dolger, a little below his soaked pants knees.

But the 300-pound convert was still too tall and hefty to be dipped here either. Most of the crowd could see the difficulty clearly now. There were nervous murmurs. Dolger's old buddies seemed delighted with this new wrinkle, possibly laying odds about its outcome. From the waters the reverend addressed us: "Well, folks, looks like we got ourselves a dilemma here." He walked further downstream up to his chest. With the water slightly below his waist, Dolger could be dipped.

The reverend placed one hand behind Dolger's back, and then standing on tippy toes and having to lean his forehead against Dolger's massive chest, he reached up with the other and tried to cradle Dolger's head. The maneuver might have worked had the reverend been a few inches taller and had he not slid off the rock he'd found to take his stand. God's emissary lost his balance and went sluicing down the creek, yelling bloody murder. Some of the congregants shouted to save him; some just stood there, apparently frozen at what was happening, but not Dolger. He dove in and after lots of splashing, groping, and "help me's" (it turned out that the reverend could not swim), Dolger grabbed him by the collar of his suit. Then scooping him up and cradling him like a baby, he slipped and stumbled over the rocks, and eventually, after falling a couple of times and cutting the fabric of his own new suit on a rock, he slogged out onto our bank to be welcomed by a relieved congregation and a few excruciatingly amused good ol' boys, the potter's former posse.

Dolger set down the reverend, who was shaken and shivering but undaunted. The crowd wrapped each man in a towel; an oversized one that had been readied for Dolger and another that had been used by a luckier, less traumatized, younger recipient. We all applauded in relief at what turned out to be both of their successful efforts at salvation as the reverend proclaimed through chattering teeth and a good natured smile, "I th-th-think we've had j-j-just about enough of the w-w-waters for one day. I hereby p-p-pronounce this feller baptized."

A proud Christie kissed her convert, this time, I thought, not so shyly at all, to more applause from the congregation. And I whispered to Jan that if religion could be so spiritual and this much fun all at the same time, I'd consider signing on right now.

A LITTLE
OL' CODICIL

EXHILARATED FROM OUR PURCHASE AND OUR river exploits, we returned to Florida a few days later. But our exhilaration was as quickly dampened as the solemnity of Dolger's conversion. Most of our friends were incredulous, or convinced, as they'd always been, that we were pleasantly lunatic.

"At your ages, you did what? Where? How many acres, did you say? How big is an acre?" asked one.

"Personally, I don't want to own anything that eats or requires cutting. And that reluctance, my delusional friends, truly defines Judaism." said another.

"Well, we can say one thing for sure. You two sure shoot from the hip. Mr. and Mrs. Wyatt Omansky badged with six-pointed stars."

"What are you going to do up there in Li'l Abner Land for amusement? Join the local branch of KKK? Seriously, what the hell are you going to do?"

"Have you run into Snuffy Smith?" This last was a reference to an old-timey comic-strip mountain moonshiner.

Our kids were either indifferent or fascinated or frantic.

"Well, we thought you guys were more condominium-at-the-beach people," said Mike, our most conservative son. He's our Republican MBA, who as yet won't trust us to drive with the grandchildren in the car.

"It sounds like the perfect place to bring women," said Steve, our as-yet-unmarried son, who persistently longs aloud for a nice Jewish girl and children, but instead dates tall muscular tattooed ladies who do pantyless cartwheels down State Street in his reclaimed Chicago. He's brought ex–Dallas cheerleaders home to dinner in skintight short-shorts and skimpy translucent tee shirts. Jan thinks it's a ploy to see what reaction he can get from us. Her reaction is different from mine. After all I'm old, but not immune to the female form. We tell him he's looking for love in all the wrong places. But that he's right on target for lust.

Our youngest son, Joe, who at the time was leaning toward serious Conservative Judaism in New Jersey, had just been elected treasurer of his synagogue brotherhood. He was even considering a move with his little family to Israel, possibly in reactive religiosity towards his heathen father and bohemian mother. His was a less moderate reply. You could call it apoplectic and be close.

"Mom, Dad, that's the South! People up there are backwards! They hate outsiders! They despise people not like them. Forget about this. You've got no realistic idea how dangerous it might be. It's the Bible belt. Those people have really peculiar idea about Jews. And they eat chitlins, for God's sake! I want you to go right back there and sell!"

He's the one who takes care of us.

We tried explaining that this wasn't our experience at all. The people we'd met all seemed pretty much like, well, people, although it was true that the proclivity to own lots of guns and odd bumper stickers had given us pause. Our sweet son snorted in frustration. His wife was muttering in Hebrew or was that a prayer for us as she hovered in the shadows close to the phone? In spite of our assurances, he remained adamant and worried.

"Go back up there and sell, at a loss, if need be, but sell."

So much for the reactions of our friends and relatives. By the time we were ready to go back up and close the deal at James, James, James, James, and James, Attorneys at Law, even we were doubting our sanity or, at the very least, our capacity for solid decision making.

We'd always taught our kids that people were people, but our kids were pushing us to see America and the world in a new 21st-century light. Joe's argument that the rampant fear of immigrants gripping the country was just another sign of growing intolerance, simply adding fuel to the old angers against the age-old scapegoat (guess who), didn't help our mood, nor did daily reports of suicide attacks by Palestinians on Israelis, Africans on Africans, and the almost daily disavowals by the President of Iran of the

Holocaust's ever having happened and his oath that he was determined to push the Jews off the face of the earth.

With all the talking heads flooding us with news mixed with opinion and innuendo, it was harder and harder to separate the dancer from the dance. Maybe we *were* nuts. The ride back to the mountains was less ebullient than the post-purchase ride home.

Closing day arrived, a bad-weather day of threatened storms. We had with us Bagel, our 85 pounds of German Pointer, a solid mass of muscle, fearsome bark, and Alpha ego who was frightened of nothing—except rain and thunder. At lightning, he would turn into a wailing child, pacing, cringing, and generally inconsolable, begging to get inside and hide in a closet. It was pitiful to watch.

We hadn't the heart to keep Bagel in the car during what was shaping into a really angry mountain storm, so we asked if it might be okay to tie our dog up in the law office alcove, protected as it was by a large canvas awning, creating the feeling of an inside space and offering a vantage point where he could see us.

The receptionist refused, explaining that it would be far better to bring him right into the outer office where she could keep an eye on him and settle him down if he needed it. And so we did, with both of us thinking this sort of canine hospitality was unlike that of any law firm we'd ever been in. Most Orlando firms we knew were dog friendly only to the point of displaying those oil paintings of aristocratic English hunting scenes, perfect dogs and mounted masters in posed harmony hanging above butter-soft leather chairs placed by the decorator atop designer oriental rugs. Anyone who can afford these digs, the atmosphere suggests, must be worthy of your trust and your money. A real dog would be about as welcome in those law firms as an impoverished client.

We tied Bagel to a doorknob closest to the receptionist about the time the senior James' secretary came out, apologizing profusely to all of us for Mr. James' being a little late returning from lunch. "He does that sometimes," she said with resignation, "and I'm not the one about to try and set that man straight." But she didn't want to keep us waiting in the lobby, so she invited us all into his office, which turned out to look like a 1940s Jimmy Stewart country-lawyer movie set, complete with stacked wooden filing cabinets, a beat-up old oak desk, and a few mismatched upholstered chairs that had long ago seen even decent days. There wasn't an oriental rug in sight. She asked if we might like some cold water (what, no Perrier?), delivered four glasses for us and a bowl for Bagel, and excused herself.

The Simmonses were nervous, especially Monroe. We were too. All of us were a binding contract away from brand-new territory.

After a few minutes of polite chat, with Monroe interrupting a couple of times hoping nothing was going wrong, the door opened and in came not Jimmy Stewart but a completely different representative of the legal arts. Unlike the model of successful upscale high-priced attorneys I had often seen in Orlando, this country counselor was not only not Perry Mason—he was not even Atticus Finch. Lawyer James was a large man dressed in a suit that had seen better days and displaying a spot that seemed suspiciously like a remnant from a previous meal. Puffing over to his desk, he eased himself down into his chair and without missing a beat offered us an uneven selection from a box of chocolates he produced from his lowest desk drawer.

"Y'all can each have one. Eunice, isn't it, you can have two, if you promise not t' tell anybody," he warned, palming a couple himself which he popped into his mouth with a deftness that could have come only from long practice. Delighted with the secret dessert and wiping his lips of any telltale chocolate with a tissue he removed from and then put back into his top drawer, he called in his secretary and formally began the closing.

"Well, now, let's get down to important business." He paused and I got myself ready for battling country-style legalese. If your experience is anything like mine with lawyers and physicians, the trick is always to slow them down before their language softens or anesthetizes your brain.

"So, what's that beautiful pointer doing tied up out there like a common cur?"

Not what I expected. Now, for the second time in a short while, I saw a mouth agape. Jan's.

"If it's all right with you folks, let's get her in here, so's we can commence with these proceedings."

"Him."

"Hmm. Something wrong with your throat? Y'all need some more water? A hard candy?" He reached back into that drawer.

"Bagel's a him."

"Bagel? Sorry we got no real food in here. But you're more than welcome to another chocolate or…"

"Bagel's the dog's name. He's a male."

"Him, then. Funny name for a fine dog. Sally, my dear, will you kindly go out there and bring that handsome fellow in here?"

All smiles now, Sally practically sprinted into the reception area and returned with Bagel, escorting him in with clucks and coos and inviting him to "set" next to Attorney James Sr.'s desk. Usually a wild and happy dancing lunatic around people, Bagel had never met a soul he didn't love, yet today he shocked us by walking in with subdued majesty. I didn't have to tell him to behave or to sit. I didn't have to calm him. Somehow, he knew he was the star of this legal show, safe and happy to lie down quietly and without a command, close to Attorney James' desk.

We, his parents, were forgotten. So was the storm, which we could still hear outside.

"Now, aren't you the specimen?" This time it wasn't chocolates that appeared from some place in that desk but rather a large carton of Milk Bones, fed one at time by our barrister to Master Content. I've seen first-born children treated worse on their birthdays. Bagel was now on his back, all four legs pointing at the ceiling, his deep brown eyes locked in mutual admiration with those of his newest admirer.

Attorney James, while scratching Bag's belly and head, proceeded to explain the details of the closing, reminding us that the firm's fee was to be split between us as agreed and pointing out that although this was a little unusual, it was fine with him. He went on to say that he had found "a foolish varmint" in the official land survey, delivered to him just that afternoon.

Varmint?

Over his lunch, he'd reviewed all the documents and sniffed out the "rascality." The house itself appeared nowhere on the survey, a pretty sizable error, and he was ready to postpone the closing if we, the buyers, wanted the correction, but that it really was not necessary since according to North Carolina law (he cited the exact code), all buildings on the surveyed property were automatically included in the purchase price. And he would have the survey redrawn that week.

Without looking once at the papers in front of him, he told Sally that in the meantime and for the signing, just to double protect everyone, the error needed to be noted in "a little ol' codicil on page eight in the third paragraph just to be 'pluperfect.'"

Pluperfect? Rascality? I loved it. And he wanted Sally to call and give a talkin' to that survey boy that very afternoon and have him redraw the survey, "not this week, but today."

"And you remind them over there that it's to be done with their pennies. Won't be real happy, but maybe it'll make them more careful on the next one they do. Business is getting too good around these parts lately. Sloppy brains an' sloppier hands. And you tell him that if he has any objections, him and me are gonna have to go a few rounds." He fed Bagel another biscuit. By the way Bagel lapped it from his fingers, you could tell that our boy was in full agreement with Attorney James' assessment of the situation.

He turned to Monroe. "It is my understanding, Mr. Simmons, that you recommended that feller and we agreed. It's not a company we've used before and it isn't one we are likely to use again. I surely don't like us being flummoxed."

Flummoxed?

Lawyer James had his own version of the lexicon. I liked his better than any lawyerspeak I'd ever encountered. Monroe was embarrassed. Talk about flummoxed!

"Yes, sir, he's k-k-kin: my second cousin Molly's boy. Thought he'd be jus' fine."

"Just." Eunice was still in the game.

"Well, cousins are good for some things, I reckon. Huntin'," he said, looking at King Bagel and offering him another biscuit. "But personally, I like doing business with strangers. Makes fussing at 'em a whole lot easier." Attorney James clearly was not all chocolate, extended lunches, and gravy stains.

"Well, now, if we're all agreed, let's get down to the finish line. Mr. Omans, do you folks have the cashier's check for the correct purchase amount? I see you do. And Mr. Simmons, I guess you've got your share of the firm's fees and the closing costs?"

"Yes sir."

"Well, except for the formalities, dottin' the i's and crossin' the t's I think we're just about through here and…"

The intercom buzzer interrupted us just before the exchange of monies. I assumed the interruption must be about something very important to break in like that. Even in this unusual legal office, money changing hands with the lawyer's poised in the middle readied to pluck his share from both ends had to be the name of the game—right?

"Yes, honey," he said. "That's right. You surely have heard right. Well, certainly you can. No time like the present. You come right on in here now. And bring along Lewis."

Whatever the problem, it looked as if it required the presence of two more lawyers, one of whom senior James addressed with familiar affection.

Through a door at the back of his office came two absolutely beautiful people straight out of central casting for Law and Order. And there was no mistaking the faces, although they were significantly thinner. These were two more Jameses, a son and daughter, and, unlike their father, they were dressed to the nines. And they were visibly agitated. Something very wrong must have just happened. Now what?

The daughter—it wasn't honey, it was Honey—was the first to speak.

"Oh my! I've seen a few beautiful pointers, Daddy, but I swear this sweetheart takes the pie. He's as solid a pup as I've ever seen, as good as Jewel or Penelope. When I heard you had one in your office I just couldn't wait another minute to see him."

She was bent over Bagel and now, though he was still on his back, he was activated, wagging his lower torso back and forth and banging the side of the senior James' desk, beating it like tympani and reveling in her tummy scratches. His loss of composure was more embarrassing than his ignoring us.

"Oh my. I'll bet you can hunt, sweetheart!"

He nuzzled his nose right into her grey-tweed designer crotch. I was chagrined. She seemed not to be at all. Her brother, Lewis, was in line behind her, waiting his turn, and as effusive in his affections as she. "Well now, just look at you! Look at you!" We were in the midst of a love-in.

Before you could say "impossible," the office was filled with the other Jameses as well as three law clerks, the receptionist, and two architects from the office next door, all of them adoring our dog while the Simmonses and the Omans sat with checks poised in respective hands.

And to no one but us did this interlude seem the least bit strange. It most assuredly seemed proper to the German-Jewish-Newly-Mountain-ized Lord Bagel. In a Southern law office, during a storm, he'd found the Promised Land.

When the legal and architectural throng finally filed out, after asking us their remaining 22,000 questions: how we got him? how we named him? who the breeders were? didn't he seem a might big for his breed?—no insult intended because he was beautifully proportioned and colored. Did we know that these mountains were filled with coyotes and bobcats so that we must be extra careful about where we let him run? Would we ever consider breeding him?

In their jubilation they'd somehow missed that he was neutered, and we weren't going to volunteer the information at this point. Attorney James finished the proceedings in record time, assuring us that the platting error was already under correction and would be filed with the County Clerk by the end of the week, with copies sent directly to us in Winter Park, Florida.

After signatures and the exchange of documents, all six of us—Monroe, Eunice, Jan, I, and Bagel, at Attorney James' heels—were out the door.

We said our goodbyes. Monroe and Eunice were off to the bank and then Atlanta to begin construction of their new home. We three were heading back to Florida to ready ourselves for the move, and Attorney James, I suspected, was bound for an early dinner and a long walk in a real woods to tell his precious Penelope and Jewel about a new friend.

Bagel.

Ol' Man on a Mountain

WHAT HERB GARDENS?

DRIVING BACK TO ORLANDO AFTER THE closing we talked about our upcoming trip to Italy. We had been imagining this trip for years. In two weeks we'd be walking the hills and vineyards of Tuscany. We'd be sampling olive oils, visiting villages with exotic names—Testrofina, Andoxia. Now, though, we had our own land waiting to be plowed; our own seeds waiting to be purchased and planted. To tell the truth, my heart was not in Italy. It was in these mountains. But I wasn't about to tell Jan.

"Stu, I've got to tell you something. You know how much I've wanted to see Tuscany. I still do. But now my heart is all over that land... it's so beautiful. I don't want to wait a day longer than it will take for us to get back up there and start the fun of making a mountain home. I know it must be disappointing for you to hear this. I'll still go if you feel you still want to. How do you feel? Tell me, so we can be together on this."

Mind link. Her words, my thoughts. We decided to forgo Italy and go where our hearts led.

Two weeks later, after looting our Florida house and piling our car to the ceiling with the stuff Jan required, we arrived to take stewardship of our new home. We arrived in time to say goodbye to Monroe and Eunice and their three sons, who were just about finished with all their own loading. Many tables and chairs, rugs, tools, suitcases crammed with clothes, even what looked like a large bundle of old burlap feedbags—thirty-plus years' worth—filled a large U-haul and a long-bed pickup. And, Monroe complained, this was the fourth trip they'd made to and from Atlanta.

We had arrived just at the tail end of a smoldering-but-repressed conversation about whether they should take the old church pew that sat on the front porch. Monroe wanted it, arguing that it was worth good money and should not be left behind. The oldest two sons were exhausted enough by this time to resist. From the looks of her, Eunice was tired enough to restrain herself from controlling the discussion. They'd been packing for three solid days. And despite her inability to move anything physically, I was sure she remained the major order giver when she could summon the energy. It wasn't worth the effort to load, the boys said. "It's too danged heavy. We ain't moving it." There were a few disgusted glares from dad, but the dispute was over.

At the very least, I expected muffled sobs or a grudging reluctance at their parting, but there was little of that. These were tough people, and they did what they had to do. The difficulty of leaving was softened, I think, because Monroe had retained about 100 acres up the mountain behind us where he was already planning to keep a double-wide trailer as a family retreat so they could visit on long weekends. And they all knew, as we'd repeatedly told them, that they were welcome to visit us any time they wanted and without an invitation.

Another possible explanation for the lack of demonstrable sadness at leaving, at least from the boys' point of view, was probably a few not-so-rapturous memories about growing up here. One son had told me that ever since he could remember they'd worked up here like mules, especially in the summer, year in and year out. "I can't ever remember working so hard, and Stu, believe you me, I've worked at plenty of hard jobs."

"So long to slavery," was the subdued whispery growl I heard from another son after he'd helped to triumph in the pew battle by sitting on the front steps and refusing to move "one more single danged muscle."

"Watch that mouth of yours, boy, and shet up" was Eunice's response. Her body may have grown weak, but her will wasn't and her hearing was acute.

"Boy"? He had to be thirty. No matter. He "shet" up.

With the last carton loaded, Monroe gently lifted Eunice into a second pickup's front seat; then before climbing in himself, Monroe turned to me. He had something in his hand. "Found this here up on the mountain yesterday when I was walking on a little break; thought Jan might like t' have it. Know what it is?"

Here was the second of many mountain quizzes.

"Well, it's a little too big for a shot glass; too small for drinking."

"No sir, Stu, you sure wouldn't want t' be drinkin' out of here. It's a spit cup."

"A what?"

"Spit cup, spit jar, for snuff an' tobacco. Real ol' one too. Coulda been my granddaddy's from the look of it, but she's still in perfect condition. Not a crack in her."

He handed it to me. "Don't be afraid of it. Won't bite you. Well, good luck—and remember, if y' need anything, call on Noah. He's a real, real good boy."

With that, he got into the driver's seat and they were on their way back to Atlanta, where he and his boys had already framed out the new house.

Almost.

"Oh yeah and remember that ol' plow down there at the side of the road next t' the fence is mine. Was Daddy's. We'll come get it next time we're up." He'd lost on the pew, but the plow was not negotiable.

They waved. Jan went to Eunice's window for a last hug. And the caravan was gone.

Finally, we were there alone and ecstatic again, roaming together from black sponge pattern walls to black, red, and purple sponge pattern walls, shaking our heads, clucking our urban tongues, and trying to figure out where to start. Where would we find painters brave and skilled enough?

Then we were outside, walking our property again, front to back, side to side, ogling our fruit trees, our black walnuts, our blueberry bushes, the thick thorny blackberry brambles surrounding our slanted basketball court-wide lawn that the family had managed to carve out, plant, and cultivate over so many years.

After an hour of wandering, imagining our harvest, I left Jan in the kitchen examining the cabinetry as I climbed up behind the house to the little outbuilding that we considered our special bonus. From a distance, we'd already decided that with only a little work we could convert it to a double studio, me up above, Jan below. Now was the first time I'd really looked at it since the house, all by itself, had dominated our attentions. Our bonus looked solid as a rock and was built of the same weathered oak as the framing of the main house, situated downhill about seventy yards away.

"Stu! Stu!"

The future Omans' studios were far enough away so that to be heard Jan really had to turn up the volume, but my quiet girl (when we were first going together my parents asked me if there was something wrong with her voice since she rarely spoke, and when she did it was in a whisper), after living with me for so many years, had no problem with that. She'd learned to yell. This was a category-four yodel, indicating a crucial discovery of some sort.

We'd already created house fantasies. Sure the house was relatively new, but it was also on land that had been settled from before the Civil War. Had she discovered some old secret passage? That was improbable. But she could perhaps have found a farm antique left behind in the attic? Hand-made quilts in the root cellar were a long-shot possibility. Could there be Confederate coins buried in the overgrown garden she'd uncovered at the edge of the woods? Given Monroe's thoroughness, it was not likely. But who knew. My expectations made just about anything possible.

When I got up there, hoping she would greet me with sooty hands full of treasure, I found her instead standing in the kitchen, nose to nose with the ten-foot-long oak cabinet that dropped from the ceiling to within a foot or so of the kitchen counter. I found not a museum curator but my determined and now vocal Mohammed Ali toeing it with a wooden Joe Foreman. I'd admired that cabinet the first time we'd entered the house. Built of two inch oak, it was fabulous and gave us a real storage space. And unfortunately for Monroe, it, like the fireplace insert, was unmovable.

"I know, I know," she cooed in a new voice, reading my mind, while at the same time running her hands along my perfect and imposing oak cabinet. "You love it. But it makes no sense at all." Within the coo was a seasoned command disguised as an innocent plea. "We don't need it for anything we have, and it blocks off all our air and any view between the rooms. It stifles. It makes everything dark. Look," she said to demonstrate, sticking her head between the counter and the cabinet bottom, "you have to scrunch down to speak with someone on the other side. It's smothering. They must have had too much wood left over."

"Remove that gorgeous cabinet," I tried, "and we'll have to refinish the ceiling and the wall."

"And just look at this," unwinding, she was moving now with the speed and energy of the wonder woman I knew, loved, and occasionally feared. My father used to say that Jan was like my bubbe (grandma), so fast she'd bump into herself coming around a corner if she didn't watch out. She was past the cabinet, redrawing and replacing the three windows in the dining area and living room by magically tracing her arms through the air. "Get rid of that cabinet and replace these with large picture windows that open and we get outside light in both the kitchen and living room.. Light. Do you hear me?" She was doing a darn good imitation of Gene Wilder's Dr. Frankenstein. The "life force" transformed with a few simple alterations, and we would be the possessors of a renewing "light" force.

"And this way you'll have a view of your herb gardens."

"What herb gardens?"

"The ones we're going to plant as soon as the windows are replaced."

My knee jerk response was a Capital N, followed by an even larger Capital O.

Echoing my father's child-of-the-Depression mentality, which, by the way, I have always denied having, I was already silently adding up the costs and hidden costs in her small remodeling job. And I was perspiring.

Jan knew the signs of a genuine freak-out when she saw it. "Get hold of yourself, boy. Get a grip. Get a life." She had long known me for the scared neurotic I could become when I thought I was threatened with failure or poverty. I am thankful that she's got the opposite intelligence. "Things work out" is her abiding belief. The morning of my Ph.D. written exams, for example, I was so nervous I drove the three miles to school, more on than off the sidewalks and arrived panic-stricken, begging my advisor to let me off the hook. I was sure I would fail. I was sure I was about to ruin my life. My kids' lives.

My bizarre driving pattern was predictable, since I'd spent most of the previous night traveling from bed to bed, clutching my two little boys and literally praying that I would not fail them. Finally, at three in the morning with the help of a tranquilizer, I was able to fall asleep. So, by the time I arrived at my mentor's office, I was a reasonable facsimile of Woody

Allen on his worst night. He calmed me by making me a cup of tea and promising that if I took the first morning exams and felt I'd done badly, he would cancel the rest. That's the way he wheedled me through for three days. Each morning, the exam got easier until the last question, for which I had no answer at all. I wrote a promise in the margins—if the examiners passed me I swore I would crack new books and learn the answer. After all, how could anyone survive without knowing the ABCs of 19th-century German Romantic criticism of Shakespeare! Later, the examiners told me that they'd had a good laugh at that final desperate answer. I passed.

In contrast and ironically, the calm guy who took the exams alongside me flunked three-quarters of them and had to redo them six months later. If there's a lesson in all this, aside from that fear is a great motivator while at the same time a trait some people like me need to work on their whole lives, it's how debilitating it can be.

So back in the kitchen as I was freaking out, Jan continued, "What would Bubbe Choma say? 'Live it up, kids.' That's what." That did it. She had me stopped before I really dove off into the deep end. Invoke Bubbe in Jan's voice, and I could return to sanity. I got hold of myself. From now on, I resolved, I would not give in to my fears of bankruptcy or old-age penury. How could I even think about trying to dampen this enthusiasm and really first-rate Wilder/Transylvanian accent? Hell, how much could a few more cosmetic changes really cost? And she was always right when it came to sensible, financial decisions, wasn't she?

When Jan and I were first married and she wanted to replace the old rusty knobs on our kitchen cabinets with glass knobs that cost $1.50 each and I went bonkers, terrified of insolvency, wasn't she right in the end? And anyway, I rationalized, even if these remodels ended up costing a few more bucks than my in-head calculations had registered, the big expenses were already over—weren't they?—thanks to my shrewd bargaining, Monroe and Eunice's eagerness to sell, and the efficiency of Attorney James?

"Okay, so long as we don't go, pardon the expression, hog wild, and can get it all done at a fair price." Bubbe notwithstanding, I reminded her that we'd agreed to live with the place "as is except for the paint job," for a couple of years.

"Agreed. Agreed. A few splashes of paint here and there and a little minor carpentry, and we're ready to move in." A reassuring motherly kiss plus a semi-sexual hug are worth a thousand words and even a few dollars to a guy my age.

And so, we kissed, spat into our palms, a joke we've been doing for a long time to seal important decisions, and shook on it. "Agreed." A few essential changes would satisfy us both. And we could rip out the cabinet ourselves in just a couple of hours, saving labor costs.

GOOD FAITH HOUSE PAINTING

Now ALL WE NEEDED WAS A reliable painting and plastering connection. We found one that afternoon, posted on the bulletin board at the general store.

GOOD FAITH HOUSE PAINTING

QUALITY WORK

REASONABLE, HOURLY PRICES

25 YEARS EXPERIENCE

CHURCH REFERENCES

Shelly Sue, the store's owner, said she knew this man and his wife and that they were good people. We called and agreed to meet in four days at our house, and if all seemed right we'd have them paint. If they couldn't replace the windows, they said they knew someone who could. They'd come up right after church on Wednesday evening.

Together, Jan and I ripped out the cabinet. It took us a full day and left deep scars in the wall and ceiling and not a few oak splinters in our fingers. When the brothers built this place, they built it to last. Jan talked about how lovely the room looked without the cabinet to clutter the space, but all I could think about was how scarred the walls and ceiling were now that the cabinet was gone. I also worried about how I'd get rid of the ten-foot monster that was in the living room, looking much larger now that it was unattached. Neither of us slept well that night.

Early that Wednesday morning, after we had once again walked through the house, both of us trying to avert our eyes from our handiwork and surveying the rooms that absolutely needed painting (and agreeing that with the exception of two bathrooms the entire house was in need of more than a splash of paint), I sneaked away, leaving her imagining colors. I would find peace by walking up to the double-studio outbuilding. Here was my escape from recalculating over and over the potential cost of gallons of "good" paint and an unknown labor force. I had read Jan's expression. Her dream only began with a splash of paint.

Escape? Not as it turned out. An unpleasant surprise awaited me when I reached the outbuilding. The studio renovation was not going to be a case of plastering scars or even turning stables into studios; rather, it was looking like a case of catastrophe to questionable rehabilitation. Once inside, I was looking at an above-ground dungeon. To be kind, the place was a sty, every corner strewn with long-dead bees and shriveled wasps and other unidentifiable dead things. There were also very alive spiders, cans, shards of broken glass—origins unknown—shredded comic-book covers, McDonalds wrappers, and strangely bespattered walls punctuated by suspicious looking cannonade-like holes. The worst of all was a 20' x 20' piece of filthy wall-to-wall leftover shag carpet crusted through with what appeared to be old half-eaten food. Pry loose a corner, raise a lethal cloud.

Outside behind the building, up close, the scene was as devastating. For some reason—and for a long time—this little piece of lawn had been used as a garbage dump. Here, half buried, lay rusted somethings, lots and lots of them, poking their tetanus-crusted heads out of the earth, rain-soaked newspapers that had become amorphous guck, and big scraps of partially buried plastic sheeting coated with something else that was still brown and sticky. The demonic pinnacle of this mess was countless—and I mean countless—empty chewing-tobacco tins crushed flat as frisbees. And it looked as if all this crap was not merely a top skin or even a pile, but rather the top layer of a deep excavation, lying just outside our "studio" doorstep and stretching for at least fifteen feet to the edge of the woods.

How could I possibly have missed seeing this catastrophe not even ten feet to the side of the path we had used to climb the mountain on our first idyllic walk? Even Wordsworth wouldn't have been able to convert this place. Clearly, this was one of the property's features Monroe, that sly dog, had overlooked during our tour. I am sure that seeing it wouldn't have deterred us anyway. We were too far gone. But I am equally sure I would have asked them to help clean it up before leaving.

On the other hand, I thought, looking down the hill toward the main house, Wonder Woman might now be pleased. Here was old-timey mountain decay. Here lived challenge. Here was the sort of disheveled sporting event she craved. Here was "dilapidated" at its grungiest. It would take weeks to clear. It would take multiple trips to the dump, a face mask, and a firm resolve to throw out or, better, burn all the clothing used during the attempted rescue. Here was a project she could sink her teeth into!

Mrs. Clean meet Mr. Shmutz: rough translation: Mr. Absolute Filth.

"Holy Shit! Could anyone believe this? People do this kind of thing and aren't ashamed of themselves?"

Was I losing my grip? I was standing here, atop a mountain garbage heap, talking to myself.

"A real slob ain't he?"

And now I was hearing answers, in dialectal Appalachianese, no less. Time to head for the hills. Hold on, I was already deep in the hills. I was trapped here with my voices and not just the usual ones.

"I said, he sure is a slob, and that's a fact. Jacky Lee, my cousin: he's the one done all this. You musta seed him when they was leaving. Sort of a big fat boy."

This was no neurotic inner voice. Sitting on what looked like a green, box shaped, sort of four-wheeled squat motorcycle, a handwritten license plate "Noah's Ranger" on its bumper, a rifle carrier strapped to its side, the entire affair covered over with a yellow metal roof, was a grinning young man in work clothes, staring at me through the bluest, most friendly eyes I think I have ever seen.

"Hi," he said and stuck out his hand. "I'm Noah," as if this was as complete an explanation as anyone might need.

"This here place was Jacky Lee's poolroom. Had a table in here and everything. A stove, too. We use to eat up here, too. And he kept all his NASCAR stuff too. You wouldn't believe how much stuff he had. All them models. About all he'd do seemed like was collect NASCAR an' play pool. NASCAR an' pool. He sure didn't like to work much. Lazy. I had t' do all the work. He never lifted a single finger."

He pointed at one of the holes.

"And he sure could get riled when he missed a easy shot. Like t' throw one of them balls plumb through the wall. Couldn't get too mad at him though after he had that accident, though, poor feller."

I shook his offered hand. "I'm Stu."

"It's a good thing he didn't get angry at you." Noah shook his head smiling, "Well, that's a fact."

For his square stature and the strength of his grip, Noah's hand was surprisingly small although thick and powerful. My own fingers are long and tapered, girlish or artistic, depending on the kindness of your point of view. I noticed I could wrap my entire hand around his with no trouble. I felt sure his could crush mine with even less. His physique matched those peculiar mitts. I remember thinking later that when we first met that day he reminded me of a full bag of cement with the impish smile of an elf. We were exact opposites, Mutt and Jeff in a mountain meet. He looked as if his torso had been chopped off when he was a child; mine as if it had been rubberized and stretched too long in adolescence.

"I heard you was moving in today so I come on up to meet y'all. See did you need anything." He just sat there looking at me. But it did not feel as if he was really wanting or needing a reply. I had no sense that he was uncomfortable by the silence, just that he was there. More, I had the sense that he was waiting, holding back a joke or a trick or a little surprise, or to have me or anyone else who might happen along deliver one.

"Mama and Daddy told me t' wait a while," he smiled. "But I guess I was a might too excited t' meet y'all. Mama's gonna be fussing at me." His voice rose in an upward pitch.

Another pause. I still wasn't much help. So, my newfound friend filled the gap again. "You got a wife?"

The light dawned. "Noah. Monroe's nephew! Your uncle told us about you. He was very complimentary. Said you'd be up here any time. Told us you might even be persuaded to help around the place."

"I sure don't need no persuading. Happy t' do it, and you don't have to pay me nothing neither, but what you want to. Mowing and weed-eatin' is what you're gonna want most. Takes a long time t' do this place. Daddy's got our own riding mower and I can use it, least ways till you get one for your own self."

"Noah, we're gonna need all the help we can get. Thank you. And thanks for coming up so soon. It must be hard having strangers up here after your uncle and aunt and cousins."

He looked at me with a candor I'd seen before only in little children. And now that elfish twinkle had vanished, replaced by downturned lips. "That woman!" His voice dropped. "I don' like her. She can be downright mean. I surely don't like mean people."

No further explanation. No qualifications. No excuses. He knew I would know whom he meant.

"I ain't been up here in a long while. And neither has Daddy much. He says it don't make sense to go where you ain't wanted."

This was turning out to be the most candid introductory conversation I'd ever had.

"Looks like the grass needs getting to now."

"If you say so, Noah. You're the expert."

"You got gas?"

I let that one go. Already in a few minutes I was learning to anticipate the unexpected question from Noah—and prescience from him. How could he know my entire family was prone to flatulence when upset and that this cesspool was upsetting me. But too personal is too personal, right?

Then the more likely explanation intruded. "Oh, you mean gasoline for the mower? Unless your uncle left some, I don't." He smiled what Jan and I came to call "that Noah smile."

"'I reckon you don't then. I don't reckon he left much anything he could tote. I see that old lawnmower under the overhang's still there. Don't reckon that old thing's worked in ten years. If'n I was you, I'd get rid of it. Can't be fixed... we all tried a hundred times. Even Mark tried." This was apparently the ultimate test. If the person named Mark could not do it, it was not doable.

"You can get you some at Shelly Sue's or down at the Bridgewater. I got an old gas can you can use till you got your own. Start just as soon as you get some. Don't wanna be too long though. Taller it grows, the harder it is. And they're a-giving rain for later on. Can't mow if it's wet. Never right though, they aren't. Them fellers don't know much about nothin'." He nodded, agreeing with himself. "Tell you what: I'll go down to the shed and get the can now. I think I know just where it is." He started the Ranger, and I noticed there had been an attempt at printing his name on the side.

"Hold on, Noah. We haven't talked about how much you want to be paid to do the work."

"Well, like I said, you don't have t' pay me nothing, but people usually give me six dollar an hour, more for setting baccy. But like I said, you can pay me less if'n you want."

"How about eight dollars?"

He grinned that grin. 'Well, that's more, ain't it? So that'll be just fine. I'll do you a good job, too. I'll tell Daddy I'm mowin' for you. He'll be real happy 'bout that. And he'll be up here real soon I reckon. Mama will be too, after Daddy. You got a wife?"

Noah was a guy who didn't give up until he got an answer.

"Yes, her name is Jan."

"Jane?"

"Jan."

"I don't believe I ever have heard that name before. It's pretty ain't it? She about?"

"Half an hour ago she was in the house, but I'll bet she's gone off some-where now. When you get back I'll try and make sure she's here to meet you. I know she'll like that. And Noah, thanks again for coming up. I feel like I just made a new friend."

"See you in just a little while. I think I know just where I put that ol' gas can. Be back in just a little while."

He backed a few feet down the slope, did an expert three-point turn, and started down the hill. I noticed that someone had started to print his name on the other side too. After ten feet or so, he slowed to a stop and looked back.

"See ya, friend!" he waved. And down the hill, onto our road, and homeward he went.

True to his word, Noah came back with the gas can. Not in a little while though. Actually, he didn't return for about four hours. When he came, it was from the opposite direction on a shortcut road that connected his Dad's property to his other uncle's that, in turn, connected to ours. This time he was on his Dad's riding mower, which he was riding slowly and more carefully.

I'll admit here that before he returned I was first a little worried and then, when I saw him safe, more than a little annoyed. After our conversation, I'd dutifully jumped in the van and headed for the general store to buy our own five-gallon gas can. Buying it was simple. Trying to figure out how to get the top off and fill it while being watched by some of the locals was harder.

"Say, sonny, just give that there lip a hard pull and she'll come off. Then put the gas hose in the hole and turn her on." This was advice from a grizzled, ancient farmer sitting out front with several other men. I'd often see them all in the same spot later, no matter how early or late I'd arrive. As summer passed we got to be sort of buddies, and my original "helper" always had the same exact question for me. "Well, sonny, have y' got the hang of it yet?" I'd nod and ask how he was doing and always received the same answer, no matter how tired he seemed. "Looks like I'm makin' it, thank the good Lord."

Mission accomplished, a mere iota of pride still intact, I came home with a partly filled gas can and waited for Noah. And waited. And waited, thinking that an accident might have befallen him on the short piece of two-lane highway that connected our properties. Or perhaps he'd come up without his parents' knowledge, and they might be angry that I hadn't called them. Truth was, I would be angry at myself for not being more cautious, since even on first meeting he'd seemed an innocent and at the same time also immediately important to me. I already really liked this new person in my life and already felt some responsibility for him.

Well, at last he was back: here he was and he was obviously fine. No cuts, bruises, or other signs of accident. Later in the year I learned on numerous occasions that waiting for people who said they'd be "right back" was a habit you needed to get used to in these mountains: "right back" could mean a few hours or even a few days here. If something more important came up, they simply made a decision to take care of it first, trusting you'd know they'd return when they could.

Noah had his gas can aboard when he returned and was not only surprised when he saw mine but disturbed that I'd bought one.

"What're you totin' there? A can? Did y' buy it? You surely didn't need to go a-buying you a brand-new one. That's too expensive. You must be rich, doin' stuff like that. From Florida—that explains it."

Labels, even here? From Noah? I do not recall anyone before this ever accusing me of being rich as if it were a sin. But when you think of it, the accusation makes sense. I have heard locals call Sunshine Staters "The Floridiots" as if they were a rock group, responding to visitors who got upset and then rude when their expectations of service or menus were not met.

"This here's plenty good." He was holding up a rusty old can that once had been a color, probably red, "Works fine." He wasn't accusing. And he was not labeling. He was just saying that spending without need was silly and wasteful. You had to be too rich to do that.

"I suppose you'd better get started. The sun's already going down." I couldn't resist. "I thought you were coming back right away and that we'd get started earlier."

This was the first time I was to see hurt in his eyes. "Late, ain't I? Don't worry. I'll work till after dark if need be. Daddy's got lights. And, if I don' finish, I'll be back tomorra'. It's better for me not to work in the hot sun. You know, with my sugar and all. Looked all over but couldn't find that danged can, so brung this one instead. And Daddy was in town at the doctor again; Mama went with him this time and by the time they come back, it was real hot. Figured it was best t' wait. Hope you got some diet soda in the frigerator, case my sugar gets low."

"Your father's not feeling well?"

He shook his head.

"I hope that whatever he has, he gets over it soon." Now, I wished I'd kept my mouth shut about his late return.

"Daddy's knee's just a-killin' him. Terrible pain. Sometimes it runs plumb all the way down his leg, and most nights he can't sleep. Just lies there on the couch watching television. He's takin' a lot of pain pills too. He says they don't do him no good though except t' make him sleepy or sick to his stomach. I'm real worried about him. Mama thinks he might have t' have surgery again."

He thought for a moment. "I don't know what would happen t' me and Mama if something was t' happen t' Daddy. As much as I worry about him, I know he worries more about me." His eyes teared over.

He lifted his tee shirt. Next to his sheathed pocket knife, Noah wore a rectangular device attached to his belt. From it ran a thin transparent plastic tube connected to a shunt that seemed to go through a round rubber patch and directly into his stomach.

"I got this here computer and I can give myself a shot if I need it, but sometimes I need t' drink a Coke or something sugary real fast. Need t' keep it with me right here on the Ranger, on the mower too. Always have one with me on the Ranger, and a candy bar or a small cake too. Unless sometimes I forget. Sometimes I can forget. One time I fell right off a the Ranger when my sugar got low." He pointed to a nasty scar on his forehead.

And I was annoyed at him for being late?

I said I'd check to see if we had the right supplies. Looking at the taped-over incision in his stomach, I was so shocked I couldn't speak. This was a very sick young man. Then, it struck me as extraordinary that a person I hardly knew would so openly talk with me about his familial worries as well as such a devastating personal detail. His revelation struck me, too, as the most profound and admirable kind of simplicity. An elf he might be, but he was an elf with a beautiful, compassionate heart.

"Hey, and Noah, if we don't have what you need, I'll remind Jan that we have to get it just as soon as we go shopping."

"Diet and regular Coke and some cakes too, small ones. Y' know I got t' watch my carbs. I surely do thank you. That'll be a big help. I really like Moon Pies best, if you please."

"Wait a minute, aren't those awfully sweet?"

"Well, yeah, but I can eat just a little bite."

"You've got them."

"I'm obliged. Reckon I'll start down at the gate an' work my way up along the road. When I finish that, I'll start down in Monroe's tater field. Then I can get the garden and the big field, side of the road." He spoke as if I knew the plan would work and as if I knew it was as solid as his mountains. "Come around and do behind the house. I'll cut you the paths last. Gonna take a while, but don't you worry none; we'll get 'er done. Then if'n I got enough energy left I'll start in a-weed-eatin'. Now that's a job I really hate. I can teach you how t' do that real easy." He hated it, but I would like it?

Noah worked for four hours, stopping only to drink, refill the gas tank, and check the engine oil, telling me several times, as if to remind himself as much as to inform me, that the one thing you don't ever want to do is let the oil get too low.

"Always be sure about the oil if I ain't here, or else you can ruin the engine, burn 'er right out. And never mix the oil (he pronounced it 'all') with the gas. That's for the weed eater and the chain saw."

Shortly after first dark, he came to the door to tell me that the mower was in the garage, washed, and he was stopping to go home for supper and that he would be back the following day to finish. He was covered head to toe in grass clippings, dirt, and sweat.

"I'm right tired," he said, lingering in the doorway in one of those wonderful pauses I was already coming to expect.

"Would you like a diet drink?"

"Don't believe I do right now. Thank you, kindly. I'm just about fixin t' go home and have my supper." He still hadn't budged.

Jan came to the door. "You must be Noah."

"I am." That smile. "And you must be… his wife."

She took his hand and invited him into the living room, mess that he was, even after she'd spent most of the day cleaning. I was less forthcoming. I mean he was filthy. I tried to warn Jan with a look, but she scowled me off. With Jan an invitation is never an empty affectation and never given lightly. Hers is always a genuine welcome, and on this occasion she was welcoming this young man into our home, and she did not care about how many dead bugs or how much cut flora he was wearing.

I tried again. "Noah's been working all afternoon. He's hot and sweaty. I think he just wants a shower, supper, and bed."

"Nonsense. Noah, I've been waiting all day to meet you."

He grinned at her sweet acceptance. I think he recognized in her as honest a soul as his own. I've read somewhere that there are natural moral souls who refuse to understand anything but goodness. They are without guile, without masks. Loved, they love; harmed, they are wounded but forgiving.

"Stu told me about your visit and how you kindly offered to help us up here. And from the looks of you, you've been doing just that and more. Surely, you can come in and visit for a little while."

"I'm awful dirty though."

"Not so dirty as me. Look, I'm covered with white paint. If it will make you feel better, you can brush yourself off on the tile there in the kitchen. Stu'll sweep it up later." If you're stingy in my wife's house, you get a job. "You come in and have something cold to drink and don't worry about a little grass. They tell me that chlorophyll's good for everything."

Noah came in, but not before he'd carefully unlaced his work boots and left them outside. He brushed himself clean as best he could there on the porch. Still, when he came in, he refused to sit on the sofa or anywhere else even after Jan beckoned him to, protesting that he would make a real mess of everything, finally accepting a glass of water as all he'd take on this first visit.

He looked around as if seeing the room for the first time, although he must have been up here countless times over the years. "Place looks mighty nice. Clean. Mama and Melanie was up here to look around after Monroe an' them left and said that they never did see such dirt, 'specially in the pantry. Said it was gonna take y'all a year t' clean it and that was a shame. Mama says it is dis-re-spect-ful to leave a house like that, but that was the way she was."

"She?"

I knew what was coming. "That woman!" he groaned. Whatever offences Eunice had committed in the past, they were big, still fresh and raw in this branch of the family. And Noah mirrored them.

Jan looked at me for clarification. What was going on here? I shrugged.

"It's not so bad, Noah." This was Jan being gracious after telling me not an hour ago that we needed a professional cleaning service armed with blowtorches, even before we needed a painter.

"You planning t' paint the inside?"

"As soon as we can. We'd do it ourselves if we had the time, but Stu's got to get back in a week or so to finish some teaching."

"You're a teacher?" The smile vanished.

"So we're going to hire a husband and wife who do painting around here. Maybe you know them. Mr. and Mrs. Elton Jones?"

Noah paused. "He's a good painter. And she helps him. Trouble is, she sure likes to talk and get into your business. If'n it was me, I wouldn't leave nothing around you didn't want them t' see. An' they got the reputation of being real, real, real, real slow. I hear tell that they charge by the hour, but don't never tell how many hours it's gonna take and I hear tell it takes a lot longer'n that."

"The lady down at the store says they're good honest people."

"I ain't saying they ain't, but all a them belong to the same church, and they're good friends too."

Was this a discreet country warning? "So, Noah, maybe it's not such a good idea to hire them?"

"I ain't saying that, exactly."

"You know lots of people around here, and your Mom and Dad must know practically everybody."

The Noah pause.

"Right?"

"I reckon." He looked Jan square in the eye. "You know, Mama could do it for you. She's a good painter. So's Melanie. I bet if'n you asked them, they'd do it and they'd do you a good job, too. And I know they wouldn't charge you too much neither." This was not a sales pitch from a guy who, at the moment, looked like the local God of Vegetation. It was a warning to keep us out of trouble.

"Noah, could you do us a big favor? When you get home, would you ask your mother if she'd be interested in the job? It would make life a whole lot easier for us and when you come up to finish the grass tomorrow, maybe you could let us know?"

"I surely could do that. Yes, I surely can." The smile was back, bigger than ever.

Noah left our house that evening, covered in grass, freckled in dirt, but looking a little taller and, I think, feeling very proud. He was about to negotiate a business deal for his mother and someone named Melanie.

And he was relieved that in so doing he'd be keeping the new people out of harm's way.

When we went to bed, we were talking about our charming new friend, and we were pretty certain we had found our painters.

I snored the night away. Jan, it turns out, hardly slept at all. She woke me at 5:30 just before sunrise. She was sitting at our bedroom windows, sipping coffee and looking out the windows to the east.

"Stu, honey, you should have seen the moon last night. It was so full I couldn't take my eyes away. I cried and prayed. I've never seen anything like it and the stars were… a painting. Now look: the fog's in and the sun's just beginning to rise."

Even if you're still sleepy, when you're married to a life poet and she asks you to look, you look. The fog filled the valleys and blanketed the meadows. Far in the distance we could see only the slightest outline of our mountains. Then as the sun came up, we could see the ranges, first as lines then gradually in their full shapes as silhouettes.

And as the sun began to burn through and the fog thinned a little here and there, leaving thick small patches like lakes in scatterings of valleys, we could see colors emerging: hundreds of wild daisies punched out of the fog like buttons of pearl. Every apple tree wore light pink blossoms, and the white flowers of the dogwoods were just starting to appear.

Daylilies in our far garden took their bows of introduction in yellows, pinks, and even powder greens. Hollyhocks looking as if lit from their inside glowed in deep reds and pinks. Some colors we saw, some flowers we saw, we had no names for yet—just brightly beautiful gifts. We had seen much of the beauty of this place, but as the fog cleared that dawn, we were astonished at so much more. If there is a feeling of awe you can taste, we were in that awe. Was this what Wordsworth meant by the glories of childhood reborn, when he talked of the wonder he felt in Nature's presence? I'd read it. I'd taught it. But I don't think I was ever close to understanding it before.

"I'll need to start a flower journal."

Awe is not new to my wife, who is the universe's specialist. But this morning's scene wasn't describable even to a lady who specializes in magic visions. "I need to start a flower book. I need to start painting again."

If anything could make a skeptic believe in a great Design, this was it. Charlie was right. Only two kinds of people in this world: them that live here and them that want to.

Mountain flowers.

MUSH THE BUTTON

By 8:30 a.m. our private showing of the birth of the world was about over. Downstairs we continued to watch the day through the windows of Jan's soon-to-be-transformed kitchen.

Noah arrived at 9 to finish the mowing, all set to teach me the art of weed eating. He came, excited with good news. His mom and sister-in-law Melanie were happy to do the painting and would do it while we were back in Orlando during the following couple of weeks. His brother would repair the scars left by the cabinet. His dad planned on coming up soon to meet us.

Our new world was taking shape and getting populated.

Noah took another four hours to finish the lawn and paths and after carefully washing down the mower again and after proudly asking us how we liked the job he did, he was ready to show me how to "eat" weeds.

If you're not familiar with the device, as I was not, a weed-eater is basically a hollow steel shaft about five-feet long with a small gasoline motor attached at the operator's end, while at the business "eating" end is a metal cup that contains a spinning plastic cylinder. That cylinder contains a heavy-duty reel, much like the line-holding disk of a spinning fishing reel. This reel is loaded with a tough polyurethane or flexible steel line that protrudes through two separate holes in the outer cylinder and spins at sonic speed when the motor is activated. That line, spinning like crazy, so fast it is invisible, slices through weeds as it edges around lawns and trees and cuts just about any other plants in its way. The line breaks off as you work, but by simply tapping the cylinder on the ground, new line feeds through to replace the old, at least theoretically. The whole device weighs about six pounds. The engine runs on a mixture of gasoline and a tiny amount of two-cycle oil.

It all sounds simple, and in the hands of an expert like Noah it was. As he demonstrated, he was a master, waving his wand back and forth over our turf, cutting with precision and efficiency, extracting new line when it was needed. After a half hour, he invited me to give it a try.

Now understand, it is a supreme understatement to say that I am not mechanically inclined. My deficiency seems clearly to be genetic or a matter of mythic pride in most of the Jewish males of my generation—no, I suspect, rather in most Jewish American males of all generations. When faced with an automobile problem, for example, our typical response is to grapple around inside the car, where the steering wheel has its home, eventually to find the lever that releases the latch that mysteriously seals the hood to the rest of the car, to serrate our knuckles until we can "pop" the car hood, look inside, touch and even jiggle a few wires, shake the battery (the square box with plus and minus signs on its rounded stubs), shake our heads, close the car hood (trying to avoid harming our fingers again), and call the Auto Club. In fact, in my division of the human family, in my old Chicago neighborhood, to be mechanically competent was looked on as a severe learning disability. If you could fix something there must be something wrong with you.

But there would be none of that here. Noah passed the Grail to me.

I took hold and drew it back and forth over a virgin patch of weeds just as Noah had been doing. Absolutely nothing happened, not even the loud droning sound I'd already learned to associate with this remarkable machine.

Noah, standing just behind me, watching, saw the problem immediately. "You got t' start 'er first." Blank look from me. "Mush that there little rubber button a bunch a times, get the gas runnin'. Pull out the clutch. Then pull on that rope real hard an' press the trigger. If she don' start, jus' do it all again."

"The clutch?"

"Don' you know nothin'? I see I gotta start from the get-go with you." He'd picked up on my hesitancy. "Don't be a-scared. You'll see; it'll start. And once she's a-goin', don't get your hands anywhere near the line. It's real easy to cut off a finger before y' even know it."

That was reassuring.

After more than a few tries, with Noah showing me how to adjust the clutch, I actually got the thing running. I was exhilarated by my success. I was also winded from yanking on the starter rope. I swear one would have thought I'd just come up with a cure for Irritable Bowel Syndrome, so proud was I of my accomplishment. I began to think that being able to operate a contraption as efficient as this might not be a punishable crime.

I waved Noah off, and then I waved the weed-eater back and forth again, and this time it worked! Where before my silent efforts did nothing but make me feel foolish, now there was sound and almost nothing left in my wake.

True, my method was less than perfect. The swath I cut looked a lot like the first attempt of a drunken novitiate at the barber college, a clear patch here, a space of bald, gouged red dirt there, and then a stand of missed vegetal cowlicks; but I got it done, sort of. Where was it written that this city-raised boy couldn't cope with machines? Didn't some of my friends learn to be surgeons? Was doctorhood an exception to the unwritten rule of mechanical ineptitude?

Of course, Noah missed my ruminations and also my exhilaration. "Don't you worry, Stew" (he pronounced it Stee-yew). "You'll get the hang of it real soon. It don't really look that terrible." And then he said something I am sure his Dad must have said to him many times as he was growing up and which over the next months would become a shared semi-serious mantra between Noah and me. He placed a hand on my sweaty shoulder, stared straight into my eyes, and with Noahian kindness assured me. "Heck, Stew, if I c'n do it, you c'n." This time, Noah's open smile went straight from his face into my heart. This wasn't irony or a joke. He was perfectly sincere, and that sincerity got me then and never fails to move me to this day.

This was fun. I was on my way to an alien adventure. With so kind a tutor, in short order I would be astride a riding mower of my very own and then who knew what might be in my future? Maybe even a chain saw. My own Ranger? Dare I think it?

But first, I'd have to master the essentials, like starting the motor on the weed-eater "all by my big self."

Stu's work boots on the old church pew.

WHADAYA THINK
YOU'RE DOIN'?

ABOUT THREE THAT AFTERNOON, AS I was working in the heat with my
new spade and hoe to begin clearing ground for a garden, Noah's father,
the twin of introvert fame, he of the telephone-pole personality, arrived,
driving up our road on his own four-wheeler. His vehicle sported none of
the paraphernalia of Noah's. It was stripped down and rugged and ready
for work but obviously in the same family of vehicles and the third such
similar to Noah's we'd seen in three days. Did these things mate?

Like his son, he didn't seem at all reticent, "Hi, I'm Lorne, Noah's Daddy. You must be Mr. Omans. Thought I'd best give you folks a little time
to settle in before bothering you. Told Noah to do the same, but when that
boy gets something in his mind, it's awful hard to change it." He looked
me up and down. "But now I see it's a good thing I come up here when I
did. Might be some help getting you settled. Guess I better ask you right
off. Whadaya think you're doin'?"

If this guy is an introvert, I thought, I'm the mountain reincarnation
of Eli Whitney. "Why thank you, Mr. Simmons. I'm happy to meet you."

"Lorne."

"Lorne, then. We're doing pretty well so far. I'm getting ready to put
in our first garden. Not making much headway here though. I've done a
little digging in my time, but not in stuff like this. This soil is rock hard;
it's like trying to dig in dried concrete. To be truthful, I'm beginning to
get a little discouraged. Does anything really grow here?" Score one for
diplomacy. His family had been farming the land for over one-hundred-
and-fifty years!

He climbed off the four wheeler. "Hasn't rained for a while. That's why the earth's so hard. Heavy rain and then you'll be digging in the stickingest mud you ever did see instead of dry cement." He pointed at my little pile of tools that also included a square-head shovel and pickaxe. "Keep that up, you're gonna have yourself some mighty sore hands," he said, politely unprying my fingers from what felt like their permanent imbedded residence within the hoe handle and laying the hoe to the side of the tiny weed-free patch we had hoped would become the beginning of our garden.

"Thirty, forty years ago my Daddy and us boys used to break up the earth with oxen and after that with a hoe and pick, but up here of late even we got sort of modern. Called 'plows.' Fact is, you'll have a hard time getting in even a small garden that way. Might manage something by December though. Whyn't you rest a while?"

He turned me toward the house, as if he were helping an invalid. "I'll call my brother, Will" (he pronounced it "Wheel"). "He's got a place just down the hill. He's got a tractor—I think it's fixed—and a plow head and a disker. I'll bet he'll come on over after work and break up the soil for you. Then you can plant. It'll be a whole lot easier."

Seeing as how I already had ripped skin and some ugly blood blisters, this sounded like a reasonable suggestion, even if, as I suspected, I was about to be soaked some sizable amount of cash when brother Will entered the picture. But, by golly, we were here to put in a vegetable garden that would be nothing short of splendid, and the only way I could accomplish this would be to make many holes in the earth first. And so far, after several hours of backbreaking work, I'd managed a space of about four sad feet and a few sorry indentations, with nearly as many in my hands as in our land.

So I retreated into the house to rest my embarrassed and weary bones, to soak my hands, and to await the arrival of the third and youngest brother.

A guy who had to be Will arrived that evening around six o'clock, riding atop a large tractor, which he parked down our driveway. He didn't get off to come up to the house. He just sat there, so after waiting what seemed to be twenty minutes, I decided I'd better go out to meet him and see if something was wrong. He's probably calculating his fee, I thought. Oh well, live and let live.

"Will Simmons is my name, sir. Lorne's my brother. He asked if I might could help you break up this dirt. It surely ain't a problem, but…"

Other than looking very uncomfortable with his calculations, he appeared to be a polite, friendly sort of guy. Physically, he fit my idea of a mountain man. He was gaunt, heavily bearded, and pretty rough looking, the sort of guy that would look just perfect in an old western with a shotgun under his arm, masked and standing at the side of a stagecoach. He looked tired and ill at ease, shifting his weight from one leg to the other. I was uncomfortable too, thinking about what waited on the other side of that "but."

"Is there a problem?"

"Hate to tell you this as you're the new neighbor and all," he began, "but I'm afraid I got to charge you, what with the price of fuel these days. It'll take me a couple hours to get it good and broke so's you can work it." Under his coal black beard I thought I saw this desperado blush. "Would forty dollars be all right with you? About the best I can do and still come out close t' even."

Forty dollars? The national debt had suddenly shrunk to the size of a dinner for two at a modest Orlando restaurant. And the fee was accompanied by a gracious apology to boot. I surprised myself by telling Will that it sounded more than fair for so much time and work, suggesting that he raise the price some.

His color deepened. "Couldn't do that, even if I had a notion to. And I don't. We're neighbors now. We share a fence line down there and, the good Lord willing, we'll be sharing His bounties, too, for a good long while. Ain't right to take money off'n you no how. Forty dollars is a-plenty."

I started to protest. He held up his hand. "Now that we're settled, you best get out the way and let this old tractor earn her keep." With that, he drove into the field that was to become our first garden. Three-and-a-half hours later, we had plantable earth. Will had broken up over double the space I'd anticipated.

"That should do you. You can plant to your heart's content. Figured I'd do more than you'll probably use. Really should disk the whole thing too, so's it'll be even easier, but just don't have the time tonight. Could come back tomorrow though, after work, if it's not too much trouble. You know, you might want to borrow Lorne's hand tiller." He thought a second. "Ask Noah to show you how to get her going and how to work it. Heard you already got a handle on the weed whacker. Noah told me he's proud of you, that he learned you real good. That boy's a notion, ain't he?"

If that kid—why did I keep thinking of him as a kid; he was a grown man—thought I was a fast learner, he was far more generous with his praise than he should be, or that I, the yiddisha (Jewish) all-thumbs had any right to expect. Will and I shook hands and he left, and the next evening he returned with another attachment of sharp wheels hooked onto the tractor to break the earth into yet smaller pieces.

So we thought we were ready. The next few days were filled with the thrill of visiting local nurseries and buying seeds. Many seeds. Noah looked at the field and judged that it wouldn't hurt to do a little bit more. He arrived with his dad's cultivator, further prepping the land, breaking big earth clods into littler clods as I picked out rocks and set them to the side of the field.

It was exhausting, and it felt great.

As for the gaunt desperado, we learned later that summer that he worked the night shift in a local old folk's home, helping care for the residents, most of whom he'd known all his life. So when he had come over to plow and disk our land, he'd already put in a twelve-hour shift. Later that summer, when I asked him what he did there, he told me, "a little bit of everything—feeding them that can't feed themselves, cooking, running for meds when they need them, and when I have to, wiping butts. Proud of it all." So much for the desperado.

KIDS IN THE GARDEN

AND, OH, THE SEEDS! AN INUNDATION of seeds. A veritable sea of seeds. After all, we reasoned, Will prepared plenty of garden space; why not use it? Oh, and onion sets. Reds, whites, yellows. And cute little zucchini seeds and plants. Warned by friendly nursery proprietors that zucchini seeds, once they got growing and the plants got large, produced a big crop and that two or three plants would be enough for a large family, we disregarded this time-tested, prudent advice and bought twenty plants so we could fill up a couple of rows. After all, the seeds were tiny, so how big could the mature plants be?

And, ah, the tomatoes. Over ten varieties of tomatoes, with homely, exotic, and even romance-promising names: Red Zebras, Green Zebras, Caspian Pinks, Big Boys, Bigger Boys, Rainbows, Biggest Mamas, San Marzanos, Tomosas, and—my favorites—Sweet Baby Girls and Cupids. We'd plant those last two alternately and romantically close. And in our ecstasy, we bought five Gardeners Delights! We even bought some in dubious honor of the then–United States President: the Bush Steak. We agreed to plant that one in the last row, insulated on all sides by our garlic. There was even one variety with the sinister, piratical name of Black Krim. That baby scared us. It was the only variety we held back on lest we curse the whole crop. How could anyone with a little imagination resist these names and the visions they conjured.

And cukes, watermelon, cantaloupe; a full flat of kale, six varieties of corn; even a variety whose package promised it would come up purple! And beans and peas. Following our long time marital motto "If it is good to do, it is far better to overdo," we went berserk.

We were like kids in a garden.

Jan and I even invented a new country sport in our preparatory zeal; we called it poop walking. Equipped with brand new leather gloves, hiking boots, shovels, and extra large plastic bags, we traversed the mountain paths used by our neighbor's cattle herd, filling the bags with dried cow patties and subsequently dragging them down to the garden. In keeping with our madness, Jan created a brewed tea by mixing cow paddies and water in our wheelbarrow, adding crushed garlic cloves and letting it steep and effervesce. When the time came, we would lovingly ladle our savory brew over the earth around each new plant.

On our expeditions, she became the spotter, I the curator. "Here, look here," my adventurous partner would shout. "Look at the size of this beauty!" And I, as equal enthusiast, would virtually leap upon it as if protecting our claim from some hidden interloper out to steal our treasure. Down below in the garden, she ladled while I gently hoed around each new baby plant, all the sweaty while envisioning the vegetables that would appear soon and grow into giants by summer's end.

We spent entire days in this enterprise, laughing like kids at one another, particularly when her dried nuggets nudged by my suspicious toe, turned out to be less than dry. According to all local authorities we consulted, who looked at us with awe or pity or the fear that only staring into the eye of the mad provokes, only the driest of the dry is useful.

"If you're really gonna do that, check and make sure it's old stuff. Real old. Mix wet cow paddies into your garden and you will burn up anything you've planted."

We learned that toe-tested discrimination and practical knowledge were key to knowing which crap you could exploit and which you had to leave for future "walks." Come to think of it, that's good advice in a variety of endeavors.

Lorne, when he heard we were at this job (via Noah, who was now keeping a vigilant eye on all our increasingly odd activities), thoughtfully told us he just went to the local Lowe's and bought bags of 10-10-10 for $2.95. "Whole lot easier and works just as good. Not so sloppy neither."

We were not to be dissuaded by our neighbor's rationale or his newfangled ways. It was bad enough that we already had to resort to all kinds of machines to cut the grass, smite the weeds, and till the soil, but in the case of planting our garden we would honor our Sacred Oath of the Organic.

So gather, drag, and mix the poop we did. And after all our preparations, finally, plant. I laid a grid using stakes at either end of twenty-five-foot rows between which I strung taut twine. This, I figured, would give us a nice straight set of lines to follow. Then, at six-inch intervals I dug holes in the Will–double-softened, Noah–triple-prepared earth to appropriate depths as directed on our little packages.

And lovingly, I began to bury our darling seeds as I kneeled on my 62-year-old knees. The creaking and popping could probably be heard in the next county. As the sun rose higher, the day waxed hotter, and my knees and I arrived at the start of the fifth row, the twenty-five-foot rows had somehow magically elongated, and now my vegetal love, although not diminished, was dulled by the shooting pains in my groin, back, and bird-like, badly jointed legs.

Jan emerged from the house after getting our lunch ready and stood on the porch watching me. She was not happy with what she saw, mostly, I suppose, because I was having some difficulty rising after only a tiny portion of the garden was planted. As usual, she was fast to offer her help and I, still macho after all these years, was fast in refusing it.

"We agreed, we would divide the work," I said from my stoop. "You would take care inside and I outside. I'd do the garden. We'd harvest together. You'd supervise the house remodeling and cooking and canning. I am a man of my word. I am nothing if not fair."

"Forget fair," she said. "Too hard, O Pioneer. Need revised plan pronto, my aging warrior. Need save body for other tasks." Then she switched dialects.

"Saichel!" (smarts) she said, pointing at her temple. "Remember that documentary we watched on the settling of Israel? You know how they designed irrigation systems that pinpointed the exact spot to water the baby fruit trees so that not a drop of it was wasted? Well?"

I was missing the point. But to my relief, I was, with her help, now standing partially erect.

"Are we not descended from the same ancient, innovative gene pool? Why do all that bending?" She disappeared for a couple of precious, rehabilitative minutes into our root cellar while I wiped my brow and worked at straightening the remainder of my spine, vertebra by vertebra. When she reappeared, she had a knowing smile on her face and a five-foot piece of PVC in her hand. Now I was standing almost straight, unaided.

"I'll bite?"

"All we have to do is sharpen one end. The earth is soft enough now that we dig the point in only an inch, maybe two, and simply drop the seed through the PVC—no bending, no heating pad, no chiropractor, and best of all no dislocated knees for you. I can't believe no one has figured this out with the size of the gardens people put in up here." She wasn't Wonder Woman, she was Sabra Sarah, a Jewish agricultural sage, right here in Appalachia.

So, we did it. With a hand saw, I managed to sharpen one end of the PVC without severing a single digit. I poked the sharpened end into the waiting earth. She dropped a seed or two into the top of the PVC. I nudged a little dirt over the seeded hole and, without bending but simply using my toe, gently tapped it. She watered. I poked. She dropped. I tapped.

A fabulous new methodology was born. She had innovated and together we had invented. As we worked, we were already envisioning our patent, counting the money we would make, picturing ourselves on the cover of *Gardening Today* or even *Mother Earth News*. For fifteen glorious minutes and for about a 175 feet we worked like a well-oiled machine until for some reason I looked down into a PVC indentation onto some corn kernels to find that... there were none. Let me repeat: there were none. The little hole was vacant!

We retraced our steps, uncovering the last few indentations in Mother Earth to find equally empty wombs. The Method, not to be confused with Stanislavsky's, had a flaw. Clay soil, even slightly moist, enriched, clay soil, acts like CLAY SOIL and, so we discovered, clings to the inside of a small sharpened, smooth cylinder stabbed into it, creating a sticky, solid plug.

We now had a piece of PVC pipe layered at its digging end with five inches of clay, encasing corn, bean, pea and sundry other seeds. The plug would not come loose even as I, like a chimpanzee working his stick into a termite nest, dug into the PVC with my new pocket knife. My jabbing grew frenetic, as my language deteriorated into disgusting grunts. As I alternately banged it on the ground and dug in with the knife, trying without success to loosen our cornucopian seed clump, we reconsidered filing that patent and in its place considered filing for a quick divorce. We also swore an oath to tell not one soul about our invention.

Jan was quick to suggest a workable modification of her innovation. I objected. "Let's just leave unwell enough alone." Undaunted, she disappeared into the house and a moment later reappeared like the genie she is with a large bottle of Vaseline.

"For me?"

"Always a solution, big boy. Think! When you manage to clear the plug, all we need to do is coat inside the digging end with this. Slip an' slide, baby. Slip an' slide."

It was just after the lubricant suggestion that I launched the constipated PVC over the fence into the realm of Spirit, Will's magnificent three-year-old three-thousand-pound quarter-horse stallion that its owner swore up and down was beautifully hand trained and as gentle as a lamb (except when anyone tried to come near, touch, or mount him).

Jan put down the Vaseline. Spirit was clearly as mad as an equine Hatter. Jan asked me if I was upset. Yes, I thought, yes, yes, yes, you could say that. This latest idea was just too nuts, but Spirit answered her before I could. He preferred solitude in his space, except when Bagel visited in the evening to race with him, and he took exception to having the PVC flung into his private territory. He was now crunching it underfoot like a length of dried pasta. The other animal in the field, a dusty tired bay of indeterminate age, munched grass and paid no attention. I could just as well have lobbed a live grenade over there, and she would have been as undisturbed as she was now, calmly watching Spirit furiously pawing the ground.

As I remember it, Jan's and my subsequent conflagration went something like this. It began quietly enough with Jan wearing her look of disappointment as she stared out at the sailing and then splintering PVC. Then as she had learned over our years together to do, she lowered her voice to just above a whisper and calmly asked the question whose answer she already knew. My wife can pass as a veteran trial lawyer, although her degree is in humanities and fine art.

"Why-did-you-do-that?"

"Do what?" I played the innocent. I'd learned a few tricks myself over the years.

"Throw the pipe. Frighten Spirit."

Why? Why? I was grasping for a rational answer. "Because," I offered, "we've just wasted precious time, not to mention seed, on this hare-brained idea. I was doing just fine, but then no, you had to butt in. Anyway, that animal spooks a hundred times a day." I knew even at that moment how stupid I sounded and that it was the exactly wrong answer.

What the hell was I so mad about, anyhow? Not really knowing what I was doing? Macho, macho, machooooo! And so, true to my old hated habit of trying to find someone to blame, I latched onto the one person available and the one person who would in the final court, forgive me.

But not quite yet. She knew me and I knew she had me cold. A good trial lawyer has the answer before she asks the question, n'est-ce pas? Even more quietly and with more control, she went on to the big summation.

"I was trying to help you, prevent your getting hurt, unnecessarily— you big baby. You're still making a big deal about nothing. We could have better used the Vaseline on you, Mister Tight Ass. Laugh a little."

Why, oh why, is she always right? For a micro-second I managed to entertain an unsavory thought about the Vaseline, trying to invoke that life-loving spirit of Bubbe Choma. So what would be so terrible? Live a little. And as always, the situation was Jan's Aquarius to my Leo; her tolerant resignation to my overly dramatic, defensive self-involvement. She turned with a dignity that always drives me cuckoo, brushed off her hands, handed me the Vaseline and headed for the house, with a single last thought.

"When you get rational, you can come and apologize, and maybe I'll accept. Maybe."

Stu in the garden.

.

MAYBE

WHEN JAN DROPPED THE DREADFUL "MAYBE" on me, I knew I was in double trouble and I had better pry my self-indulgent head out of my ass—quickly—and get on with a big contrite and sincere apology. Why? Because she's Jan. In usual circumstances her forgiveness was without qualification. "Maybe" forgiveness meant she was truly irked.

To my credit I walked after her, managed to get in front, fall on my already pain-riddled knees, and admit that perhaps I had been a tad rash in my responses. She was not amused. So, I just said what I should have said in the beginning: that I was sorry, that I was a dufus of grand magnitude and honestly grateful for all her help every hour of each day. And, that unfortunately for her, she was the antidote to my every neurosis.

She took away the "maybe" and relented.

We hugged, kissed, and spent the rest of the afternoon working the old fashioned way, guzzling water, sweating, and on our knees carefully hand-planting our many seeds together. That night we watched the stars through our bedroom window, and before kissing goodnight at around nine o'clock, we laughed about the greatest agricultural invention of the decade whose time had not yet come.

In the morning, over a breakfast of organic oatmeal with raisins, I reminded Jan that Lorne's wife, Bitsy, would be up today to see the first part of our garden. Even the few visits we'd had from our diminutive neighbor had already made her dear to us. But for Jan the visits meant more than they meant for me. She and Bitsy had somehow discovered a kinship. I think it was that they shared tolerance, maternal understanding, and a deep capacity to care about people. They were both soft spoken but strong. And smart, very smart. I think that they already recognized in one another an independent strength that drew others to them. People trusted them with personal secrets and pains. Who knows? Maybe it was because both had plenty of experience with their own traumas and pain.

Both Jan and Bitsy had experienced mastectomies at almost the same moments in their lives. Both had had chemotherapy. Jan had also had lung surgery and a variety of other physical traumas. She not only came through them with dignity but turned the experiences into ways to help others. As a result of the breast cancer, a month following chemo she turned around and used her talents as a potter to create a national fundraiser she called Cups for the Cure, soliciting, via email and an extended trip through the country, original art works from potters all over North America and raising tens of thousands of dollars for research.

Neither Jan nor Bitsy was pushing the acquaintance farther than it was ready to go. It never was instant hugs or pledges of fealty. It was as if they, too, were planting seeds, but sparingly and without unnecessary fancified money-making innovations. Their connection was based in deepest reality, not banter.

Strange, but though I could recall the exact moments I'd met Noah and Lorne, that wasn't the case with Bitsy. I told Jan I thought that was peculiar.

"So much man stuff has been going on here with you boys, it's no wonder! But I remember. It was a big event for me so I made a journal entry that day. I'll look for it if you want."

We went upstairs to the closet where she kept her books and returned carrying one of those spotty covered black-and-white composition books she'd begun as her farm journal. We sat back down at the table as she read:

MAY 2, 2004

Yesterday a white Toyota drove up the driveway, surprising me because we weren't expecting repairmen and we rarely see visitors. I saw a tiny woman about my age walk toward the front steps. I guessed who the visitor was.

"Hi, I'm Bitsy." Sweet smile. Her face is tanned and weathered. "Lorne's wife and Noah's mother."

I invited her in. She refused my offer of tea or anything else to drink. We sat at the counter on stools I just bought from the consignment shop. She liked the stools and told me so. I had met Lorne and Noah a few days earlier and I immediately liked them but her presence was somehow like a gift just for me. A quiet, small and farm-fit woman holding the key, I think, to my survival on the "land." Her face reminded me of a pencil drawing I did years ago of an old Indian woman.

When she smiled she looked sad to me. Noah had said that his mama had lost her mother recently, and I felt I should say something to her about it.

I said I was sorry and wondered if she was having a hard time. My statement felt so feeble and inadequate. I said no more.

A long silence followed. I am reminded of folded thin sheets of dough made with butter. When preparing to make strudel, the paper thin sheets must be very carefully unfolded and separated or they will tear.

She told me her mama was her best friend. After their daddy died she lived alone in the house where Bitsy and her sister were raised. She saw her every day. The house is near the Carmel Valley where I walk. Bitsy goes over there now when she feels lonely and sits in the house or sweeps, or dusts. She and her sister meet at their mama's house to cut each other's hair. Lorne and his sons just painted the house and soon they'll be putting on a new roof.

I asked if they were getting it ready to sell.

She shook her head. No. She told me that the furniture is just like it was when she was small. The bedroom she and her sister shared is exactly the same as sixty-five years ago.

In the week after we arrived I noticed on my long walks in the valley a few houses that appeared unoccupied. Some had concrete front steps, which had separated from the porch, looking as hazardous as the rotted porch floorboards. Mailboxes were dented or missing parts, leaving the rusting metal doors to hang open where I could view the empty interiors. Mail had not been delivered here for years, but there were no 'For Sale' signs.

Some homes seem lovingly cared for. I think this is a big difference between Winter Park, Florida, and Maple Run, North Carolina.

Here property is valued by your connection to the place through love and years spent as family, for remembering when the apple tree was hit by lightning and still produced apples on its remaining branches. It seems like some people could not take care of the house after their loved one died. Maybe they couldn't afford to or they lived in another part of the country. I may have this wrong though, but selling the home place was out of the question, whether it could be kept up or not. The empty houses are called 'Daddy's' or 'Grandma's' or 'Mama's' or whoever was the last relative to have lived there. You don't sell your history.

I understand the reverence Bitsy has for her childhood home and how by keeping the rooms clean and polished she is tending to the life she lived when her mother and father were still alive. I moved four times before I was sixteen years old, six times before I was twenty-one. Mom and Dad were always looking for something, bigger, something better.

I told Bitsy about Mom and my own conflicted feelings about leaving her for months so I could spend time up here. I told her how independent Mom is living alone and still driving all over the place in her old Volvo. Even as I write this I am torn by the fact that I am here and she is there. Even with Robin there I still feel guilty for being away.

Bitsy and I shared a lot of personal stuff on just our first meeting.

I found out that like me she'd had a mastectomy five years ago. Pretty amazing! I hope we will share better experiences over years to come.

We each have sisters though and so it doesn't feel like we need or even want another one. Bitsy watched long into the nights as her mother made patchwork quilts from scraps of old clothing. My mother made cotton pinafores for Lonnie and me. Whether out of lack of knowledge or patience Mom never put buttons or zippers on our dresses; she'd fasten us in with a safety pin, removing it at the end of the day when she undressed us. It was pretty much the way she did everything. Fast. She just didn't take on any long projects. If it couldn't get done in a day, it wasn't going to get done. I am fascinated by Bitsy's childhood stories because they are so different from mine. I wonder what she is thinking about me.

Jan hiking with Bagel.

I MUST HAVE
THAT TRUCK!

SEVERAL WEEKS PASSED. JAN WORKED IN the house. I cleaned the poolroom garbage dump, loading all the gunk into heavy-duty plastic bags so it wouldn't leak and pollute the interior of our van. Each morning we walked into our garden, waiting for our seedlings to pop. It was June, already blistering in Florida but just mild enough here during the day to warm the earth and just cool enough at night for us to use a blanket. But the cool evening breezes didn't do a thing to change our garbage problem, and that remained an aggravation. The plastic bags did not work. Even doubled, we had smelly seepage. The moment I finished loading, I was on the road to the dump, racing to get there before the odor became permanent. A few more drives to the dump with runny garbage bags and I'd ruin our van.

To function up in the mountains, we needed vehicular muscle, preferably a four-wheel pickup with a long bed that I could wash out. With one of those babies I could haul to my heart's content. Jan reluctantly agreed, holding on at the same time to her belief that we could get along for a year with what we had. After all, we'd agreed to tighten our financial belts.

"Can't you use more plastic bags, double them, vinegar and water?"

"Vinegar? Dynamite! Couldn't we at least look around?"

"Okay. You caved in on the windows; on the cabinet. Let's look."

We found a dealer on the outside of town. His lot consisted of a single row of used pickups and horse trailers. He did not even bother with cars. Now this, I thought, was a mountain place.

Glenn, the owner, was the only salesman. His brother–partner was their car buyer and sole mechanic. Together, they washed and detailed the vehicles as they came in. Their office was tiny and messy. That was the work force. The lot was immaculate.

He showed us a long-bed Dodge in our $10,000 price range. It was fire-engine red with a double cab and a silver running board. It looked brand new. To me it looked like the pickup's pickup. As he was busy washing another truck, Glenn allowed through the spray that the long-bed seemed a pretty good ve-hi-cle. The word was pronounced in three distinct syllables by everybody up here. His total sales technique was explaining that he tried to buy good clean vehicles exactly the way he'd like them.

With no more fuss, he suggested we take it home and try it for a day. He needed only to look at a driver's license, slap a tag on it, and we could be on our way.

I was astonished.

Off we went. It was smooth and powerful. I gushed to Jan that it was a pleasure to steer. The four-wheel drive worked. It had a winch on the front that looked barely used. I could pull stuff. I could haul stuff. I could put the dirtiest load in the elongated bed and after unloading, just hose it clean.

I loved that truck. I wanted that truck. How could I do our work without that truck?

Jan didn't love it or even like it. It was too big, too garishly red, and it had a huge running board that I was sure to trip over. She reminded me of my propensity to back into cars and smash into shopping carts in the grocery store parking lot. And, she said, it had a "sound" and a weird habit of leaving the roof lights on for too long after you closed the doors.

Reluctantly, and with the petulance and disappointment of a candy-deprived child, I agreed to take it back the next day, knowing that we were about to miss the bargain of a lifetime.

Glenn listened to us both, Jan the skeptic and me the dashed enthusiast, without saying a word. Instead, he took the keys, got in, asked us to wait in his office and drove away.

When he returned, he called his brother over and asked him to take it for a drive. "You know, I never even noticed that sound." His brother returned a half hour later. He put the keys on their shared desk, shook his head and went back to the garage.

"Can't sell it to you. We'll be taking it back to the auction on Tuesday. Nothing big he can see, just a couple of little things. But signals."

Was I broken? No. Fractured? A little. After all, practically every guy up here with more than a quarter-acre of land and a doublewide trailer had some sort of truck. Befuddled? Plenty. Glenn and his brother never exchanged a word as far as I could tell. Yet, Glenn knew what his brother was thinking. And when was the last time a car salesman told you he'd decided he couldn't sell you a car because he wasn't 100% sure it was fine?

"You look like one sad feller. Got the mountain-man bug. Yep." He talked to Jan as if I were out of the room. "He'll never be the same now till he's in a cab, but we can't sell you this one. Tell you what, though. I'll loan you mine… until we find something I like better for you. Got to do it for him," he told Jan. "Cannot stand to see a grown man cry." Like the compassionate woman she is, she took pity. And then he handed her, not me, his keys and walked us to a small nearly new Ford pickup at the corner of the lot.

"By next week, I should have something good. If not, why for sure the week after. How about you call me around next Wednesday."

I reentered the picture. "Glenn, the reason I wanted a pickup in the first place was to haul all kind of really dirty stuff. And I need to do it now."

"Well sure. What good's a pickup if you can't load it? Have fun. Just don't crash it will you? Don't know how that danged sound got past us." With that he left us and went back to begin washing a horse trailer.

On our drive back to the farm we talked about how this was just another one of those Appalachian "can you believe it?" experiences.

We used his truck for two weeks until we got the okay on another good possibility. And again Glenn insisted we try the new candidate and take it to an independent mechanic for a separate evaluation. The Fair Fellas Garage confirmed its name. They put it up on the rack, drove it, judged it as sound but in need of new heavy-duty shocks. And charged us—nothing.

"Don't worry, if you buy it, we'll get you on brakes and shocks."

Jan and I drove home sure that this place was inhabited by Utopians.

NEIGHBORS

As we came up the driveway, we noticed three cars at the little house below ours. One of them was a sheriff's squad car, the roof bubble flashing and turning; one appeared to be Lorne's old Chevy; and one was an old Buick sedan we'd not remembered seeing around before. We hadn't looked at that house much.

We didn't know much about the person who lived down there either, only that it was a woman who seemed to be gone much of the time. We had tried to call and introduce ourselves once or twice when we first moved in but got no response and then got busy with the excitement of our new life.

We decided to go down and see if we could learn anything about what was going on just as soon as we parked the truck.

Suddenly Jan spoke. "Where's our license plate?"

"What? Where it's always been, on the back of the van."

"Uh-uh, it's gone. The van's where we left it, but the plate's gone and the side window's broken."

She was right. Jan jumped out of the truck and pulled open the passenger door of our van to discover safety glass all over the seat, her new Nikon gone from the glove compartment, and the radio half ripped out and hanging from the dash. The operator's manual was gone too.

Inside the garage, all of the small power tools, my power drill, jigsaw, circular saw—gone. So was a box of spark plugs and a battery charger, all the items Lorne had suggested I would need up here to get along, which I'd purchased only after he agreed to teach me the fundamentals of how to use them.

Jan was shaken; I was furious. Eden was not Eden after all.

We phoned Lorne and Bitsy and got no answer. I drove down.

Lorne was there. He and the deputy were on the bottom stair talking softly. Lorne's face was tighter than I'd ever seen it. A woman I took to be our neighbor, seated on a rocking chair on the front porch, was weeping and between sobs repeating over and over, "What are we going to do now? What shall we ever do now?" It was as if she thought repeating the questions out loud would provide an answer.

I knew the feeling. I'd done much the same thing when I found out five years previously that Jan had breast cancer. Except I did it with the support of our devoted youngest son, Joe, who'd rushed to our side and stayed with us for weeks, having left his demanding job as a trader on the Chicago Board of Trade and telling his boss he did not know when he'd return and that they could replace him if they needed to. I did it in a comfortable living room, sipping from a bottle of scotch, in a mortgage-free home, until I passed out and he put me to bed. Me, the novice lush. And I did it with the support of two other devoted sons. Each came to our aid in different styles.

Mike, our middle son, was stoic, as he usually is in times of crisis. As a little boy, he had a hard time saying the word *love*. When his beloved grandfather died after a long illness, he refused to cry, saying it would betray the memory of Papa if he did. Only after Jan pled with him did he manage, and then just a little. How he ever got the idea that mourning was somehow a betrayal, I don't know. I do know that he feels deeply and that his apparent stoicism is betrayed by a recurring nightmare that his children are kidnapped. When he called me, he was more a listener than an advice giver. He helped us get through in his private way.

Steve, our eldest son, more demonstrative, called about every day, often twice a day, from Chicago, where he'd moved to be with Trami, his then-girlfriend. Each call brought his offer to come to Orlando and stay with us while Jan underwent chemo.

Our neighbor woman was keening, we learned, not only because she'd been robbed, but because she was living day to day with the terror of a devastating illness, in near poverty, and with no health insurance. A slender and pretty girl of 18 or 19, who turned out to be her daughter, Laurie, cared for her by taking an administrative leave from North Carolina State nursing school, and she was there as well. But she was the only one, and although she was shaking with fear, she was trying to calm her Mom. "We'll be all right. I promise," Laurie said over and over again, but she was having little success. Her mother knew better.

The deputy sheriff was a well-spoken young black man in his early twenties. His head was shaved close in a style that I remember thinking was old fashioned. It's crazy what thoughts run through your head at moments like this. He appeared well intentioned and as appalled by what he was hearing as were we.

As far as he could determine, the break-in had occurred just after lunch when our neighbor was in Daneville receiving her once-a-week chemotherapy. Her daughter had gone with her, knowing she would be too sick to drive herself home. The thief must have just driven down their road, kicked in the door, grabbed whatever he could find that looked valuable, and taken off.

When they returned after the chemo, our neighbors—their name was Jensen—found the front door off its hinges and all her medications gone. Two-hundred dollars that she'd been saving for rent was gone. Her two handguns were gone. The old TV was gone. Their dog, a ten-week-old German Shepherd puppy called Pretty, had been clubbed unconscious and then dragged into a closet and locked in. A bloody path ran across the floor from the front door to the closet. He was now lying next to his mistress, whimpering as she stroked his neck, trying her best to console him and calm herself.

Mrs. Jensen managed to explain between sobs that she was on "relief" because she could no longer work. She'd been a librarian but had received no retirement pension. Her biggest immediate worry was that she didn't think the government would replace the expensive medications, at least not as quickly as she needed them. Could the deputy see what he might do to help? He said he would try. But from his hesitation before agreeing, I didn't think he had much confidence in his ability to make good on anything but a sincerely offered promise. He was very young. To me he looked plenty scared too.

Later, after Laurie put her to bed, we explained to him that we'd had a robbery as well. The deputy said he thought that whoever stole her property knew her medical schedule and knew she had expensive drugs in the house. He robbed her house first and figured he would drive on up the road and see what else he could grab.

The thief found our side garage door open, took whatever he could carry easily, then smashed the van window, grabbed again, stole the license plates to be used later, decided it was too dangerous to take the time to break into the house, and left. We were lucky, the deputy said. He didn't know how lucky. We hadn't locked the door. After all, who would invade Eden.

We were more outraged by the ruthless robbery of our neighbor than by our own, although the idea that anyone would just drive up to our house in broad daylight, here in the middle of what we were coming to think of as an idyllic place, and rip us off made us both sick. What if we'd been home, Jan asked. Would the thieves still have broken in?

Lorne said little except that he'd be back to repair the door as best he could. The house was his property. It had belonged to his daddy. He assured our neighbor's daughter that he would adjust the rent just as long as they needed. That they should not worry. All the while, he looked sicker than Jan and I felt, like someone who'd had the wind knocked out of him. Sucker-punched. Like someone who was working hard to keep from throwing up.

We drove back up to the house, realizing we barely knew this woman. She was living below us and we didn't even know her or her daughter's names. We didn't know she was critically ill. We didn't know she was living close to poverty. Noah's innocent words came back to me. "You don't know much of nothin', do you?" Some neighbors we were!

We agreed that we should write a check to help, somehow. We began visiting them daily; volunteered to take her in to chemotherapy. We offered to write letters to the government if she needed help with them. Jan made her grandmother's challah (egg bread). I volunteered to run any additional errands, and Laurie told us that Lorne had come back that same afternoon to fix the door and tell them he was suspending the rent. He also had called his church and they would take up a collection for the family.

Noah came to mow the grass even though he'd just done it a few days before and even though they'd asked a week before that he not come around so much. They'd been spooked by his looking in the window. Knowing

Noah, the irony of their fear is that I'm sure he was looking in to see that they were all right. He'd been devastated even after I explained that some people really wanted privacy. And that sick people did some funny things. I don't think he was convinced by my explanation, but still he came.

We were becoming neighbors.

What sort of person would steal medicines? Bludgeon a puppy unconscious? If the deputy was right and the thief was waiting for her to head out to the doctor for her treatments, how would he know her schedule?

Two days later we would find out.

I drove down to Lorne's with the new pickup to see if he would look it over, listen to the motor, and give me his opinion on whether it was a good buy. It sounded and drove fine to me, but my opinion about mechanical welfare, as all had come to know, was as useful as "teats on a bull," to quote Will. I made a point of telling Lorne how much we admired his willingness to suspend the rent for as long as necessary. He waved off the compliment. I guessed it embarrassed him.

Looking over the pickup, Lorne, as usual, was willing to help. "Let's drive 'er and see what we can find out." We headed up the highway toward Tennessee, both of us listening for ticks, murmurs, knocks, or any other sounds that might indicate a serious problem getting ready to happen. The way we were tilting our heads this way and that, him first, me following as if I really heard something, I got the picture of an experienced country doc and his raw assistant trying to set a diagnosis. He hit the brakes on sharp turns, stopped and started, used the four-wheel drive, and turned off onto bumpy steep side roads to see what the shocks were really like—anything he could think of to find weaknesses. After a few really jolting side trips, he pulled the truck over, got out and sat on the front fender, rocking the truck up and down by jumping on and off and watching as the truck righted itself. "Way too slow." he said. "In these mountains she needs t' come right back." Except for the shocks that he said were pretty worn out and should probably be replaced with heavy-duty ones, exactly what Fair Fellas said, Lorne thought it was a good buy at a fair price.

Most of our road-testing ride was without the usual banter we'd already developed as part of the way we were feeling a path toward a friendship. I figured the silence was simply because we were on a mission and he needed all the available time for listening, but even after we'd finished, he was uncharacteristically quiet, as if something was really eating at him.

We rode back from Tennessee, testing the radio, some country boy lamenting how his girl had left him for another and how sad he was in his big empty bed. And that was on the FM station! I found myself humming along and singing a couple of the repeated lyrics. That got Lorne smiling for the first time since the robbery. "Watch out Stew. You're becomin' a mountain man. Pretty soon we'll have you a-chewin' and a-spittin'." I told him that would be the final conversion.

As we drove along, I was fascinated by the road signs. Around here you cannot travel more than a mile without reading handwritten admonitions warning you to obey God's laws—or else. Peculiarly, the closer you get to the Tennessee border the more severe the admonitions.

At first, the signs in North Carolina were almost soothing. "The Lord's Love is patient. The Lord's Love is kind." "With joy will you draw water from the well of salvation." "Let your hearts be turned from sin for the kingdom of Heaven is near."

But the messages grew spikes as we went north. "If you're going to curse, use your own name." "The wages of sin are death."

I told Lorne that all these messages, both soft and harsh, had gotten past at least one local resident. Lorne slowed the truck. Since this didn't seem like a likely spot to stop, I figured he was doing one last brake test. Or that he'd heard something I'd missed. "Look down there." He was staring into a hollow.

"Where? Something interesting? A baby deer?"

"No, down over there, by them raggedy pine trees."

Below us in the hollow squatted a rundown house trailer near a burned-out car. By the shape of its charred carcass it looked to have been an older model of '50s vintage, probably sitting in that same spot for years. You couldn't really tell what kind of car, because it was so badly charred. Scattered around the yard—if you could even call it that as there was no grass or vegetation, just beaten down dirt—were some old auto parts, chunks of rusty metal, an old washing machine, and junky, indistinguishable rubbish of one sort or another, plus a couple of kids' bikes.

"That's where your stuff is. Drugs are gone. I'd bet this truck on it. Right down there."

I guess I was plain astonished. "Stop the truck, Lorne. If our stuff is down there, I'm going down and get it." I probably sounded like a poor man's superhero.

He said nothing. Then it occurred to me that he wasn't guessing. He was absolutely sure. He didn't stop. He kept driving; in fact, he sped up.

"Wait a minute, slow down Goddamn it!" He looked straight ahead. "How do you know?"

"My nephew and his no-good wife live down in there with their two children, poor little things. You ain't goin' down there. Them people are dangerous; they're crazy. Drugs, meth. No telling what they're into. I knew it was them the minute I got to the house and heard that her meds was missing. That's what they was after. And anything else they could sell. His wife, she's the one beat the dog, just 'cause she could; she's mean as they get."

"Well, I'll be damned. Go back. Now."

"No use cussin', Stew. Won't help nothin'; just get you to feelin' worse. And like I just told you. We're not goin' down in there."

We drove a while in silence. He pulled to the side of the road. We'd traveled about a mile by now. I guess he figured he'd gotten us out of ballistic range, theirs and mine.

"If you know they did this, then the deputy must have known."

"Don't think so. Not then. He's new around here. But I'll bet you he knows by now. And I'll bet you a nickel he ain't going nowhere near that place on orders of the sheriff."

"Lorne, I want to tell you, Jan and I grew up in Chicago. I even got to know some of the mafia when I was working for Jan's dad, but I don't think I've ever heard anything like this happening, even there."

He stared right at me. "Sheriff's afraid of them, too. I told you they are plumb crazy. She's been in and out of jail; him, too. Last time they got arrested, she fought so hard nearly tore out a deputy's eye. Three weeks later, she was back in that trailer. I don't know why or how, but there she was."

"Then she and him got into a fight, probably over drugs, and he hit her good; blacked both her eyes. Know what she did? Shot him that night while he was sleepin'. Hurt him real bad. Then she ups and calls the sheriff herself and charges him with assault and damn—sorry—if they don't go and arrest him and take him to a hospital jail. Him. Two days later his prize vintage car, '48 Chevy, he's been restoring it for years—that boy's got good hands when he's sober—burns to a crisp. She's out braggin' to everyone she done it."

"That did it. When he got out of jail he took those kids and moved to Georgia, with Monroe's son and them. Said he wanted to start over a new life. Go back to church and follow the Lord. That he was tired of livin' like that. Didn't want nothin' to do with her no more. Monroe told him they'd take him in just as long as he did what he said he'd do, stay off the drugs and drinkin'. And he did, too—for a while. Even started a business with his cousin trimming trees, bought a truck and some equipment with money Monroe loaned him, and was doin' good. That boy's a real good tree man."

"Then, wouldn't you know it, after four months she showed up, sayin' she wanted him and them kids back; then before long, got him to drinkin' again. One day Monroe comes in, finds them both in the house drinkin', kids running around like a pack o' wild dogs, the baby in a filthy diaper, and Monroe gets his shotgun out of his truck, tells him to pack up and get out and get her out of the house or he's gonna shoot them both. And he meant it. My brother's a lot tougher than me. He can be real strong when he wants to be."

"Anyhow, here they are back again, raisin' Cain, makin' trouble everywhere they set a foot. Doin' the devil's work. Like I said, I'd bet the truck all your stuff is down there if they ain't sold it all by now or hidden it in the woods. If I was you, I'd just start lookin' around big trees from your place till here. I'll bet some of the stuff got hid."

"So we just sit still and let them get away with this, stealing and raising hell? Taking a poor woman's medicines and nobody does a thing?" I was righteous. "And you don't say anything?"

"Everybody tries to do what they can. I'm givin' up all the rent. Noah told me he's gonna keep going around there and fixin' the place, mowin', makin' sure they got fuel. Church is raisin' money. Not much more we can do. By the way, the girl told me you give them a check. That was right good of you."

"Lorne, I think you're my friend, so I'll take a chance and ask you right out. Why didn't you at least hint who could have done this to that cop?"

His answer was thought out, one that goes deep, I think, into a cultural psyche that I can barely comprehend. "Well, first, I know them and I know that if it got out who told, it could come back on my family. Then who knows what I'd have to do? Second, that boy is still kin. No matter what, he's kin. He's my sister's son. She's had terrible trouble from him her whole life. She even moved away from all of us, all the way to Knoxville, just to get away from him and that wife of his. And now she's just about eatin' herself to death. Must weigh four-hundred pounds. I can't make her more trouble. Just can't. I knowed him his entire life and he wasn't always this way. Smilin' little boy. Mostly happy even with a bad daddy who drank all the time and whipped them kids something fierce. Once, his daddy even came after me over your fence gate with a knife. Drunk. When he saw my shotgun, he backed off, ran away cryin'. Crazy as a rabid coon. But the boy wasn't bad till he got to be a teenager. Started runnin' with a rough bunch. Then he found her. Truth is that when he isn't high on something and with that woman, he's right nice. Heart of gold. Would give you the shirt off his back if you needed it."

We were coming up to our road, driving past Yancy's, a local preacher's house. Lorne looked out the window at a beat-up van. "That's a good man down there. Still runs the local mail. It surely is a shame about that boy."

I said nothing. The real shame was that the guy and his wife were out on the loose. The shame was that they'd probably stay out. The shame was that eventually somebody innocent was going to be severely hurt.

Lorne looked at me as he got out and climbed back on his four wheeler. "Well, I got some work to do up at the garden. Stew, we never had nothing like this till the drugs got hold. Nobody robbed nobody else. We left our doors open, unlocked. Even when we went away, we never bothered to lock up. Now, now it's no good. Drugs. Meth labs all over these hills. Even your own relatives are rotten." He looked grave. "I never said this to anyone but you and Bitsy, but it'd be better if that boy was dead like his big brother. Found him floatin' in the river, beaten to death. Down by the low bridge, near Steve's. Some friends of his did it. Can't even imagine. They're in jail now. Be better off dead like his brother. Then maybe everybody'd have some peace. For sure my sister could come back."

I wanted to hug my new friend, but didn't.

He went on, "I truly do believe that the wages of sin are death and the Lord will take care of that. He is a loving Lord, but he is also a vengeful Lord. You'll see."

"I hope you're right, my friend. But you should know I don't believe it for one second."

"I know you don't; I can tell. But it's true."

"Meanwhile, Jan and I are going to start locking doors and first thing in the morning I'm going down the road and buy the biggest heaviest farm gate, chain, and lock there is."

He took out a handkerchief and blew his nose. "Bad allergies this time a year; never know when they'll act up." He blew again as if to convince either himself or me. Probably both of us. "I'll send Noah up in the morning around nine to go with you. He'll know what to buy. And I'll be up after a while to help you put her in. Be sure and buy a couple of treated 4-by-4s too, and some cement, and some heavy bolts and nuts. Might buy an extra length of chain, too, that we'll put around the gate post so's no one gets the notion to steal the gate."

"You're kidding, right?"

"Wish I was. Surely do wish I was. Don't believe they'll be up here again. Too smart for that. But just in case, the gate's a good idea. And I'd buy a shotgun too. Might even be persuaded to sell you one of mine. Don't need as many guns as I got anyhow. Don't hunt no more like I used to. Don't like killin' deer. Love lookin' at them though. No, I ain't kidding. Wish I was. Surely do wish I was."

He looked weary. "Stew, I think it's a good truck. I'd buy it if I was you. That fella's got a good reputation. And remember. You stay away from that holler."

Well, paradise is altered now, and we're about to drift a little further away by adding a heavy farm gate and a 12-gauge.

IF YOU WANNA
KEEP THEM OUT,
YOU GOTTA KEEP
THEM OUT

THE NEXT MORNING NOAH CAME UP on the Ranger, saying his Daddy wanted me to borrow their Dodge Ram to pick up the gate. Our little pickup was too small.

"Daddy says he already knows exactly how we're gonna do it, too. And it ain't gonna cost you too much neither. Once we're done, Daddy says nobody, not even my cousin, is gonna mess around up here. You and Jan's gonna be safe and that's for sure. And Stew, you know what I'm gonna do if'n I find anybody messin' up anymore around here?"

"No, but I'll bet you're gonna tell me."

"Shoot them, that's what!" He was grinning at the idea of his really shooting anyone. We both knew he couldn't hurt anybody, but he truly was angry at our invasion, even if it was his cousin, probably precisely because it was. As protective as we were starting to feel about Noah, I sensed he was feeling every bit as responsible for us. He'd work as hard as necessary to build us a protective barrier.

In Chicago, as apartment dwellers, and even though we lived in close-knit, safe ethnic neighborhoods, it was still Chicago, and so we guarded the portals too. On occasions teens from the gentile neighborhood across Montrose Avenue would raid our neighborhood, looking to catch and beat up Jewish kids. Once, when I was cornered and scared out of my wits, I escaped only because I knew the gangways and alleys and could sneak my way back home.

To this day, I remember locking the front and back doors and checking every window, even though we lived on the second floor. Every door had at least a couple of locks. Some had more than two, ingeniously contrived. Gerry, my beloved brother-in-law, the big brother I never had, who put himself through dental school pumping gas and who was raised poor and without a father from the time he was eleven, learned early to avoid spending money unnecessarily. He also learned to be insecure. As the elder of two boys and without a dad, he worried constantly about protecting the family.

Gerry was convinced they needed better security than the ordinary locks on the front and back doors. But good locks cost, so he improvised. He took an old broom handle and attached a deflated volleyball on one end and a fifteen-cent rubber end cap from a walking cane on the other. Then before going to sleep at night, he'd wedge the volleyball end under the front doorknob, with the broom handle at an angle so that the cane cap was secure on the floor. He had invented a non-slip safety lock, a poor man's deadbolt; solid protection against the nefarious house invaders who had their crooked eyes on his mother's tiny apartment. I never understood why he thought any crook in his right mind would want to invade his mom's apartment. The few times I was there, as far as I could tell, they hadn't a thing worth stealing.

On the occasion of my sister's and his engagement, Gerry's mom invited us to their apartment for a celebratory meal. In my seventeen years, I'd never seen so much food gathered on one table. My parents had talked about how hard she worked and how difficult earning money was for her. But for this occasion she would not be reasonable. And so there were several roasted chickens and cabbage soup and stuffed cabbage and brisket with potatoes, along with sweet potatoes and carrots and peas and many different types of bread in overwhelming quantities. Her explanation was that they were Hungarians!

Gerry told me years later that he'd been embarrassed by the quantities of food his mom served when they had guests, mainly because he knew they could not afford it. He admitted, too, that his mom would go so overboard with this kind of generosity on other occasions at the cost of meager pickings later in the week. Insecurity was a way of life for them. So was overeating. The two were intricately connected.

Wherever he went for the rest of his life, whether it was to live with his own young family in the fancy northern suburbs of his childhood dreams or to vacation at the Hilton or Ritz, where there were doormen and superior locks, or to drink Dom Perignon or Slivovitz (plum brandy) with neighbors who often had inherited family businesses and an easy life, Gerry carried his broom handle with him. And neither my sister nor their kids thought it the least bit odd. Nor did they think it odd that he filled the closet shelves with toilet paper and bottles and bottles of wine and liquors. In private, he would tell me that all of his wealthy neighbors were amazed that he could afford to go out with them to the most expensive restaurants. Even then, I remember wondering whether it was their amazement or (more likely) his own. I don't think any of them gave it a second thought. Gerry's childhood in Chicago followed him, regardless of where he was or what he had.

Gerry died at fifty-two from heart failure, having lost all his girth after a long painful struggle and a heart-valve replacement. I lost a good-hearted, neurotic, brother who looked after me, taught me to study, loaned me his dental office where I could go late at night and crack the books without the intrusion of a loud TV in our small apartment. My sister lost her first love.

Now, back in our tarnished Eden, I found myself going out to buy the best country gate I could afford, in part because I feared that the raid on our property was not the one-time thing that the deputy and Lorne suggested. Or even that it was as simply motivated as they suggested. If the word had gotten out about our neighbor's medical schedule, had word spread among others about the new "rich" city folks moving in? Were there even other dark cousins as yet unrevealed, malingering just beyond the tree line? Who else might be waiting to get us?

So off we went, Noah and I, in Lorne's real truck.

The general store up the road in Sistas specialized in farm equipment. In the back room, you could buy about any size nail or screw or bolt you needed. They sold dog food in hundred-pound bags, and they stocked chicken feed, deer corn, and fertilizers in as large or larger quantities. Even the proprietor was big—300 pounds or so. Strangely, for so large a man, he was soft spoken and extremely polite. You had to lean across the counter to hear him.

Outside, piled high was a small mountain of farm gates. On this day, Noah eyed them and, with the meticulous care of a Venetian jeweler searching for the perfect stone, lifted each one, eliminating this one as too flimsy, that one for a bad dent, that one for too much rust, that one for some flaw I couldn't see. And he made sure he reported the flaws, all the flaws, to the proprietor, who just nodded and told Noah to keep looking until he found the one he liked. Finally, after almost an hour and a half, Noah chose one—a mega gate, to my eye the Jurassic father gate of all farm gates. My brother-in-law would have been envious.

"That big, Noah?"

"If you wanna keep them out, Stew, you need t' keep them out."

Wisdom speaks out in the mountains, and if you've got a brain, and even if you're not smart but are already neurotic, you listen. Noah was my mountain maven: translation—a guy who knows his business. So I listened. Jurassic Gate was ours for $90.00.

"Well now let's get us them bolts, hinges, screws, and don't forget the nuts."

The nuts? He was the one who took over an hour to pick a gate. I resisted.

"Oh yeah, an' a chain an' lock."

"Whoa, whoa, what about 4-by-4s, pressure treated?" Now, if I only knew what 4-by-4s were, I'd have a tiny bit more authority in all this.

"Changed his mind. Said to tell you he remembered a couple good ones up in the high barn and you could just use them. Just sittin' up there collectin' dirt anyways. No sense spendin' more money when you don't have to."

He was eyeing the chains, sold up here, like everything else, off enormous rolls by the linear foot. Big chain here was Big Chain. We're not talking bicycle-lock-for-when-you-run-into-the-supermarket-for-milk chain. We're not talking plastic-sleeved-cable-to-secure-your-racing-bike chain. We're talking serious linkage. Steel to secure your average work elephant's ankles. BIG! We're talking keeping T Rex at bay. We're talking Rambo. We're talking Dante in hell to secure the world's most heinous offenders.

"Noah, don't you think maybe this is a little overkill. I'm not expecting Soviet tanks."

He looked at me with those trusting eyes. "Don't know them people. Do know bad folks come up there with a chain cutter they're in for a surprise at Stew an' Jan's. Nope, this is what you want."

Could we even carry it without developing a hernia? "How about a compromise? That size, for example."

"You're stubborner than Cousin Norbert. I swear you are. And that's a bunch of stubborn. All right, but keep the receipt." He wasn't through yet. "Cause with that there chain, somebody's likely to just come up one night an carry off the whole danged thing."

I chose a large combination lock.

"Won't work neither."

I bought it anyway. So there. We didn't talk much on the ride back. When we returned home, Lorne was waiting, large square posts from the barn—aha, so that's what 4-by-4s are—on his ATV.

"We'll put it right here between these boulders and this drop off. Either side's like to be a might discouraging to trespassers who take a notion to try an' walk around. Deep drop down in there."

We unloaded.

"Good gate. It'll do just fine. But Noah, what were you thinking, son? What did you think we're gonna do with these?" he said, holding up my sizable chain between thumb and forefinger, as if it were a sticky child's toy. "I thought I told you to get the big one," Lorne asked, more as a rhetorical question than an accusation or reprimand.

"I tried, Daddy, but this Ol' Man, he's real stubborn."

I think this was the first time Noah used the title "Ol' Man" on me. Coming from anyone else I would have been highly offended. I was after all, newly retired from what to the world is a prestigious job. I can remember that for several years after I received my PhD I signed my name with Dr., and God help the student who didn't add it.

When I now reported my newest title to Jan, she laughed and said anyone else would have gotten a tongue lashing from me. By 63, the need for title prestige had long ago worn off, but age had started to become a touchy issue. Nobody called me Dr. Old, but coming from Noah in this situation, I liked it. I'd heard him use it on his dad, respectfully, affection-ately, and kiddingly. It was a lovely familiarity.

Bitsy used it, too, when she was fussing at Lorne after some physical indiscretion or other, such as overworking himself in the garden or get-ting angry at somebody's discourtesy in the grocery store parking lot. "Ol' Man, whatever is the matter with you? I think you just might be entering your second childhood before you're out of the first one."

'Ol' Man' became Noah's and my shorthand like a playful punch to a friend's shoulder.

"Won't do," said Lorne.

"Told him," said Noah.

"He did," admitted the Ol' Man.

"You two get back in that truck and tell Jesse you made a mistake. Get you the real heavy link, hard steel. And while you're at it, exchange this here," he said, handing Noah the lock, "and buy you the biggest steel key lock they got."

"I told you."

He had.

"If you wanna keep them out, you gotta keep them out." It was Lorne this time, not Noah. "Meanwhile I'm gonna start on these postholes."

Noah was upset. "Daddy, you want me to run back t' the house and get the posthole digger? Won't take but a minute."

"Thank you, son, but by the time you're back, I'll be half done. Now get!"

So it was that I learned several mountain maxims.

1. Don't buy it if you don't have to. 2. But if you have to, buy the best you can afford. 3. Buy big, and buy right—the first time. Gas is expensive.

Oh, and Noah's most important maxim, drummed into him, I think, from birth: Always keep the receipt. It's always been Jan's principle too. And my parents'. I, on the other, hand…

At the store, Jesse was "as nice as he could be," another mountain ex-pression I've grown to love that often proved to be true up here.

"Figured you might be back. How's your Daddy, Noah?" I'll be damned, but he already had a new length of heavy chain cut and lying on the coun-ter. "You're gonna want this. Don't worry about the other. I'll sell it to somebody. Probably need a new lock too. How about this one?" Coiled steel; one half pound; three keys. "And Noah, tote them two bags of cement out to the truck. You'll be needing them."

"Daddy didn't say nothin' about no cement." He nodded to me for confirmation. This time I kept my mouth shut.

"You just take them. Tell Lorne if he don't use them to bring them back next time he's on the way t' town. And don't be getting those wet neither."

Six other men dressed in overalls, two of them my usual country critics, were sitting on card chairs in front of the store near the register, saying nothing but nodding their heads in agreement.

Back home, Lorne was almost finished with one of the holes.

"We're gonna sink these 4-bys a good five feet. Say, son, good for you, you thought to get the cement. Drop the 4-bys nice and straight now, dump in about 50 pounds of that cement and pour in the water."

Noah said nothing about the cement and neither did I. Let us both seem at least a little prescient.

"Son, you go on up to Stew's and fill us a couple of buckets full of water."

"Daddy, I can still make a run and get the posthole digger. You know all this shovel work ain't gonna do your back no good. You'll be hurtin' later."

"Son, just go and get the water. Please. And let me worry about my back and this leg. I'll be just fine."

Noah was still reluctant to go.

"Oh and Noah, get me the big hand drill and a couple of bits—big ones, one or one-and-a-half. Can you remember that?" Noah shook his head, tried another warning, then drove off, leaving us alone.

Lorne kept digging into the rock hard clay, readying the second hole. And Noah was obviously right. With every foot strike on the shovel, Lorne's face registered pain. Noah couldn't stand it and neither could I.

"Lorne, enough already. Genug!"

"What?"

"'Enough', in Yiddish. Give me the shovel. I can use one of those things. Dug my way through college tuition for three summers. Not as good as you, but good enough."

"Well, I could use a little rest. What's it again?"

"Genug."

"Like it. You sure you're up to this?"

"Hand the darn thing over."

Reluctantly, he gave it to me, watching me with what I hoped was a little mountain respect, as I started to dig. Like granite. Butter-soft hands. Too much moonlight, too many libraries, for so many years; not enough sunlight.

"You know Stew, Noah told Bitsy and me about him mowin' up here. And about your givin' him more money than he asked for. He was tickled t' death. My own brother never did that. And it ain't necessary. But I want you to know that we appreciate it."

I stopped digging. "Yes, it is necessary."

We stood there looking at each other. Quiet moments are more frequent and seem to last longer here; during this one, I thought of another Bubbe Choma recipe for living I didn't even know was still stuck in my head. It's not funny, but it's essentially her just the same.

When we used to visit the Jewish cemetery where her 'Mann,' her beloved Reuben, my grandfather, was buried, an old Rabbi would inevitably find and approach us. The place seemed to me, a kid of 14, to be teeming with them, ancient men from the old country—dirty, a little smelly, with scraggly beards, always dressed in old shma'te-dicha suits; translation, near enough to rags to be rags. To a teenage kid, they seemed frightening, like aliens from another world.

And, of course, they were. The reality is that many were learned men in the old traditions; many had been rabbis in Poland or Germany or another European country. Fifteen years earlier their congregations had been murdered by Hitler or sent to the concentration camps all over Europe to die. Once respected rabbis or teachers, these men, who had somehow escaped or survived the camps, found their old worlds destroyed. They were the closest thing to working Jewish beggars in America. I think that even then their eyes looked empty to me, and that's why I was scared. I wondered if this is what they did all day long, wandering around the cemetery like ghosts themselves, asking to say prayers at the graves. I never expressed my fears to my grandmother, but she must have sensed them, because as one approached, she wrapped her arm around my shoulder.

"Mrs., you want I should say a prayer for your husband?" he offered in Yiddish.

And she, as inevitably as his appearance, agreed, always agreed.

"Nu (well), so say a prayer."

Then she would give the ghost a dollar or two. Sometimes, when she'd had a really good week in the bakery, she'd hand over a five-dollar bill.

At fourteen, I was already something of a skeptic. "Bubbe, if you don't believe," and she made it clear she did not, "why give him money?"

She shrugged those little world-toughened shoulders. "So, an old rabbi also has to make a living. An old man also needs dignity. Remember, 'zein besser, nit erger.'" (For him we can make it better. Let's not ever make it worse.)

My mind turned back to Lorne, who was saying, "You know Stew, in a lot of ways he's like a child. He ain't good with money. But that boy's got a real good nose for people. And he already sees you as his friend. When he calls you Ol' Man, he don't mean a thing by it except love."

He thought for a moment before he went on. "I ain't never seen him cheated, not by nobody around here. Well, maybe one time by that lady down by the river. And she's kind of nutty. But strangers, that's a different story. Wanted to let you know while he was gone. You're no stranger."

"Lorne, you've my solemn promise. I'll never do a conscious thing to hurt him. Only try and make his life better. Fact is," I only half joked, "I think that boy of yours and I are in love. I know my wife is in love. He's a special guy."

"And he thinks the sun rises and sets on you."

I went back to digging with those sentiments deep in my pocket. And to make things even better, Lorne went on. "I'm lettin' some fellers from Georgia put some beehives up on top. Sourwood trees. You ain't never tasted honey like that. If you and Jan want some, I'll keep a couple bottles for you. Don't usually give it up to nobody but Mark."

Noah arrived about then with the drill, bits, and six five-gallon buckets filled with water. We finished the holes, dumped in the dry cement, poured in the water, and covered it all over with clay.

"In twenty-four hours ain't nobody ever gonna pull these posts out, ain't that right, Daddy?"

"As sure as the sun rises tomorrow. Not with a team of horses."

We were ready to finish. Lorne took the drill, fit the bit, and began. It's tough work. The drill was shaped like a sharpened 'U'. At one end was a doorknob-sized ball. At the other, the drill bit. The middle of the 'U' was a turning handle. You worked this contraption by pressing the bit against the wood and turning the handle. You needed plenty of traction to get a bite in the wood, and the best way to get it was by placing the ball against your stomach and leaning in hard. Noah and Lorne took turns drilling, but Lorne did most of the work. I did a little, but after several turns, I pooped out. Butter belly too.

"Can't be a mountain man in a month 'r two, Stew. Give it time."

With the holes drilled, we slid the bolts in place to secure the non-locking side of the gate and threw our second chain around the post 4-by-4s, connecting them to the gate. Noah fastened the nuts as tightly as those thick muscles could turn them—and believe me, that's tightly—locking them down using a special wrench I didn't recognize. Then to my dismay, he sledged the hell out of them, purposely destroying the threads.

"Just let 'em try and take them off!"

This gate was here to stay.

Last, we fastened the hinges with the galvanized screws literally coated with the sweat of Lorne's brow—another mountain trick. Pressure-treated wood is rock hard. Screws will barely go in, but you can get them to go in if you lubricate them. And unless you're prone to carrying KY jelly or a jar of Vaseline around in your watch pocket when you go out into the field to work, the sweat of your brow will do just fine. Even if it weren't true—which it is—man oh man, what a metaphor it is for the way of life up here.

By the way, next time you see an old John Wayne western as he works out on the range with his hair all slicked down, you'll know a mountain carpenter's trick he could use to fix a fence nobody else in the theater, even the Duke, had even an inkling about.

First dark, and we were finally done. I was tired and was sure they had to be, too. Lorne and Noah loaded the tools and went home to supper and probably some additional work. I went home to bed.

The following day about mid-morning I called again to thank Lorne, and Bitsy told me that he was flat on his back in bed.

"He ain't feeling all that good this morning."

"What can I do?" The question sounded feeble. I was definitely the wrong kind of doctor.

"Well, just wait a second, he can come to the phone." I told her not to bother him, but she said it wasn't any bother.

I told Lorne I was sorry, sure all that digging was responsible.

"Don't fret none. Wouldn't have done it no other way. Nobody's gonna come up and bother you no more."

Later that morning, Jan and I walked down to our gate. Something new had appeared. Perched atop the post that secured the gate with its dinosaur-proof lock and its pachyderm chain was a miniature lean-to house made of rough-hewn oak siding and topped with a sloped, tiny, bright red, corrugated metal roof.

How? Leprechauns? A visit from friendly Appalachian Mitzva (good deed) Sprites who'd ventured out in the dawn, lost their geographical way, and transformed themselves into carpenters?

An incoming phone call around midmorning solved the mystery.

"Did you see it? So when it rains or snows, that lock won't rust up on you." It turned out that Noah had come at the crack of dawn, carrying the little house he'd shaped and pieced together the night before out of scrap wood. He had salvaged and reshaped the tin roof from an old chicken coop. Noah seemed to always have a hidden source for a needed ingredient. Later that summer, for example, he came up with an unexpected stash of bicycles in the lower barn when Jan decided she wanted to try riding the hills.

"Noah, thank you," Jan said. She kissed him over the phone and told me afterward she could hear him blushing with pride.

"You really like it? I made it all myself."

"Like it? We love it!"

"So I got it right, didn't I ? It's a real good job ain't it?"

"Good? No, it's perfect! Noah, I think you are an artist and you don't even know it. Thank you, again."

Jan said he was laughing with what we used to call glee. Just before she hung up, she heard him yell to his Mom, "Mama, she liked it!"

Noah's gate.

HONEYMOONING
101

WE HAD COME TO ENJOY SUNDAY visits from Lorne and Bitsy after they came home from church. When they first started visiting around midsummer, we would begin by talking about the gardens and the prospect of good weather—safe subjects—but as we'd grown more trusting in one another's company, less afraid someone would make a mistake, the visits got longer and more open. It became the time when we could all relax and share our stories, mostly about when we were young. We'd laugh at ourselves, looking back at how goofy we were, especially, say the women, our men.

One Sunday we were sitting in the spot that had become the meeting place we all loved, right beside the huge flat-topped boulder. Jan had had it carried down the mountain by a road excavator, a grizzly old man who owned a bulldozer. He had been hired by Monroe's eldest son to put in a gravel road paralleling our road so that they could reach the acreage they'd put aside up the mountain for their trailer retreat. Monroe had explained that although we'd given him permission to use ours, he didn't want to intrude on our privacy.

When Jan saw what was happening she was not only agitated at a new pathway through her woods but intrigued as well. She walked up to the excavator and asked if she could have one of the giant rocks he was moving. He told her he didn't understand why she wanted to bring one part of the mountain down to another part of the mountain but was glad to do it for her if, as he said, "it'd make you happy."

The spot where the rock ended up overlooked the garden and the woods where I found and rescued a newborn faun that was being attacked by a hungry local dog. I had shooed off the dog, carried the wounded faun down to our garage, and put it into Bagel's unused crate until such time as Noah and I could bring it to a local lady who rescued hurt wildlife. When I located it in the woods, it was crying, sounding eerily like a distressed human baby, wailing "Mommy, Mommy," over and over again. I lifted it next to my chest, and the terrified little thing's heart was beating as if it would jump out of its body. By the time we got to the garage, it had stopped crying and calmly lay in my arms. I don't believe I could have had such a privileged moment anywhere else.

Day by day, our rock built memories and became the perfect place to just sit and talk. With most of our friends we had a glass of wine. With the Simmonses we munched pistachios and sipped lemonade.

This day we were talking about the time just after our marriages, both, it turned out, in 1962 and both, it turned out, followed nine months later by the births of our first sons.

Bitsy, who as I'd gotten to know her often looked to me as if she'd got a wise secret or joke she just might reveal, looked at Jan,

"Pretty darned fast, weren't we?"

Did she mean in a hurry to be moms, or naïve, or plain dumb? I hadn't a clue, but from the looks they exchanged, I had the feeling she and Jan knew exactly. I also had the feeling that Lorne and I would never know.

I started to tell our honeymoon story, and as I got into the first details they were both smiling and shaking their heads in disbelief.

"The day after our wedding, we left for Kennebunkport, Maine."

"Where the heck is that?" asked Lorne.

"About 2,500 miles from Chicago. At the time, though, we really didn't understand how far. And we didn't care. We were going! The farthest either of us had ever driven was one-hundred-and-fifty miles."

"Mmm-hmm." Bitsy laughed. "We took a trip, too. Right up that highway, about a mile, to Lorne's granddaddy's house. Of course, back then it wasn't much of a highway. Come to think of it, it wasn't much of a road neither."

"Not us. We were too smart for staying close. Both sets of parents warned us. They practically begged us to take a plane to Miami Beach where almost everybody our age went. Stubborn? I'd have made Lorne look like Gandhi. I was taking my bride to a swanky resort—and that was that."

"You hear that, Lorne?"

He spat out some shells. "I hear it, but I can't barely believe it. You're always tellin' me you didn't have no money. You sure must've had some."

I let that one pass. This was not the time for our continuing debate about who was poorer when we were young.

"So we got into our brand new Chevrolet, already named 'Bluie'…"

"Law! You named your car?"

"… like a king and queen. We bought it with a gift bond Jan had been given as a baby. All the real money we had. Smart, right?"

"Druther not say."

"We were in heaven. All our dating had been in my uncle's old laundry truck, a Dodge with all its seats stripped out except for the driver's. Jan perched on a card chair next to me. We could watch the street go by because most of the floorboard was rusted out. The heater didn't work, and off and on I couldn't get the transmission into reverse. We were either going forward or we weren't going at all."

'I don't recall even havin' a car.'

"You did so! You and your brother tearin' around these mountains like crazy men."

Lorne let that one pass. "So you was feelin' rich."

"We *were* rich! I'd worked all summer on a construction gang for $6.50 an hour. I had a pocket full of money. No more college expenses and a fellowship to go on to graduate school."

Jan remembered, "We must have gone through every tourist brochure ever printed about New England. We spread them all out on your Mom and Dad's living-room floor, until we picked the one and only place that we were going."

"$6.50?" Lorne was astonished.

"So, after four days of driving, one really scary moment when I drove up a down ramp, and a million wrong turns, we arrived in Kennebunkport, on the coast, and we found the road that led up to The Colony Beach and Yacht Club."

"You brought your yacht?" The man could not resist.

"We brought our bottom of the line, road-dust covered new Chevy Biscayne. And we drove up the hill when we got our first glimpse of the Colony, looking just like the picture on the brochure in Jan's hand. It was a beautiful white building with spires and curlicues, encircled in a sea of mist—perfectly like what we'd been singing for three months. Do you guys remember a song in the '60s—Old Cape Cod?"

"Don't believe it got up here."

"Every station in Chicago was playing it. It promised sand dunes, quaint little villages, and salt sea air—and love, love, love on old Cape Cod. We bought it hook, line, and sinker."

So we rolled up this long winding driveway and stopped. Out of the Inn came an elderly, bent, black man in a red uniform with brass buttons, and white gloves, I swear, white gloves. He approached and asked if he could help us? Were we lost? When we explained that we had reservations, he asked if he could help us in with our luggage."

"$6.50, a new car, a yacht. A servant. High cotton." Lorne again.

"Will you hush up and let Stew tell the story?" This is about as harsh a reprimand I'd ever heard out of Bitsy. She was usually quiet and patient. Where Lorne would "fuss" at the dogs that got into trouble and even beat one who disobeyed, she'd pet it and talk to it and end up giving it a biscuit. She'd find a similar way of smoothing over arguments with her sons. She worked by understanding and kindness and sometimes just efficient silence. So in the few instances she "fussed," it stuck.

"We couldn't believe it. We were there. Against my protests—he was old enough to be my grandfather—he took the bags, but he had a look on his face as if he'd swallowed something funny that was making him sick. So, I was trying to help him with the bags and he was sort of trying to keep me away. I guess I was breaking a main rule of the club. 'No helping the hired help.'"

"I remember Jan gesturing for me to look around at the parking lot. It was all Mercedes and Cadillacs, with a Rolls sprinkled here and there. No Chevys. Not even an Olds to be seen."

"No Ford pickups neither?"

"Not one. Then we got why the poor man was so shaken. And it wasn't our inappropriate car messing up the scene or my mistake in trying to help. He politely asked us if we wished him to remove the garments from the antenna. Jan's bra and panties were hanging on our radio antenna."

"Law!"

"She'd washed them the night before and discovered they weren't dry in the morning when we left our motel. So she hung them on the antennae and we'd gotten so used to them fluttering there and so excited about finally reaching our destination that we'd forgotten all about them."

"Well, sure. Makes sense to me. Doesn't it to you, Bitsy?"

"Jan was out of the car in a flash, red-faced, politely thanking him for his trouble and frantically gathering her underwear."

Both Lorne and Bitsy were delighted.

"So, having made fools out of ourselves, we followed the bellman up the stairs onto the porch in what was becoming our personal parade to the lobby. But before we got there we saw a sight the brochure pictures didn't include. The entire length of the porch was lined with wicker rocking chairs, and each was occupied by a very old person, all of whom looked to us as if they were well past 90 if they were a day. The men were dressed in white linen slacks and seersucker or navy blue blazers and the ladies were in immaculate tea dresses. The few who weren't in their chairs staring at us were at wicker tables playing bridge, looking at us over the cards. And as we passed, we were probably the most interesting event to occur all summer: a little girl rushing by clutching her underwear and a boy wrestling to help an old black worker not do his job. Anyhow, we went in, registered, and followed an even older bellman down a dimly lit hall paved with worn old carpets to our room. We were sinking fast."

"You know, I do believe you two was dumber than us—and that's saying something." Bitsy was prying open a pistachio and doing what I've seen her do before, accepting the foolishness of others as just fine.

"Wait. That's just the beginning of the Omans' honeymoon journey."

"You mean there's more? Think I would've killed him right there and then, Jan," offered Bitsy.

"Believe it. What looked quaint in the brochure looked now to be just decrepit."

"Don't believe I know that word."

"Old, really old. And worn out. The room was tiny and so ancient it had pipes hanging down out of the ceiling. The wallpaper was peeling. The place was musty with the song's promised salt sea air. Every step we took, the floorboards creaked. And for this gorgeous, expensive "honeymoon suite" we had single beds and they looked none too clean. And there were two rockers and an ancient old chest of drawers. That's it. Oh, and the toilet was down the long hall we had just navigated. This was what I had spent our ditch-digging money on."

Bitsy was shaking her head in disbelief and sympathy, as if she'd been watching a show about alien life. And, of course, that was exactly what she was watching. But she was also smiling that "Noah smile" that accepted you no matter what.

"This boy had you spending your honeymoon in a nursing home?"

"Granddaddy's doesn't sound so terrible now, does it?" said Lorne, grinning.

"The bellman left with a quarter tip in his hand, and Jan and I sat down in the rockers. We were both exhausted from the trip, from being away from home, from trying to get to know each other, and from realizing that we had made a big, big, expensive mistake."

"And?"

"The truth? Just between us kids?"

"Sure."

"Sitting there, I was crying and she was trying not to. I was asking her forgiveness for making such a dumb mistake, already trying to take on the responsibility of a manhood I didn't have and she was consoling me, saying she was as much a part of the decision as I was. We promised each other not to tell anyone when, and we were feeling if, we got home."

"Just a couple of babies."

"Exactly."

"The next morning, after a night of tying the beds together with shirts and having some drunk try to bust our door down insisting we were in his room, after the phone rang in the middle of the night and I couldn't find it because it was under the tied beds, and after we discovered that the rocky ocean shore was too freezing to swim in, we moped our way downstairs to the dining room where we were the only diners—everyone else was still sleeping."

The waitress, a college girl about our age, leaned over while she was serving us our fancy lobster omelets and whispered in Jan's ear, "What on earth are you two doing here? It's a morgue. They're all boozing themselves to death. An ambulance arrives at least once a week. Get out! Get out before it's too late!"

We got up, went to the front desk, and told them we'd made a mistake and asked for a refund, and the Manager—who maybe had kids of his own—charged us for one night, refunded the rest of our deposit, and asked if we needed help with our bags.

"That colored feller was dyin' t' help you."

"Probably he was. No help needed. We were out of there, down that hill, speeding for New York City. We figured it couldn't be too far away; after all we were already on the east coast. Eventually, after about twenty hours of hard driving, we made it, but not to New York."

Jan picks up the story. "We were driving in a rainstorm after crossing and recrossing the same bridge. It was awful. I felt lost and alone. I longed for the familiar; I didn't know where we were going or how we'd find our way to a hotel where we could get in out of the rain. Seeing signs for a hotel was nearly impossible, yet somehow I was able to see the warmth of lamps in countless apartment windows, where I was sure people were inside preparing dinner and feeling the coziness of their families and homes. I remember thinking that back home my mom would be cooking a great meal for my dad and my three younger sisters. The house would be noisy with our sounds. Instead, I was driving in the heavy rain, the darkness of the night, wandering unfamiliar roads alone with this boy I didn't feel I really knew. And I was not so sure I wanted to know. What I wanted was my little sisters, my mom and dad, my house where dinner would be made for me and I would be protected. I wanted to be back necking on the couch with this boy I mistakenly married. I could be home, and I could be back in my bed with my sister Lonnie sleeping in the bed next to me."

"I was thinking of how Mom must have felt when I left with Stu to go off on our honeymoon to a place called Maine. Was she as frightened for me as I now think she should have been? Was she able to care for Dad and the girls as before, or was she worrying about how I was? As she should have been! Did they miss me? This is very odd to be thinking of this now, forty-five years after the honeymoon. My God, just thinking of it makes me cry."

I decided I'd better take over.

"So these kids wound up not in Manhattan but in a motel in Brooklyn. Jan was relieved. I was relieved. There was a party going on at the hotel. A Bar Mitzvah."

"A what?" Lorne and Bitsy in chorus.

"Another story. We ate a lobster. The next night we drove into Manhattan. But that's still another story."

"And that's how you bought this place forty years later. Crazy as the day you was married. Straight ahead and no stoppin'. But we love you for it. Makes life a lot more fun around here," Bitsy said.

"Cuttin' cans," Lorne said in a really odd segue.

"Sorry?"

"While you was weepin', eatin' lobsters, and playin' rich, we was cuttin' cans. $6.50? Up here we was makin' 85 cents—if you could get a job. You tell 'em, Bitsy."

"First off, we didn't have much of anything. So when Lorne's granddaddy offered us the house, we grabbed it. It was pretty much like it was the day he built it. All rough boards and a floor that had holes all over from where the knots had dropped out. So, like Lorne said, I spent my honeymoon cuttin' cans and nailin' the bottoms over the holes to keep out the critters."

"And it worked pretty good most of the time."

"Most. You ain't lived, Jan, till you wake up in the middle of a winter night and see your groom a snorin' next to you and feel somethin' else movin' against your leg under the covers. I've been 'fraid of snakes ever since. And scream? Law!"

Now it was Jan and my turn to be aghast. Jan couldn't resist. "Is that the way you grew up?"

"What? No! We had a nice house, electricity, runnin' water, inside toilet. I didn't get such luxury until I married this here feller."

Lorne began another story. "You should've seen her back then. Long hair down to her back—and quick? You think she's fast now?"

He was talking about the weekend before, when we were all out together in the back yard picking cherries. To get to the cherries highest up the tree, Lorne had gone into the woods to cut a forked branch he could use as a hook to snag and pull down the higher branches. Bitsy solved the problem differently. She kicked off her shoes and climbed right to the top of the tree. Filled a gallon bucket by the time he'd snagged his second limb—and thought nothing of it. Just the way she'd been doing it ever since she was a girl. It didn't matter a whit that she was sixty-three and a grandmother.

"Lorne, don't you dare go tellin' that story."

But he was already telling it. "About a week after we moved in, Bitsy went out t' the outhouse one night…"

"Lorne, I'm warning you."

"I had this big double-barreled 12-gauge, and I loaded her up. Then I waited till Bitsy was real settled in and I snuck up next to that privy and let both barrels go right over the roof. Well, she come runnin' out of there in all the clothes the good Lord gave her. Fast! As pretty as a picture. Right into my arms."

"Prince Charmin' to the rescue. Don't you worry. I got him back plenty, but those are tales for another time too."

It was clear that in spite of her objections, Bitsy remembered those times fondly.

"We didn't have nothin'," Lorne said, "except each other, but that was plenty. We was in love and young, and full of the dickens."

I kissed Bitsy right on top of her head and neither she nor I were embarrassed. She said it was getting late and they should be going.

Lorne and I walked down to the garden to check for the dreaded Japanese beetles, a beautiful iridescent bug that eats everything in sight and, if you were still determined to stay organic, or at least nontoxic, must be picked off every vegetable by hand one by one and either squashed flat or dropped into a tin can of gasoline. It's either that or use poison, spraying the whole garden. Lorne longed for the "good ol' days" of DDT. He said that twenty years ago they didn't have this particular problem. Nor did they have the infestation of other insects that looked like ladybugs but were a foreign variety from Japan that would come in the fall and swarm, getting into every cranny of your house. "They bite a little too," he said. And they stink. Increasingly, as we lost plants and awaited another pest, I could see his point. DDT didn't sound so bad. Damn it!

Stu and Jan's wedding.

THE GARDEN

THE GARDEN WAS STARTING TO SHOW more and more as long as we kept vigilant with our insect war. Each morning, as soon as there was enough light to see, we were out spying on what might be about to come up next. Sometimes, in our anticipation, we didn't even change out of our pajamas before we were through the door. I imagined we must look like two geriatric kids out of Peter Pan—John and Wendy adventuring into our personal Never Never Land. Neither of us cared about how we might look to the saner world of our more adult contemporaries going about reasonable activities in town, bidding in bridge games, scouting the latest movies, attending dinner parties. Come to think of it, even before the farm neither of us cared much.

If we found nothing new we would be disappointed, but like the excited kids we loved being again, we returned several more times a day, walking the rows, checking and rechecking the plants, lifting their leaves, to see if they'd made any progress, and whispering to one another, so as not to disturb the just-waking kids and their attendant bees, if one of us should discover a new blossom or hint of a vegetable.

We knew we were not behaving rationally, but our quiet garden walks were incredibly full of mystery and so much fun. I think that the slow progress of everything made for part of our fascination. For someone used to speeding through events and needing to have control, I was happy. I think that it's more remarkable for me than for Jan, because she long ago discovered the value in tiny moments. The new garden was my teacher's confirmation.

For someone who had lived much of life pushing towards what many, including me, defined as achievements—running this committee, establishing that program, scheduling and redoing schedules for other people, evaluating their effectiveness and not really feeling justified in doing it—the feeling of just walking through our garden checking the new growth of each tiny seedling was a precious lesson in observation and patience. One day you planted a seed, and for days, even a few weeks, you saw nothing but soil. You waited. You took care to be sure the weeds didn't take over. You took care not to step on a spot where you had planted. You were on the watch for lurking Japanese beetles and slugs and the dreaded potato beetle that does not restrict its taste to potatoes. You checked and rechecked the places where you placed the seeds. Sometimes you found yourself revisiting the garden three times a day. But there is no way you can burrow under the earth and hurry up a thing.

Then magically, a little green something would push its way through the hardened earth, and then the next day a few others at the other end of the row. And even though we couldn't even remember what they were supposed to be, it really didn't matter. Just that they were coming up was the excitement. You can't will a cucumber to produce on your time schedule, can you? And if you could, would you want to?

So we walked, waited, and watered. And stood guard.

The onion sets were first to appear, sending up their green tops all standing stiff almost a half inch in just a couple of days. It didn't seem to matter how we planted them or how close, they managed to push through and thrive, indifferent to everything around them. And somehow, some way, a few had migrated into other parts of the garden. Nothing bothered them. Then the zucchini plants started coming on, and in a week they were already twice as large as every other planting. Our tomato blossoms were tiny, but there. I'd bet they'd be the most temperamental. Lorne warned us about fungus, other bugs, blight, you name it. As usual, he was right; all the enemies were on the attack, and since we were still determined not to use insecticides or chemical fungicides, we experimented. We came up with a super concoction: garlic, hot peppers, and Dr. Bonner's peppermint soap, all brewing and bubbling for a week and then strained and sprayed.

Peppermint and garlic is a new aroma you'll probably not find any time soon in the cosmetics department of your local gourmet food market. But it actually worked! Nobody liked being near it. The experimental row of Bush Steak tomatoes seemed to be doing well in their own space. Not much seemed to bother them either. What I thought were the squash were producing the most beautiful leaves and the hint of yellow blossoms. Or they may have been orange. We'd be able to tell when... we could tell. For the moment they were spreading their vines across everything else.

And we had the first hints of corn.

Most plentiful was the kale. I'd never heard of the stuff before, let alone eaten it. But Jan told me it's great for you, packed with vitamins and listed in every nutrition magazine. And the fact that we were its parents made it even more promising of nutritious salvation.

Jan insisted on watering each sprout in the garden using a rusty old sprinkling can she found while walking in the woods. Long ago there must have been a garden back in there. She went back and forth to the laundry sink for refills. Twenty-five refills just about completed the job. Happily exhausted, she returned to the house for a nap. I told her she needed to compromise and use the modern device called a water hose so we could keep our principal laborers in good shape, since we were the principal and only laborers. She just looked at me with pity and refilled the can. She made the trips morning and just after sunset. Inefficiency was no problem to her. But you know a new part of me loved her attitude. I thought she was so persistent because it meant more time in the garden with the plants, and she loved tending to each one slowly and individually, alone. She was teaching me to see the subtleties in color and texture, the differing shapes in the leaves. She said it was in keeping with the pact of THE ORGANIC. She was right.

Bagel made his garden contribution, seeing himself as our vigilant care-taker. If he sensed something in the woods just beyond the garden, he would charge out to investigate. He also added to his efforts by waiting, one foot in the air, intensely focused on me as I weeded. If I tossed a clump of weeds, he would catch it on the fly and then carry it out to the field, shaking it free of dirt, dropping it, and returning for another load. Bagel was happiest when he had a job he loved. Lorne said he'd seen a lot of dogs, but never any critter that acted like that. He also said that Jan watered like his mama used to and it was fun to just watch her.

Our neighbors warned us that as soon as green really appeared, so would the deer, before sunup when Bagel would still be asleep. The raccoons would arrive after dark and the rabbits whenever they saw an opportunity—and devour everything they found. They advised we begin to try and keep them away by attempting to fool them with decoys or by hanging brightly colored pieces of cloth on wires strung across the rows. Some folks hung up old compact disks or aluminum pie pans to reflect shards of sunlight, or they went back to the "old timey" scarecrows. There was also some horribly stinking, chemical stuff that you could spread around the plants that was supposed to keep everything away. You could even put up an electrified fence. Or you could lay in wait at night and shoot them. Shooting for our neighbors was a last resort.

With Bagel's nose on the job, combined with his terrifying bark, we thought nothing two- or four-footed would choose to cross our garden line. Just so long as the wild critters did not realize that his bark was one-hundred times worse than his bite, which is non-existent, we felt he had us covered.

Even the cows from Mark's farm who wandered down the mountain trying to get a few morsels of our grass on the slope behind the cattle grate were chased right back up by our fierce, barking sentinel. He saw it as his sworn duty to keep any intruders at bay. He was particularly fierce with docile, domestic heifers. And to give the boy credit, so far he had been remarkably successful in discouraging the entire herd except for one stubborn intruder, a giant, determined young bull with very long, sharp horns who ran from Bagel several times until one late afternoon when he decided to stand and have it out.

I happened to be looking out the back bedroom window when the showdown occurred. Lowering his head, the bull trotted straight toward our canine matador. Bagel countercharged, leaping from side to side, barking madly. When the bull kept coming, Bagel, in less than a graceful turn, jumped back in astonishment, stopped barking, and decided that one retreat was no defeat, and that his beautiful, unblemished, and unpunctured chocolate hide was more important than his honor or our grass. The bull stood, front legs splayed, staring straight at our formerly fearless watchdog while Bagel decided he had something more important to do. Bagel now began to steer clear of that particular opponent.

My suspicion was that word of the standoff and retreat had gotten around and that some of the other less brave members of the herd would follow El Toro's lead and Bagel would find out that giving way one time would mean the possibility of continued humiliation. But so long as he kept the other critters away from the garden, we pretended not to notice his increased backing down from what we suspected would be a growing number of unimpressed members of the herd.

A few garden vegetables.

HOW BAD CAN IT BE?

I THOUGHT I HAD A NEEDED alternative to Jan's sprinkling-can method. As the garden grew and even though we both were willing to continue the slow watering, we just could not afford the time, even up here and in our present slowed-down disposition. I'd read in one of the organic gardening magazines we'd both been devouring that you could build a watering system out of PVC pipes, connecting them like tinker toys and then drilling tiny pinholes parallel to your plants. This, according to the authors, satisfies the wish to conserve water and treats each plant as a unique individual. All we needed was a simple, efficient design.

Jan and I agreed that watering wouldn't feel the same but that a touch of pragmatism was necessary. "Go on," she said. "Give it a try. How bad can it be?"

"In light of my past history?"

"Forge on. It's a brave new world."

This encouragement was certainly not the result of any previous successes on my part. She could easily have thought back to a small task I attempted back in Florida. Rescreening the door of our front porch in Florida should have been easy. After all, I had the old screen lying on the grass laid out before me as my pattern. I had the required tools arranged in order of use. I'd been going in and out of the old door for years. I'd been extraordinarily careful about removing the moldings. I knew exactly how the finished product should look.

As I began, it was obvious that the news had travelled quickly around the neighborhood: Dr. Omans was laying out tools to do something! I suspected that our boys had secretly announced it to their friends. Why else would they be suddenly setting up a lemonade stand?

Neighbors gathered to watch. It was less expensive than taking the kids to Disney, and when my inevitable monologue got too filled with colorful expletives, they could take a break, go home to eat lunch or dinner or watch the Wonderful World of Disney before returning. Dr. Omans could be counted on to provide comic relief on a hot Florida day and into a sultry evening. And it was free, except for the lemonade. They could always return even later, after a moonlight swim, knowing for certain that the screen door and I would still be engaged, illuminated by car headlights, at least until Mrs. Omans took over.

Once when he was still a tyke of five or six, our future MBA environmental engineer son Mike, who I know has to be a descendant from some ancient Russian tryst infiltrating our family, was watching me grapple with a screw that I believed had fallen from under our car's dashboard. He watched me sliding my hands back and forth under the dash for a long while. Then innocently he asked, "Daddy, won't it be better if you look underneath to 'see' the empty hole?"

On another occasion when Jan had bought the hull of a fishing boat from a rich doctor neighbor and we'd spent 500 dollars, more than we could afford, to fix the motor only to discover that the boat would not move more than five miles an hour no matter what we did, Mike, staring at the disabled craft sitting on the street, asked me what the plug in its sub hull was for. Sub hull? Plug? I'd never noticed it before.

"Pull it," I said. "What can it hurt? The damned thing won't go anyhow."

He did and the most viscous stinking water rushed out—for about a half hour. Gallons and gallons and gallons of it. Our neighbor forgot to tell us that the boat had previously sunk. I had no idea a boat had two hulls. Emptied of a few thousand gallons, it ran just fine for several years until we sold it.

So Jan's go ahead for the irrigation system was an act of unequalled faith, and as a new mountain man I was determined not to fail us. I drew a diagram marking places for the pin holes. I bought all the pipes and connections and the special glue. The next day, with the help of the vegetable

Muses and the imprimatur of my incomparable spouse, I would draw a
refined schematic and I put our watering system together.

But first things first.

Our son insisted that if we were determined to live "up there" we must
do water tests. "Water tests?" you ask. "I thought your water was dee-li-ci-
ous as well as per-fec-tion."

Yes, of course. So did we.

Mike's warning that our "dee-li-ci-ous" gravity-fed water could very
well be contaminated got us to worrying about little things—like excruciating horrible deaths—and, consequently, to buying gallons of bottled
water, which Noah, finding out that he loved it, has been drinking as an alternative to diet soda. I could now practically build the proposed watering
system with the accumulated empties that were taking up more and more
space in our garage. Lined funnel to funnel we had at least 600-square-feet
of useless plastic.

We decided we could neither afford the death-watch nor the bottled-
water expenses, let alone all those plastic bottles that had taken over our
garage and which Jan despised as landfill pollutants disguised as health
vessels, and so I took a water sample to the waterworks and paid the reasonable fee of twenty dollars for the tests, which came back—positive,
meaning we had some nasty little bacteria populating our deee-li-ci-ous
water. Mike was right.

In short order, we'd become the worry-free owners of a $1,500 ultra-
violet double filtration system that proved effective in killing coliform
bacteria. Belatedly, we found out that most of the Florida transplants up
the mountain who had sealed themselves into the exclusive ski-slope communities had installed similar systems, probably on the advice of their
property managers.

In case you're as unfamiliar with the term as I was, coliform is the gen-
eralized bacterium that can contain multiple bacteria, among which can be
E. coli, the nasty variety that kills people. *E. coli* comes from animal drop-
pings, and up at our part of the mountain and very near our perfect water
source, poop is plentiful enough. Deer, cows, bobcats, bears, raccoons,
even a mountain lion or two, and many other creatures great and small
roam around the spring, refreshing themselves and pooping.

It was true that our water was delicious, icy cold, and plentiful. It was also true that for newcomers it was potentially dangerous. The testing agent who lived here his entire life was simple and direct, "I wouldn't drink it without a really good filtering system, and I'm a boy that's from here. The old-timers don't seem bothered drinking directly from the springs. They've been doing it for generations, developed antibodies, and aren't threatened unless the bacterium is actually *E. coli*. Bottom line folks—and I'll say it again—I wouldn't touch that stuff again without a good system."

That was enough warning for both of us. We hurried to the local water experts and bought what we were told was the best system available. Now as long as the little green and purple lights stayed on, as long as there was no alarm going off, we felt safe in drinking the dee-li-ci-ous water. And we renewed our appreciation that the fixed cost of living here "as is" kept getting unfixed.

After the installation of Ultima Violetta, so named by Jan in recognition of its exotic price and the hue of one of its lights, I set about building my PVC watering system—at a pittance of forty bucks and change and after a few setbacks with the gluing which I will not go into here except to remark that the advertisements are accurate when they say it sticks to everything. Once I had the elegant contraption assembled, I simply ran a one-hundred foot hose out from the garage spigot and attached it to my system, turned on the water, began to whistle (according to my kids a sure sign that I am in a state of terror based on former constructing experiences), and waited for the aquatic explosion.

No such event occurred. The water flowed evenly, gurglingly through the pipes, straight to and through the itty-bitty exquisitely drilled pin-holes. No one could have been more surprised or enraptured than I, unless it was Jan.

Lorne loved it. "Just as nice as you please."

"Proud of me, Dad?"

"I am. Up here nobody does this. Mostly, we just let it rain. Or sprinkle with a hose. I might even take a notion to build one of them myself."

Noah came down to see our demo. "It works real good, Ol' Man."

Bitsy came late, alone, to come to her own conclusions. "Law, that'll do you, won't it."

I would have invited the entire county to our flow if I could have, so taken was I with my success. Come to think of it, my first concern for subsequent guests to the farm, even before they use the bathroom after a long trip, had been to insist that they come right down to the garage and turn on the water to see for themselves, before I rushed them into the garden to see the operation. I suspected Jan to have been embarrassed by my zeal, but she humored me. She understood the pride of success, although she did hazard "I'm not sure you were as moved at the birth of our firstborn."

Aside from my 24-hour frustration with everyone's thinking I was waving to them until we discovered the right solvent to loosen and separate my fingers—the glue story I'm not telling you—we were both satisfied with all the new watering machinery. And we'd overcome the specter of deadly, lurking contamination—as well as a watering system. True, the filter had cost more than a few extra dollars, but we could sleep at night assured that we would awake in the morning. We had bought the Cadillac of filters, after all.

There did seem to be a strange little bubbling sound since installing the filter, but the water that flowed from every faucet was gorgeous and clean, and the system installation guys explained the odd sounds as a few air pockets caught in the lines during installation. A few baths and showers, a couple of laundry loads, some dishwashing, two or three garden waterings, and the noises would disappear. How about the ominous groans from the upstairs toilets? No problem either, said the foreman. They were just part of the shakedown in a new system.

Lorne was considerably less enthusiastic when I demonstrated a flush. "Can't say I like them grumblin's. Sounds to me like the whole system's full of air. There's a leak somewhere. What'd you need the blame thing for anyhow?"

"Contamination!" Here was a subject about which I could be authoritative, even erudite, as I explained coliform, local antibodies, etc., weaving an intricate explanation out of Mike's phone lectures and the water expert's warnings.

"Well, Stew, I understand all that. But wouldn't you have been better to go on up to the reservoir every couple of weeks and drop in some of them chlorine pellets? That's what I do and it works just fine. And it don't cost almost nothing at all. Seems to me you just love spending money."

His seemed a reasonable strategy now that I knew about it, but I was already committed to how precisely smart we had been in buying our system. It was done, paid for, and—except for a few odd sounds— near perfection!

[Note to self: Never give yourself a "kinahora." What is a kinahora? It's not precisely translatable, but here are a few examples of use: "Be careful, don't congratulate yourself. Especially out loud. SOMEONE will hear and get angry." Or maybe, "Don't tempt fate by being too full of pride." Or, "Don't draw the Evil Eye's attention."]

Our newborn oasis was receiving far too many kinahoras. Some sort of retribution was just a matter of time. What seemed like the angry fates struck a few days after the installation when Jan turned on the kitchen faucet and nothing came out. Not a drop. But although there was no water there was plenty of sound. I went under the house into the root cellar, where the magic filter, along with its primitive forerunner, were located and found everything in working order. The right lights were glowing. The turn-on valves had not slipped a centimeter. There were no leaks that I could see.

Lorne, sounding a bit weary of our S.O.S. calls, said he'd be over to look at it, and as good as his word, he came. This trip was the first one in which he expressed any frustration at all. "I'm getting just a might tired of this," he murmured. I didn't blame him. We were taking up plenty of his time. Then, as usual, he set himself to try and help. With me as his "gofer," scampering up and down the stairs and, at his instruction, turning on each house spigot one by one, all twelve of them, to drain superfluous air and break any vacuums, we managed to do nothing except unleash the most cacophonous combination of pipe belches and toilet explosions any plumber's nightmare has ever conjured. And still we had no water.

Jan was cursing. I was livid. Lorne was figuring. His conclusion was that they'd incorrectly installed the filter and that there was a leak that intermittently was creating air pockets not only in the Cadillac, but in the little filter that fit into the preliminary system that had been there for years. I called the filter company and made inquiry, only to be told that this was impossible—that their installers were expert, but that they'd send someone out anyhow. And so, that afternoon we were visited by two men, or rather a man and a boy, who admitted that they knew nothing about such fancy filter systems—their specialty was well digging—and after apologies said they really didn't have an answer and departed in a cloud of exhaust fumes as quickly as they could.

More calls to the company got an irate foreman who promised he'd come out himself. To our ears it was like hearing the messiah was about to arrive. By this time Jan was in despair, certain we'd never have water again. The messiah arrived and turned out to be a false incarnation. He hemmed, he hawed, he spat, he bit his lip—and told us that there was not a thing wrong with the system that he could see. I told him I was not going to pay his entire bill, especially the hourly charges for the two earlier technicians who'd come and done exactly nothing. He was not happy. He told me he was not coming out again—that no one was—so there! And I told him. And he told me. And on it acrimoniously went.

Meanwhile, Lorne kept figuring. "We done tried everything else. Let's change out the old system and see what happens. Can't get any worse now, can it?" I'd already replaced the old raggedy filter with the best one I could buy, a polyurethane device that was guaranteed to last a year. It had cost ten times the old one, but I figured it was worth the price given its safety. Lorne got the old timey cheap one from Mark, the sort all the people around had been using for years. It's a string wrapped, old fashioned cardboard cylinder and needs to be changed out every three months or so. Cost? Two bucks.

He turned off all the feeds, slipped the cheapo cardboard filter in, made sure that it was seated firmly, turned back on the feeds, and damned if it did not work! We had water! Neither of us could believe it. The entire process took five minutes, if that. Lorne suggested that maybe the old system had warped just enough that it could not take any additional changes but what it was used to. Anything else was just too good. Whatever needed sealing got resealed; whatever needed flushing got flushed. And without the messiah, and for two bucks plus tax, we had water again. And the terrifying sound effects disappeared.

MEZUZAHS, OR WHAT THE HECK IS THAT THING?

JULY 4TH IN THESE MOUNTAINS WAS still a big, bright, optimistic, celebratory holiday packed with picnics, town parades, church suppers, and, of course, plenty of fireworks that you could buy from tents that sprang up along every other main road.

People from the valleys tried to position themselves higher up the mountain so they had a clear view of the ski slopes, which were even further up than newcomers (like us), rich people (unlike us), where Mr. and Mrs. Moneybags had built elaborate houses within gated communities and where their community management organizations shelled out the big bucks for dazzling bottle-rocket displays and Technicolor explosions.

Frugality remained a prime virtue here among the farmers and longtime local residents. So a heck of a fireworks display each July that they did not have to underwrite was one of the few perks that came as a byproduct of those lavish, gated developments and the people who inhabited them.

Our place was halfway up the mountain at 3,500 feet, across from, but a couple thousand feet below, the ski slopes and, it turned out, had traditionally been the best of viewing spots. Polite hints in June made our Independence Day obligation clear to us.

Fourth of July had always been seen from Monroe's. Of course, we would carry on the tradition, inviting our neighbors to share the view with us. But my visionary bride had a more complex idea for the holiday. She had been privately ruminating on a plan for officially inaugurating our unique household here in a way that would serve to more precisely define who we were.

"We will have a mezuzah-hanging ceremony, and we'll say the appropriate prayers, once we learn what they are! I'll look them up on the computer. I'll say the prayers in English and you'll say them in Hebrew. Our friends, old and new, will come and meet, eat, help us hang the mezuzah, maybe even repeat the prayers, and then we'll watch the fireworks. It's the perfect time. With Steve and Gretchen here now and our friend Beverly coming for a visit, this feels right. I sense the depth of meaning this can bring to everyone, both Jews and Christians alike. We are all the same after all." Jan tended to get carried away with herself and what she was sure was a fantastic idea. Now she was talking about a religious icon typically affixed to the doorposts of Jewish homes. "We can each say something about what 'home' means to us. We'll keep the agenda loose. What do you think?"

I braved it by questioning if this was such a hot idea after all. We'd already explained that we were Jewish and gotten from the sellers a solid okay in the form of "Well, what's wrong with that?" and an assertion that we were the Chosen. Good enough for me. It was one thing, I suggested, to live here quietly; another to say brochas (Hebrew blessings) and chant aloud in the language of Abraham, Isaac, and Jacob.

Jan reminded me it was also the language of Miriam and Ruth and that in matters of good faith and an intuitive sense about human situations she was far more anchored than I. Her present intuition was that our new neighbors were lovely and giving and far more open than I thought. And chant we would, either before the explosions or after. End of discussion. To my credit, I stopped my Doubting Thomas routine and she started planning.

Whom to invite?

The first answer from my openhearted wife was simple. Everybody. Why not make this party an Appalachian open house for anybody in the community we'd met or had contact with? We went through a potential list, realizing after writing it that in a short time we'd actually met a good assortment of people. In other words, we had a heck of a long list. The local pastor from Sugar Creek Mountain Church, Charlie, the fiddle maker, vendors from the farmer's market, two local potters we liked but didn't really know very well, the mysterious River Lady who lived by herself in a trailer on acres of land down by the river, who was, talkative and who ominously warned Jan that we needed to be armed with an arsenal in case of bear intrusions or even more dangerous human invaders. Word of our robbery had gotten around even to her, and she lived in self-imposed isolation with three dogs that roamed her property.

The list was getting too long. Very locally, there was the family's distant uncle or cousin, Orville (we couldn't figure his exact relationship), who appeared in his dusty pickup the day after we had taken up residence on the property to welcome us and take an on-site look at the newcomers, introducing himself as "just an ol' hillbilly who lives across the holler" and who was in the habit of coming to pick our property's apples in the fall.

"Fact is," he explained, "just ate the last one yesterday. As good as the day I picked it, ten months ago!" It was clear to us that he must have picked a heck of a lot of apples. We assured him that he'd still be welcome at our place to pick apples, jokingly adding, if he'd just leave a couple for us. Later in the season we reneged, learning that our joke was more serious than intended because Noah told us that if Cousin Orville came, "he'd surely nab just about every apple on every tree." Orville's frugality, we concluded, would mean a severely limited apple supply for us. Maybe we'd better take our joke seriously and scratch Uncle Orville from the housewarming. A little distance from some folks might be a good thing.

I eliminated the River Lady. She scared me although Jan found her "intriguing." Jan suggested inviting Shelly Sue, a wonderful lady we'd just met who owned the tiny local grocery-general store, probably what 7-11s were before Corporate got wind of the profits to be made, painted the stores green and red, hired minimum-wage help, jacked up the prices because of the long hours they were benevolent enough to keep to stay open, and then got rid of Mom and Pop who'd always stayed open without thinking they were doing anything special. So far and lucky for us, there were still not enough profits to be made in these mountains for CEOs to get interested.

Shelly Sue's place was owned by her father before her, and now as in the past she worked the long hours and had a feature I'd not seen in any 7-11s I had shopped at—lots and lots of snapshots of her many grandchildren taped up around the register and thumbtacked as well on a makeshift bulletin board, photos taken over the years of baptisms, confirmations, graduations, and proms. We'd meet these same kids and grandkids stopping by to pay their granny a visit or spell her so she could rest almost whenever we were there to buy gas, a loaf of bread, or a much-needed bag of Epsom salts for our aches and pains.

Shelly Sue's was located just up the mountain and in front of Sugar Creek Mountain Church, where we'd been invited to revisit immediately after we'd witnessed the river baptism. And in emergencies Shelly Sue's was the place to get help with no questions asked. To us, used to the supermarkets and Sam's Clubs of urban America and to our local super-convenient 7-11, where indifference or an obligatory smile were more the order of the day than cordiality, Shelly Sue's was a gift in its sincere goodwill. Need to use the phone? Fine. Don't worry yourself about it. Long distance? Don't worry. Pay me later. Cash a check? "So long's it's good. Heck, I know where you live."

At Shelly Sue's you could find pretty much anything you needed, as long as the emphasis was need and not want. Further, if she didn't have the item, she would get on the phone to ask another small general store a few miles up the road to ask if they did. Such courtesy to save you a trip and gasoline was just part of the right way to do business.

To us, Shelly Sue's was also a sort of wonderland, because she had so much unfamiliar stuff that was part of everyday life here: tinned Spam, baloney cut by the slice off an enormous log, and old-fashioned ice-flavored pushups in the small antique Coca Cola cooler by the door. And the store was packed with so many old items that must have been in there for years, ranging like sentinels across the topmost shelf: tin cans for storage from a time when you stored everything. And pewter sprinkling cans, and three sizes of canning jars, and thread and needles, mouse and rat traps, axe handles and dust-covered rubber worms and bobbers for local fishing—and best of all, a dazzling array of chewing tobaccos.

I had never really noticed chewing tobacco before, but here you could not miss it. The tins sported labels: Southern Pride, Redman's Gold (and Silver), Levi Plug and Levi Garrett, Beechnut and Lancaster, Copenhagen, Hanken, and Skoal. Then there were the animal brands named for the toughest chewers: Longhorn, Grizzly, and Kodiak. Their labels combined old pleasures and new government health regulations. One side read, "This product may cause disease of the gums, falling teeth, and mouth cancers." The other side in larger letters announced, "It's as good as it gets."

Clothesline and clothespins, soaps and some basic unfamiliar cleansers were for sale. People here still conserved what they would not immediately use until they needed it. They dried their wash outside when they could, not because they didn't have dryers, because many did, but just because it made sense to hang the clothes outside when the weather was good enough. "Living green" was not new here.

The most unusual thing we found at Shelly Sue's and other family-owned local stores was the deep tradition of unashamedly requesting help for a neighbor in trouble. On a hand-penned sign we would read, "Tommy Jenkins got the cancer and needs money to help Jennie pay the medical bills," followed by details of the church supper and the date and place. You would go to the church or the volunteer fire department on the announced date and there would be hundreds of people and an array of donated food and, most important, a ten-gallon pickle jar rapidly filling with five, ten, and twenty dollar bills. You'd eat at long folding tables while a group of local fiddlers and guitarists played, their time and talent donated. This didn't feel like a community that had lots of extra twenties, but when local people were in trouble, the food, talent, and money appeared. There was no question that this was the only and right response for neighbors. Often, when we attended we wouldn't know a soul there, but we never once felt out of place.

At Shelly Sue's you would also find every single bit of information about the local community, not only who was born, sick, recovering, or dying, but who'd missed church last weekend, who was moving (including conjectures about why), and if you were an accepted member of the community, which we were not yet and might never really be, whispers about who was cheatin' on whom.

And no matter what time of day you might arrive, there was an old man sitting on a rusty porch chair in front of the store, doing nothing. We developed a little ritual.

I'd wave and ask "How you doing?" and he'd reply. "All right, I reckon. Looks like I'm gonna make it another day, the good Lord willing."

Nonetheless and as nice as she was, at this juncture we decided we'd better delete Shelly Sue from the list. How about E. Ray, our mysterious down-the-mountain neighbor? Not yet in the "friend" category. Scratch.

Monroe, Eunice, and family? They were questionable invites too. Bits and pieces of conversation and a general uneasiness in the air, plus Noah's "that woman" told us that there was more to their selling the property than first met the eye. We got the feeling of brothers unhappily estranged by a wife's possessiveness. Family spats and varying sized antagonisms were no strangers to us. We had our own family "tsuris" (troubles) and didn't need to get involved in anyone else's. We figured we'd better stay clear of what we couldn't fully understand. Besides, they had already moved and were living eight hours away, outside of Atlanta. Yes, scratch them.

In the end, we agreed to include only those people we had started to feel strong attachments for and who had already shown us their genuine goodwill, plus the few old dear friends who were here or visiting. Beyond this, the guest list boiled down to how many people we could seat on Monroe's reluctantly abandoned church pew as well as the four stairs of our front porch.

Who would be our guests? Steve and Gretchen, our oldest and closest friends, Bev, our former longtime Orlando neighbor, now a resident of North Carolina. two hours east, and, of course, our new neighbors and friends in-progress, the Simmonses, their children, Mark, and Noah and Mark's wife Melanie, and their children, Caroline and Molly.

So Jan got on the phone and told our old and newfound friends about our plans for a 4th of July barbecue and firework-watching. She asked each guest to bring a special dish. Jan anticipated a happy party, while I, unconvinced but as always fascinated by her chutzpah—sheer guts, nerve, and audacity—waited for the fireworks to begin.

Exactly at seven, the Simmons family arrived, all squeezed into their elder son Mark's van. This was the first time we were all together sharing an event, and in a show of solidarity in the face of the unknown, all three generations arrived together. We'd have done the same thing. Jan invited everyone in. The best way to describe our atmosphere might be self-conscious courtesy.

The beautiful kids were shiny as were the adults, and I felt, as they came in, that we were all wondering the same thing: what the heck would we talk about all night? But the moment Bitsy stepped out of the van carrying a gorgeous cream layered cake decorated with a red strawberry, white, and blueberry flag, any hesitation about the initial topic of conversation disappeared.

Wowing about how amazing the cake looked, we told them how much the cake reminded us of a delicious English trifle we'd eaten years ago in England. But way better. How cool it was that here it was again, adapted and dressed in its Appalachian berry finery for our Independence Day. Bitsy offered that it wasn't such a big deal, but Molly and Caroline knew better and were bursting with pride about how great their "Me Maw" was. And they couldn't have been more right.

Everybody pitched in now, arranging chairs, setting up the tables, putting out the red, white, and blue paper tablecloths Jan had bought for this, our Mezuzah Fourth. We all bustled, arranging dishes and plastic wear to get a little more comfortable with the idea of being together. Jan looked my way and, as only she can do, shrugged her shoulders and winked a wink of goodwill. And I needed it. "See," her wink said, "I was right. We're doing what neighbors who want to share lives have been doing for a long time, before the age of 'event planners,' and caterers, and DJs, took over. We're enjoying just getting together after a long, hot day of work to celebrate our good fortune as Americans who have plenty to eat, the time to eat it, and the wish to enjoy one another." Okay., I replied to the wink, but what was in store when she introduced her little surprise?

Part of the fun was to be what I'd already learned was a long tradition of mountain teasing, a first cousin of good-natured kibbitzing. Watching me fire up the charcoal, Lorne wondered if we should alert the volunteer fire department to stand by. Up here, he reckoned, we had to worry about protecting the surrounding trees. After all, it had been awful dry of late and my "squirting a fountain of starter on them briquettes…" I told him I figured an experienced mountain man like me would be all right. Together, we could manage something as simple as a forest fire. Just the same, he said, it would be good to show him where all the fire extinguishers were located. I went on soaking and stoking, not answering, but making a mental note to buy fire extinguishers soon. I was sure we could not rely on volunteer firefighters.

The reason was not only the remoteness of our location. The second week after we arrived a young man of thirty or so came up the driveway to introduce himself as a neighbor. It turned out that he was a neighbor from ten miles away, and he lost no time in letting me know that he would be pleased to come up and hunt deer on our land in the fall. I explained that there would be no hunting. He was used to hunting here, he said. Well, if he couldn't come up and park on the driveway, could he come up and follow one of the old logging roads up the mountain. I explained that we did not want any hunters anywhere. He was perturbed.

"You know," he said, "I'm on the volunteer fire brigade. It could take only ten minutes or so to get up here, but it could take a lot longer if a body got delayed." He promised that he had permission from the brothers to hunt. I, in turn, explained that the property was now ours. No hunting. He left in a huff. Later, I mentioned the incident to Lorne. He said the boy was plain and simple a liar. He and Mark and Monroe had told him and his friend on a couple of occasions that they wanted no hunting. Period. That evening he planned to call that boy and let him know that he wasn't happy, not at all, and didn't appreciate his telling lies on him. That it would be good not to happen again. We never heard from the fellow again. Still, it would make sense to get those extinguishers.

Lorne reckoned it'd be best to stay upwind for a while and we both silently agreed not to notice my nonexistent answer to his extinguisher question. In reality, it was a more perspicacious query than he realized. A couple of days earlier I'd decided to burn a pile of brush, and having trouble getting it to really ignite and not having any charcoal starter, I doused it with gasoline. It started all right. The explosion knocked me off my feet and scared the hell out of me. I did not confess to Jan what I'd done, even when she asked me if something was the matter because I looked so flushed. I wasn't flushed; I was singed.

Steve and Gretchen arrived fifteen minutes late, as usual. Some minor crisis usually came up and delayed them. But the wait was always worthwhile if just to see what Gretchen was wearing. Typically, she was decked out in a dress, saved from the local resale shop and converted into a beautiful smock along with an array of antique necklaces and beads that included a Jewish star, a crucifix, a peace sign, the Hand of God, and a Buddha on a beaded jade chain. Often, she included a Krishna. Gretchen had spent her life looking for a connection with God. I think she finally concluded that the most reliable connection was with the essential Oversoul, that there was a truth in all religions, and that you could wear them all together.

Gretchen cooked the same way she dressed—reusing, restoring, combining—creating dishes with the principal ingredients being tolerance for all kinds of unusual components and providing comfort for her guests. For this occasion, she'd prepared her corn pudding, a yummy concoction of her own invention, featuring ingredients no one but Gretchen would ever imagine combining. Cinnamon, nutmeg, several cheeses, cardamom, and yogurt were only a few of the ingredients she blended. Both the pudding and Gretchen looked marvelous. Every one appropriately oohed and aahed, as Jan gave her exotic corn concoction a place of honor on the table beside Bitsy's flag cake.

Still, with all the good-willed joking and the arrival of special foods, there was that sense of us all tiptoeing around on unfamiliar ground—especially our new family neighbors and Steve and Gretchen. Both of our old friends were self-admittedly idiosyncratic in their habits. Steve had been known to disappear into his painting studio for days on end, finally to emerge with 12-foot-square canvasses covered with Jungian images graphically depicting the fecundity of reproductive life. The penile and vaginal imagery had often startled the innocent, conservative, or uninitiated. When I was director of our Shakespeare Festival, I had one of his museum-sized paintings hanging in our reception area to announce to all who arrived that our Festival was serious about commitment to art and the honest exploration of the human condition. Some patrons and more than a few board members were put off.

Gretchen in her younger days, searching for models for a sculpture of wings she was imagining, was seen by other amazed pedestrians walking down the streets of metropolitan Orlando, a huge white swan under each arm, which, as she calmly explained, she had borrowed from the central city park lake and would return after she'd photographed and sketched them together. The astounding thing was that she carried them both home, a two-mile walk, without either bird making a sound or exhibiting any kind of objection. Anyone who knows a thing about swans will appreciate how remarkable this really was. Gretchen was the good witch Glenda with bona fide credentials.

Both our friends were naturally shy and sensitive and sometimes unaware of how beautifully odd they might have appeared. They had lived in these mountains for 25 years and seriously told us that in three months we'd met more people than they had in all their time here. This fact had a simple explanation. For most of their residence, they lived by the principle "keep apart." If these folks up here got to know anything about you, they'd know everything. And they would add and embellish more than the imagery in any of our paintings—"make things up," Gretchen explained with innocent incredulity.

It turned out that this uncharacteristic mantra was fueled by an incident during their first years here. One winter day, Gretchen had been out shopping in town and had found a wonderful, slightly ratty, waist-length old skunk fur jacket in a used clothing store and had worn it to go walking in the valley. The next day a somewhat removed neighbor had called and mentioned in passing to Gretchen that still another neighbor lady had viewed Gretchen's stroll and, misconstruing the moth-eaten hairy wrap as a Yankee show of luxury, had labeled her a "hussy," a woman flaunting herself and her wealth in public. Gossip spread, and before they knew it Gretchen was the Whore of Babylon. That did it. They would keep to themselves and resist knowing almost anyone. The possible repercussions of not doing so could be too hurtful.

So, while we were now all together inside our living room, tasting and chatting at our gathering to celebrate the implausible birth of a wonderfully diverse nation and a new household, there was ever present a hesitancy still hovering at the threshold. The Simmonses would continue to be polite and chatty and Gretchen and Steve careful. Who could know what surprises such a meeting between the Simmonses and the hussy and her consort would bring? Polite, careful; a sprinkling of joshing and talk of the unseasonably pretty weather might be the best way of safely negotiating the evening for everybody.

But nobody, not wary Steve and Gretchen, nor the innocent Lorne and Bitsy, not the bold, intuitive soulmate Beverly, not even I, could know what Jan had up her freshly ironed gingham sleeve. Emotional reserve was not on her agenda for this holiday.

We waltzed ahead. More introductions. Hesitant and shy hellos as well as polite inquiries about the remodeling Steve was doing down at their house; about the well he was digging; about how beautifully Lorne and Bitsy kept their property; and about whether Noah might consider helping him with some land clearing close to the river.

Then into this strained dance of the mutually restrained and cautiously wary strode Beverly, the six-foot-tall big-sister act both physically and emotionally to my wife, and a lady who does not believe in protectionism or quiet dances. Beverly's rhythm is more the mountain merengue or quick two-step, and here in she swept, taking center stage and without reservation began to tell her mountain tale.

After embracing Steve and Gretchen and telling all the Simmonses how happy she was to finally meet them and how happy her dear friends Stu and Jan were to be here and how many good things she'd already heard about them, and especially Noah, without, it seemed, taking a breath, Beverly explained that she now lived in North Carolina near Georgia. And she had come to the mountains ten years before during the winter as a result of dreams and premonitions that told her that if she stayed in sunny Florida she'd be lost. She'd been born there, but the mountains were where God intended her to be.

It happened, she explained, while she was lying on her stomach in her Florida backyard, thinking about her own life and unhappy marriage. Suddenly, a rabbit, who had taken up residence under her house and whom she had named Alicia after a mythic goddess she'd invented, came and crouched not two inches from her nose and communicated to her.

We all sat, staring and quiet. Undaunted, or merely unaware, Beverly went on.

"Well," she went on, explaining to us as if we were from another planet unable to speak the universal language available to earthlings, "wasn't it obvious?" Not to me, I was thinking. And I'll wager not to folks who are used to hunting rabbits rather than talking to them.

"It was a sign. Alicia was explaining how life should be lived, close to the earth and according to Nature's way. The very next day I put my house up for sale and filed for a divorce, and six weeks later I was moving. I knew only one person up in the mountains but trusted that it was the right place for me and that good people would emerge, as they always do if you give the Universe the chance to help you find your way."

"Well, to make a long story short, I moved, found a blessed place to live in a little mountain cabin. Neighbors showed up with food and blankets, and when they saw I was more prepared for a Florida winter than deep Carolina freezes, they came back with tons of clothes too. I met Skoshie, who has become a dear friend, and, best of all, I met Iggy. We married and had eight wonderful years, running his restaurant and discovering the wonders of our new mountain home and the land that we bought. Iggy died this last year." Her eyes filled with tears. "And now life goes on. I'll never leave these mountains. I am so happy to be here with all of you to enjoy this 4th."

And as corny as it might seem, there wasn't a dry eye in the Funny Farm living room. Gretchen gave Bev a huge hug. And Lorne, quiet since he arrived, with the exception of small talk and of his needling me about forest fires, spoke. "Well, we surely are happy to welcome you here. I don't know about that rabbit, but there are sure an abundance of amazing things on God's green earth. And I'll tell you something: we feel sort of the same way, like Jan and Stu were supposed to come and be here. And be part of this family."

If any ice remained to break, it was now in rapid meltdown and wafer thin. Jan called it the moment when we were all tenderized to one another. Coming out of the kitchen, Jan said there was something she wanted to show everybody and do together before we sat down to eat. She held a small package wrapped in tissue paper. Then reaching out and caressing it in the palm of her hand, she opened it and offered it so we all could see.

"This," she explained, "is a mezuzah. For us and for all Jewish people, it signifies the creation of a home and contains blessings for the family that were written thousands of years ago and have been repeated as God's blessing through the ages. It's from the Hebrew Bible, the Bible we embrace."

"I knew a few months ago that it would be the right thing to invite our friends together to help us hang the mezuzah here, because, I don't know, I felt that having community present needed to be part of this ceremony. In all the apartments and houses we've lived in and hung mezuzahs in, I've never felt the need to invite anyone besides our immediate family. Being here it seems right to share this important event with you. That you," she looked at Lorne and Bitsy, "would feel my wanting this to be holy."

"Before I say our prayers and hang the mezuzah I want to ask each of you, if you feel all right with it, to say what home means to you. I really want to blend your voices with our own."

That was final meltdown. No vestige of the hesitation waltz or even the fandango remained. And once again, as so often in our lives together, my wife's intuitive sense was spot on.

Softly, Steve began. He spoke about his love for his wife and children. He told us that he was unable to conceive of home without them. Verging on the edge of confession, he went on to say that there was not a day that went by that he had not thought of the mistakes he'd made as a young man that could have jeopardized his and his family's future, the one that he was enjoying this moment. He continued that he had gotten much more in life than he probably in truth deserved. It was a beautiful, sincere, and unmeasured response. It had the feeling of the confessional rather than the feeling of a man used to talking to classes and formal gatherings of admirers.

Beverly also expressed her love of family. "But," she laughed, "I have probably said far more than enough already and simply want you to know that wherever you are is home enough for me."

Lorne spoke next. "I want to say something, too, and I want you all to know that I'm not one used to talking like this. First, I need t' tell you that I, well, we were all pretty worried about who was going to move into this house. First time anyone not family's been up here. Then we heard that my brother'd done sold to people from Florida and we really got worried."

That one caused some embarrassed laughter.

"Well, it's true. First time I came up here, ready for the worst. And then I met Jan and fell in love. Sorry Bitsy, but I surely did. And in a little while, after I gave Stu a few lessons in gardening that he needed real bad, I found myself sharing things with Stu I ain't never shared with any other feller in the world. No one. Still can't figure out why. I need to tell you, too, that I ain't never been in a Jewish home before and I know how we have real different beliefs. So, to me it's real strange to feel so close. But there it is. There's so many experiences the good Lord prepares that not one of us understands."

"What I do know in my heart is that home for me cannot exist without the presence of the Lord Jesus Christ. He is in my heart and in every moment of my life and the lives of my dear family. And that I must tell you in anything I say about life. I also got to tell you that Jan and Stu feel as much like family as any two people I know. And we feel so grateful to have them here."

I'd already understood that this was a unique and substantial man. Now, I was doubly impressed with him.

From the very back of the room, nearest the kitchen we heard still another voice, muffled by sobs. Melanie, Mark's wife, stood there crying, great big tears rolling down her cheeks. "I was so scared," she sobbed through a thick Georgia drawl. "I thought anybody might move up here, they could chase us off the land, tell us they didn't want us here. Fence it in. I was just so scared. Then we met Jan and Stu and I felt... I felt..." She couldn't finish.

Bitsy was crying too, but in a controlled way, the way of experience conditioned by years of hard work and maybe disappointments. I don't know. But in that tiny body I sensed at that moment the person who most held that family together with good sense, strength, and decency. And abundant love.

Then Jan began the ceremony. She gathered us all around the doorway and held the mezuzah to the jamb and I began to place it with as much delicacy and grace as I could master. Which wasn't much. With her approval I began, "And you shall inscribe these words," to be joined by a second voice, "upon the doorposts of your house and upon your gates." The voice was Lorne's. He knew the biblical words better than I. But I knew the Hebrew. "Barukh ata Adonai Eloheinu Melekh ha-olam, asher kidshanu b'mitzotav v'tzivanu likbo-a mezuzah. Omein." I translated. "Blessed are you, Adonai, our God, Ruler of the Universe, who makes us holy with sanctified commandments and commands us to fix a mezuzah on our doorposts. Amen."

Everyone was quiet.

Then I discovered that I didn't have a screwdriver small enough to turn the tiny screws designed for the mezuzah. It was perfect me.

Now Mark spoke for the first time. Always practical and prepared, he volunteered that he had a set of screw bits in the van, and if we wanted and thought it would be all right, he'd be proud to help us hang the mezuzah. After some shuffling in and out and directions from Steve, who liked to give directions, the mezuzah was installed. And applauded. And the gathering shook hands as if we'd all just had a baby. We most assuredly had had a baptism. All we needed to complete the affair was a round of Cuban cigars or maybe even more appropriate, given the place and our human mixture, cups of chicken soup followed by chaws of tobacco.

All evening I'd noticed that Noah hadn't said a word, hanging close to his Mom, except when he drifted over to tell Steve that he'd think on the offer to help him clear some land. Then he'd repositioned himself near Bitsy and watched.

I'd supposed he had been overwhelmed by the solemnity of the sentiments, by his Daddy's speech, by Melanie's and his mom's crying, by the recitation of a strange language, by the newness of all of it. But now he was coming toward me with a troubled look in his eyes. He stood next to me and pointed at the mezuzah. "Stew," he asked, in an insistent voice, pointing at the mezuzah, "just what is that thing and what the heck is going on here?"

Well, I'd expected a twist somewhere in our ceremony, and wouldn't you know it, it was Noah who produced the question that came as close to summing up all our feelings as any one of us might have done. Just what the heck was going on here? I hoped we'd be working that one out for a long time to come.

Mezuzah.

ADAM HAD
HIS PROBLEMS

WHEN WE MOVED TO THE MOUNTAINS we were sure we'd found Paradise. Our house was surrounded by beauty. And its construction was endorsed by none other than our dear gentle giant, our personal Pier Gynt, Steve. When I describe his feats most people simply do not believe me. At 66, the man still moved boulders around with ease, by hand, cradled on levers he had constructed out of fallen trees he had toppled and sawed to precise dimensions. He still jackhammered, used air guns, and excavated stone rubble—without gloves. He labored with a myriad of mysterious machines. I probably wouldn't recognize him unaccompanied by grindings and explosions. All this he did with passion and ease. When Steve assured us both that in his opinion the house was as solid as the rock on which he had hand-built his own fortress twenty-five years before, well, quite simply, no testimony could have been better.

Steve's were pedigreed credentials. One of my most vivid memories was visiting him during his second construction summer and seeing Eric, his ninety-year-old father, hanging out over the ravine without a safety belt on a jerry-rigged scaffold, hammering in nails one by one. I don't know whether nail guns existed at the time, but I am pretty sure that if they did my friend and his dad would have resisted using them out of manly and craftsmanly principle.

Steve's dad was a born boss. When Eric was six years old his father abandoned the family, leaving him to try and take care of his three siblings. He went to school without shoes and with little to eat. He always had a job of some sort. When he got to high school and found out that if you joined ROTC you got a suit of clothes and shoes, he joined immediately. After high school off he went to the army. When he retired, he was a full colonel. Then he joined the fire department as a recruit. When he retired he was chief. And along the way, he taught himself carpentry and built homes.

The point is that when Steve, son of Eric, who made a believer of all the local skeptics, Steve the Super Builder, tells you the house you are buying is solid as a rock, you must believe. Period. End of potential debate.

And he was spot on for four weeks. Based on the man's endorsement and my subsequent hubris, I forgot the warnings of Bubbe Choma. Jan and I filled the air with self-congratulatory kinahoras, disaster-courting complacencies.

The house was perfect. We had a splendid paint job and had installed new windows. We added a cathedral-ceiling screened porch. Now we had a see-through, open kitchen, no obstructive old oak cabinets. Kinahora! And our acres were too beautiful for us to believe they were really ours, but there they were. Kinahora! Below the house, the apple, pear, cherry, plum, and black walnuts were thriving. Kinahora! Behind the house on the rise sloping up into our mountain woods were our blueberry and blackberry bushes and a mature grape arbor, all getting ready to drop their treasures. Kinahora! And above the slope on our mountain were our paths that wound up around groupings of monolithic boulders millions of years old under which bubbled our springs. Kinahora! And all of this was surrounded by pine, hemlock, locust, poplar, oak, and maple forests. A final chorus of kinahoras!

Surely you can see why Jan and I kept wondering at and praising our miraculous good fortune. Why we momentarily in our jubilation forgot Bubbe's warnings? It was all more than any city-born, Chicago-raised, Florida-grafted Jews could even imagine, let alone actually possess. Kina— kina—k-k-kin… everything was about as perfect as it could get.

MOTHER NATURE SURPRISED

THEN, EVERYTHING CHANGED, AND SUDDENLY. OH boy did it ever. Before you could get out the first syllable, "kin," and not even murmur "ahora," we were embroiled in a medical emergency that took the shape of an abrupt personality transformation in my usually sweet-tempered wife. Think Evil Queen's transforming potion. Think malicious alchemists turning gold into dross, and you've got it. We were all at once living with the reality of a mental disruption so severe and sudden as to turn our lives competely into chaos. And I was as lost about how to cope with her as she was about her new feelings.

Things had been roiling onward, getting worse and worse. This particular night Jan and I had a megatonic confrontation before I left to drive through a violent storm over to the Tri-City airport to pick up our son, Joe, and his son, Matan. She was insisting I needed a travelling companion in the person of Noah to ride with me, with both of us screaming at each other just before I ran out into the storm like a Jewish Lear. I suspected that the same thought crossed each of our minds: What have I gotten into, after all these good years?"

She shouted, shaking her finger at me. "He'll be your companion. He'll keep you awake at the wheel. He'll be a calming influence, a stabilizing force." Her finger, the same finger that magically reshaped our windows and cajoled me into tossing out the offending cabinet, was now madly trembling as it stabbed at me.

Talk about the charred pot screaming advice to the blackened kettle! As angry and confused by our turn of relationship as I was in Eden transmuted, I was still in my own mind a voice of reason.

"But what if the plane's late? What if his sugar drops? What if... ?"

I ran into the garage (where Noah had taken refuge) to quietly warn him off without hurting his feelings, but it was too late, because he had heard the shouting and looked terrified. By now he loved Jan. He loved me. And hearing us in what was obviously an ugly and impossible screaming match sliced him to the heart. I decided not to resist anymore. I ran back in the house to get a heavier rain jacket.

"Go!" She screamed. "Get in the damn car and go."

"I will. And maybe I'll just keep on going." Neither of us was really sane at this fissure in our marital journey. Instead of the apple, she was ready to bite me.

Me: "What is your problem?"

Jan: "You! You're my problem." She moved to turn away from me and left the room, enraging me by walking out on me while I was talking. Offended, I reached out for her arm to stop her, to calm her down. Now, our problem had taken on mega-alpha proportions.

"Don't-you-touch-me. Look at you; you're turning blue around the gills." I was sure she was right. She was grinning to let me know—what? That she'd won? No contest. I was a bewildered manchild in the land not of Eve but of Lady Macbeth, living right smack in the middle, not of a garden, but a heath, a decimated forest.

If the whole episode were not so pitiful, it, like most out-of-control emotions, could be high comedy. And even as I raged out the door, close to tears, I was not too far from laughing, too. I, the bungling, loving, peaceful gardener was now being accused of abuse by my life mate. And just a few months before Rosh Hashanah, the Jewish New Year, when we were supposed to be examining our lives and repenting of our sins.

If there was a watching God and he (or she!) was listening and on this strange woman's side, I was in big trouble. How could I convince him (her?) that I was being wrongfully accused of crimes I did not commit by this woman I did not know? Lately, I was guilty until proven innocent. In most of the modern world, wasn't the system of law designed the opposite way around? Why had it reversed so quickly on me here in what was so recently nearly idyllic Appalachia?

Though none of us could tell then where this lunacy would end, it was pretty easy to explain how it began. So briefly, here goes.

The Villain.

EVE TRANSFORMED

UPON SWEET JAN AND THEN ON everybody around her, Mother Nature played an enormous joke. As best as we can figure it, one gorgeous day Jan was walking high up on the mountain dressed in a t-shirt and shorts, picking blackberries.

"Tra la la la la," she went, skipping through our new pastoral world, reveling in the beauty all around her and trusting as only she can do to the goodness of the day, dropping her drawers to squat and pee whenever and wherever she felt the need.

Then, somehow, somewhere, and we still haven't figured out how or where, she got a lightning-quick case of poison ivy. My wife was allergic to lots of stuff—chlorine, penicillin-derived drugs, bee stings. Mother Nature, it turned out, was not only indescribably beautiful in these mountains, but inscrutable to the unsophisticated and unwary—and very dangerous as well.

At first, there was a little itch on her backside. We joked about the purple pimpernel. Then there was a little sore. Then it exploded like wildfire through dry brush sprinkled with gasoline (note my new understanding of the mountains), and she developed a spreading series of sores that literally got nastier with each passing hour. The lesions grew purple and relentless, claiming more territory, until her entire formerly beautiful derrière was covered with the spreading rash and unbearable itching.

What started as a "Gosh, wasn't I silly?" little lament turned into anguish and what we eventually agreed was becoming a frightening medical emergency. The damned stuff kept moving into adjacent areas. At the beginning we could joke about the rashes going into places I hadn't been for eons, but the jokes ended pretty abruptly with rashes, blisters, open sores, and monstrous itching all at once. And we found ourselves first scoffing at and then trying all the time-tested remedies recommended by our good-willed neighbors.

"They must know," we reassured one another in our desperation. "They've lived here all their lives." But they didn't. My favorite, in retrospect, was the famous sand-scrub ointment remedy. "Just take a real hot shower and rub this sandy stuff on and scrub till you're raw. That'll do it." Well, maybe for them! Which is not to say it was completely ineffective. It did something for us too: the infection spread even faster and further.

Next there was the "my mama used to pour straight bleach on it." We did on a tiny spot. The result? Something that looked like third-degree burns.

Then there was jewelweed, recommended in the herb books sold at the local bookstore in town that apparently specialized in tourists, informing us that the jewelweed remedy was first discovered by the Cherokees who lived in these mountains for hundreds of years and passed on their medical wisdom to the white man. I now think that the jewelweed stuff was a subtle revenge perpetrated by some very embittered descendants of those original Native Americans. Either that or, let's face it, the original inhabitants weren't so super effective in their remedies.

After failing miserably with the ordinary jewelweed applications, which, it turned out, could be purchased in an infinite variety of formulations, we resorted to less folksy means. In the interim, I decided we might get inventive and use this latest disaster to join the natural-remedy crowd by contributing our own (failed, but no one had to know that) process and adding our own prescription for application that, if we played our cards right, would soon appear on the labels of our personalized blue glass, translucent, flower-bordered bottles.

"You must Chew it, Rub it, and Soak your Disturbed areas in it. Next, you must drink a teaspoon mixed with a glass of one-hundred-percent cranberry juice while standing naked on the highest peak in the area, your arms outstretched to the four winds, your privates exposed to those same winds as you chant our culture's secret ancient incantation, "A brokh tsu Dir. A brokh tsu Dir. A brokh, a brokh, a brokh tsu Dir," which roughly translated from the language of the 13th tribe of Israel, now represented by us and in residence in these mountains, was "A curse upon You. A curse upon You, a curse, a curse, a curse upon You,"—"You" being Mother Nature, of course.

Our rationale for this adaptation was that having suffered the failed attempts of natural folk wisdom and love, we would give notice that we were here to stay and would not again be tricked into believing this world was wholly benign to our residence. We figured our own brand of magic language laced with skepticism combined with the touted native shtick (process) had to be every bit as good at turning the poisonous tide as anything we'd had recommended by our neighbors or by zealous, suspicious-looking, over-the-counter clerks at the local herbalist. It couldn't be worse, right? Wrong. More hubris. It could be and was.

While none of the local medicinals worked, neither unsurprisingly did the Hebraic cabbalistic incantations. Even a thick solution of oatmeal, calamine lotion, and honey (a last desperate attempt touted by a local bee-keeper) spread on the expansive area—the closest we had come to kinky sex in a long time—didn't do a bit of good.

Finally, we resorted to the wisdom of modern medicine, when we could get an appointment to see a doctor. And he, in his infinite wisdom, looked at her behind using a magnifying glass (yes, really!), pronounced in learned tones "Poison Ivy," and prescribed prednisone by mouth.

But even that did not work. And so off we were sent to the dermatologist, who used an even larger magnifying glass, diagnosed "Bad Poison Ivy," and hit her with a double-dose injection of prednisone plus a two-week dose by mouth.

Well, that did it. Oh boy did it ever. The medical cavalry had arrived. The poison ivy was defeated and pretty quickly too. But unfortunately we had merely traded one problem for another.

Jan suddenly went into mental overdrive. In a trice, my rational bride became a walking, speed-talking incarnation of that old TV ad, "This is your mind at work. This is your mind (picture a sizzling, burned, fried egg) on drugs."

My darling and demure, trusting, understanding, and, above all, kind bride metamorphosed into a cross between Lady Macbeth and Medea—only with a much worse attitude. Lady M sleepwalked; Jan slept not a wink. Lady seduced; Jan cursed. For her, I became the rotten Jason and the spineless, infantile thane all rolled into one.

Quick as you can say, "fiery dress," or "toil and trouble," I was accused of every marital and domestic crime known to humankind.

"And another thing, you belittle me. You've always belittled me," she railed. "You're an asshole and you're a big baby," she swiped, accompanying her words with a profusion of snarls I'd never heard before, anywhere, not even in the lion house at Lincoln Park Zoo.

All through her tirades and my inadequate responses, Bagel looked as if he was trying to figure out whose side to be on. Mostly, even when she was hollering, he tried to stay by her side. Or out of her way. She'd yell; he'd retreat then return, only to be scared away by another volley. In the end, he walked to a neutral corner, first in the kitchen, then in the living room, and watched us out of those big brown concerned eyes.

"And you were a bad father. You never spent quality time with your sons. Always wanting me along, for Christ sake." She was right. I did always want her at my side.

"And another thing... and another..."

The inventory and the catalogue seemed endless and hurt like hell, but I must admit the words impressed me as remarkably inventive, even at the moment of their delivery. Was any of this stuff true? Probably. Otherwise, where was she getting the unlimited supply of ammunition?

To add even more stress to a bad situation, all of this screaming prior to my careening out the door was in earshot of my 85-year-old mother-in-law who had come to visit us—and had been here for, let's see, three glorious, fun-filled weeks—while an awful storm back in Florida was gearing up and getting ready to rip apart whole neighborhoods. Winds were predicted to attain hurricane velocity. This disturbed her. It disturbed us all. But what disturbed me more, I am ashamed to admit now that she has passed away, was the prospect that she would become our permanent house guest, adding one more strain to our already rupturing marriage in our sinking Eden. What disturbed her as much as anything, I think, was that from her point of view *she* was supposed to be the all-powerful natural force; the ripper, not the rippee. The hurricane was trumping her act and she was not a bit happy about it.

For as long as I'd known her, Shirley's general idea of Nature was that the natural world would just have to adjust—to her. After eight-and-a-half decades on our planet she was almost deaf, but, true to form, she refused to acknowledge the severity of the problem by purchasing a hearing aid.

"I'm old and a little hard of hearing so you'll all just have to talk louder."

She wasn't "a little" hard of hearing. But on the occasion of this episode in Jan's and my marital madness, she seemed somehow to be right, damn it. She had overcome the calamity of aural Nature and somehow miraculously heard our entire fiery exchange: each word, syllable, phoneme, nano-sound particle.

Sure that her age entitled her to senior witchhood in our recently enchanted household, Shirley was equally certain that she should be even more irritating and obstreperous than usual. I'd like to be more generous by saying that her refusal to admit to a severe hearing problem was mostly a sign of her defying old age. Well, maybe that was part of it, but defiance was not unusual to her at any age.

"Is it so hard for you to talk a little louder?" she yelled.

During these last few weeks, my wife had spent time alternately either embracing and kissing her Mother, "Mom, I love you. I love you," or telling her off in fiery language, dripping with resentment, linguistic pistolas drawn and leveled and held to the head. "You can no longer insult me or anyone else." I thought that with her back arched and those green eyes focused squarely on the center of her Mumsy's forehead, my formerly sweet wife, now my feral Eve, was dangerously close to pouncing into her Mother's witch-like province. My fear was that once fully in, she would never return.

"I want to be a Bitch—and I am going to be a Bitch." pronounced my bride.

Was this a new form of perverse latent ambition? Work hard enough at a goal, rehearse intensely enough, inject enough hormonal fluid, and anyone can succeed, even someone dispositionally unsuited to the role.

During one of these episodes when Jan told me she could no longer endure the color of the downstairs bathroom toilet, or her mother, or me, and alternately begged or commanded me to flush myself down the commode or get Mumsy out of the house, or best of all possible worlds, both flush and get, a logical impossibility she could not see with her eyes clenched so tightly, Mom and I went for a ride to town.

"And don't either one of you dare talk about me! In fact, don't talk at all."

So here I was riding with another mandated travelling companion! My mother-in-law did not heed her spawn's advice to forebear. After fifteen minutes of soothing silence, she just felt compelled to speak to me, telling me that she knew "Who I Was And What I Was," pronouncing each word as if it were a proper noun She allowed that I was basically a good person, but that I had a terrible temper. Well, I thought, this was not as bad a condemnation as I thought I might receive. It was true, I did have a temper, but if I kept my lips zipped or spoke at inaudible decibels during this ride, we might both exit no more wounded or perplexed than when we began. So I clenched my teeth and chose silence.

But sealed in the car together, she took the opportunity to tell me I was goodhearted most of the time, but without empathy, without sympathy, with no gene for caring. Like most men, even the best. Only women stepped forward on a moment's notice in a health crisis; men were not able. At the moment I had no need of being excoriated; actually, I was doing a pretty good job blaming myself for my fears, my confusion, my unmanly behavior, and, yes, for my embarrassing temper. After 5,000-plus years of guilt training, she and I were an unbeatable duo.

Yet even through my guilty mist (was I truly just a rotten, unfeeling, worthless piece of cow flop?) I could see the dark irony of this particular judge and jury bringing down her gavel on me. This judgment was from a woman who had once actually set fire to her husband's mattress, using a safety match (a nice touch) and his own lighter fluid to get him out of his bed when he was in a desperate depression. Whose idea of empathetic therapy was to flush him out like a terrified deer, or barbeque him as a sacrificial ram enwrapped in his own fiery bed linen. To be fair, her incendiary impulse was born out of desperation, since my father-in-law had been sinking deeper and deeper into depression, and psychiatrists were no help.

But though her plan was extreme, it was not at all uncharacteristic. After all, this is also the woman who once objected so strongly to her husband's unsolicited, loving gift of a full-length mink coat that she tossed it out with the morning garbage. "When I say I don't want something, I don't want it!" she shouted. From a woman who once spray-painted every item in her home gold—yes, gold: chairs, drapes, sofas, a grand piano, a harp, lampshades, and even clothes and shoes—because she was feeling... creative.

This from the woman nicknamed by me "Early Shirley" for her habit of arriving three hours early at an event and then insisting she wanted to leave because she was tired of waiting for the show to begin or because of some imagined slight perpetrated on her by one of those late people!

From the woman who once, objecting to her designer husband's ward-robe, his major sin this time being his possession of too many shirts, gathered them all while he was at work, and placed them collar to shirt tail, starting in his closet and lining them up through every room of their three-story house, up and down staircases, over chairs and tables, through closets, all three hundred of them complete with matching ties! It was her demonstration that he, he, was obsessive.

This from the woman who, brandishing freshly sharpened scissors, chased her sixteen-year-old daughter around the house, threatening to cut off her bangs because she hated all that hair hiding her exquisite forehead. And would have done it if said daughter, my wife to be, had not run into the furnace closet, locking herself in and refusing to come out unless her mother put down the scissors.

From the woman who hid diamonds in the coffee grains for safety, and later, having forgotten, flushed them down her kitchen sink drain. From the woman who rented a camper for a family vacation and then kept it securely parked on the driveway because she was afraid to go, creating a motive for her reluctance by saying the kids had committed some imag-ined crime. From the woman whose patron saint (can Jews have patron saints?) was Lucille Ball.

And I'm nuts? I'm abusive? Just imagine.

But. (There's always a "but," isn't there?) We slap someone into a cat-egory and as consistently fruitcakey as they seem to be, the envelope tears.

This is also the woman whose remarkable energy and will allowed her to keep her mortally sick husband with her after every physician advised her to place him in a nursing home to save herself; who drove him around the deserted city until three and four in the morning, because riding was the only solace that could ease his crippling anxieties. This was the lady who called us with calm and exhausted dignity from her car at 5 a.m. to say that Dad had just died sitting beside her. Crazy and equally admirable.

So, she and I drove on, both frightened that our beloved, thoughtful, talented Jan was terribly sick, possibly like her bipolar father, and both wondering in our own ways what we could do about it.

LIFELONG LEARNING

AND NOW SO HERE I WAS, a bewildered Lear, wondering that same thought again, driving toward the Tri-City International Airport with my new automotive companion, Noah. As I drove and listened to the pounding rain mixed with Noah's renewed talk of chicken livers and the gastronomic wonders of Big Macs and fried onion rings, the odd justice system recently imposed by my child-bride-turned-inquisitor seemed just right for a dramatic climax. This was a night perfectly suited for an automobile accident, my sacrificial blood splattered over the highway, a fitting and semi-kosher substitute for those little packets of restaurant catsup Noah loved. Noah and I would be discovered in the morning as road food for hovering North Carolina vultures.

And although initially I objected to his riding with me, finally I realized I was happy he was along. And now that we were out of the house and on our way, he was calmer. Jan's and my ranting were in the past.

As usual, his conversation was simple, honest, and without guile. Was this because he seemed to possess almost no inclination to dwell in the past and so he never seemed to hide behind old histories? I really don't know. I did know that already in our short relationship he had told me some big things, about his sugar, for example, and that because of the diabetes almost each time he ate anything he had to check the numbers on his computer and often give himself an insulin shot. Learning to check the numbers was not easy because as he'd also explained, he'd never learned to read or write. When he needed to buy something at a store in town, he depended on whoever was with him to watch and be sure he was offering enough money and on the clerk to offer the correct change. I'd seen him offer a twenty-dollar bill for a two-dollar item and ask whether it was enough.

When he explained about his inability to read, I asked him how he felt at the time the teachers told him and he replied almost inaudibly that it made him sad. He said he was still kind of sad. Sad? With so many problems, one would think he would be gloomy or bitter or at least, to use his word, "snappy," but he was none of these. He possessed a wonderful optimism, a wry sense of humor, and, most important, he was perhaps the most genuinely open and kind human being, besides my wife, that I had ever met.

Lorne, who had always made his living with his clever hands and mind and monumental work ethic, questioned the school principal's verdict that Noah would never read and was told that he could hire a lawyer and sue the school system and then they would have to provide a one-on-one tutor, but that this would take a long time and the school system had no money for special education.

Lorne told them that he could not understand this kind of thinking. Why did he need to sue if suing would force the issue and eventually get the results? Why not just find the same money and try to help his son learn what he could without lawyers and lawsuits? I don't know what the answer was. Probably the principal said that tutors wouldn't make any difference. Lorne did not pursue his question. I suspect that going up against the system and all those suited, educated people was intimidating to him back then. I can see how this still bothers him.

Lorne's dilemma reminded me of ours with our eldest son, Steve. He was a sweet, shy boy who seemed to have some difficulty with school. But we were naïve and young, and he was our first child and we so doted on him we could see no serious problems. Added to this, we were in a primitive Florida where California open-schooling techniques were all the rage. It was not unusual for children to disappear for a while and then be found after a couple of hours coloring under a table. I'm not kidding.

When Steve was nine, yes, after four years of public school, I took a sabbatical to do post-graduate work at Northwestern, and we enrolled Steve in public school there. After two weeks we were summoned to the school and told by the in-house psychologist that our son was two years behind the curve and had a learning disability, most evidenced in reading comprehension. Neither Jan nor I had been smart enough to pick up on this, probably because he was a quiet boy who gave the beleaguered teachers who were searching out the more aggressive kids under the tables no trouble, partly because we were in love with him, and mostly because we paid far too little attention to what was going on in the school. We just assumed they knew what they were doing.

We were devastated by the news. We ran to other psychologists and received all sorts of conflicting advice and recommendations. They told us everything from that he was average, but shy, to that he was of borderline intelligence, to that he was gifted as an artist but challenged with verbal comprehension. All we knew was that he was having trouble and it was up to us now to take some kind of action. If we could not get help in Florida we were prepared to leave for a more progressive state. We cursed; we fumed, as much at ourselves as at the school system.

Luckily, we found a private school whose principal had quit the Florida public schools in disgust and frustration at their letting children slip through the system's very large cracks and started her own school for learning disabilities in a church basement. She hired young teachers who loved kids and doted on the ones who were difficult to teach. Their qualifications were enthusiasm, love, patience, perseverance, and innovation. She didn't much care if they possessed education degrees. Steve thrived there. And this time when we didn't have to, we watched and questioned all that went on. After three years, he returned to public school and, in time, graduated from a fine private college.

Earlier, when Steve was seven and I was twenty-eight going on ten, I convinced myself that in order to fulfill my obligations as a proper Jewish father, it was my duty to send Steve and his younger brother to a synagogue Sunday school.

A few weeks after the boys started, Steve came home crying, explaining between sobs that the teacher had singled him out from the class when he had trouble understanding the Hebrew alphabet. This practitioner of sweet religious education had bent over next to Steve and shouted into his ear, "What's inside there? Anything? Sawdust?" The rest of the class laughed. Steve wept. I was so angry, I was sick.

The next day, I went first into the teacher's office who told me, as he protected himself behind the desk, that it was just a little joke. Then I was in the rabbi's office, shouting into his ear, asking him when he intended to fire the stupid, insensitive, and arrogant son of a bitch. His response was that everyone makes mistakes, etc., etc., etc., and I realized that the correction of my mistake was to do what I really wanted to do in the first place and let my kids grow up as good people, learning the ethical principles of Judaism from Jan and myself, without the rituals, and staying as far from organized religion and its insulated, self-righteous advocates as we could get ourselves.

I do not think that the heartaches Lorne and I suffered as a result of people's insensitivity to our children were different. If there were any real differences, they resided in Lorne's and my fatherly responses to the pains suffered, not the pains themselves. Mine were the result of 5,000 years of training in belligerence and anger at authorities' abuse. Maybe, too, it is simply that by then I had been in the professional education business for ten years and knew from experience how abysmally stupid some so-called educators could be. I remembered that a balegolah (wagon driver) in a suit and tie or caftan or collar or yarmulke is still a balegolah.

Anyhow, for the last month, I had been trying to teach Noah to read and was making some progress. It happened this way. Noah told me during one of our conversations in the garden that he wished he could read at least some of the ads in the newspaper and that more than anything else he wished he could read enough to get a driver's license. Days passed, and one day when we were again working in the garden, I reminded him of our conversation about reading and reminded him again that I had been a teacher and that I would be willing to try and teach him to read if he wanted it, but that I wouldn't ask again—ever. It would be up to him to tell me. He nodded but said nothing.

Later that week during a visit to our house, Noah surprised me.

"Stew, you remember what you said about learnin' me to read?"

"Sure."

"Well, did you mean it?"

"What do you think?"

"Well, I reckon I'd like to give it a try."

That was one of the honored moments in my life. I may be kidding myself, but I think that for someone to say he would trust you to work with him on something so difficult and painful is a big vote. I know I could never be so trusting so fast.

As we drove, I remembered our lessons.

In his sweetness, Noah asked me at least three times during an hour session about how he was doing. He was a worker, but for him progress in this kind of work was excruciating and slow. Most frustrating for both of us was his inability to conceptualize. No matter how many times I explained that each time he sees the letters "ing" together, they have the same sound pattern as in "starting" or "going" or "fixing," he would still begin to struggle with "I"—"I," "i," (eeee), "n"(nnnnnn) and "g," trying to fit them together. I would reassure him he was doing fine. He'd smile. "I am, ain't I?" And he was. He was slowly learning to read. Determination is a powerful motivator and a big component of heroism. Noah was heroic, hour after hour.

After our first few sessions, Noah appeared with a small briefcase that his dad gave him to keep all his materials and lessons. He was scrupulous about gathering them each time he left. If, somehow, he forgot something, he telephoned and was at our house the next morning to search it out. Aside from the terrible difficulty he had in learning, one couldn't ask for a better student.

For me Noah was also a tonic. Before buying this remote farm, we lived the university life for thirty-seven years, where a large minority of my colleagues (if not the majority) were lucky enough to have the gift of high intelligence. They were equally maladjusted and unhappy, wearing their discontents and cynicism like medals they'd earned in graduate school, medals that in their own minds set them apart from ordinary mortals. And were they ever vocal about it! Never was there a paucity of words, usually caustic words, about their fates at this silly institution that was lucky enough and unappreciative enough to have them in residence. Why oh why, they lamented with scorn in many, many words, didn't the powers appreciate the degrees earned from Michigan and Stanford?

Noah chose his words. When he had nothing to say—surprise, he said, nothing!

Tonight, though, he was hungry and so had lots to say. As we wound along the twisting roads, he talked with me about one of our favorite subjects: food.

"Stew, do you like Chinese?"

"Yes."

"Me too. Do you like fried green tomatoes. Ever eat them?"

"No, I haven't."

"They're good. Mama would make 'em for you. Squirrel gravy?"

"That's absolutely a 'no.' Yuck."

"It's good, too, on top of biscuits. Don't be so prejudice!"

We'd had some talks about prejudice. He had me there.

"Okay. She makes it, I try it."

"You'll see. Chicken livers?"

"Now there's a food I know something about. Chopped liver and onions on dark rye bread or a toasted bialy with a ripe tomato. And a tiny little bit of chicken fat mixed in it. Now there, my friend, is heaven."

"What's that? I never heard of that. Do you reckon Jan would make us some? I'd like to try it."

"You bet. For you, I know she would, but maybe without the fat. We really stopped eating that about fifty years ago. And I will personally bake you a bialy."

"She likes me, don't she?"

"She thinks you're great." The truth is that Jan in any state of mind loved him. Said he was one of the sweetest souls she'd ever met. A human being with a big heart, a mensch. On this one, it's not so hard to do a rough translation. The overtones are clear. Mensch is simply a matter of fundamental character, of understanding what's right and doing it. It's not a matter of intelligence or worldly accomplishment. It's not hard to talk "mensch," but it's rare to be one.

Even in the darkened car I could feel him smiling.

Tonight, though, besides food, this mensch was also very concerned about weather. My problem was that I was getting nervous as hell driving these unfamiliar roads, and Noah had moved on from food and Jan's admiration to what I had learned to recognize as "Noahian anxiety."

"Sure am glad it rained," he began. "We sure did need it. Do you think it's raining at home?"

"I guess so." He was right. We did need the rain, but not so much, not all at once, not in sheets, and not now. Not with the wind blowing and me agitated; not with my wife being nuts. And as I guessed, Noah this night was turning out to be a tremulous companion.

"Stew, I think my sugar's getting low." The rainstorm and the long ride through foreign territory without the comfort of his parents were making him super jumpy, and when he got nervous, his diabetes seemed to get active. There was always the danger of diabetic shock and he'd told me it had happened before.

"Did you bring something to eat along the way?" I was hoping he'd say yes, but I suspected it was too much to hope for.

Sure enough, he admitted, "In all the rushin' I done forgot."

And so, though I'd learned to enjoy his company, even to love him as a kind of younger brother or son, he was not the traveling companion of choice as the night lengthened and the ride got longer and more treacherous.

With each crack of thunder and each flash of lightening, the road became more slippery. It was by then a deluge, and we both could hear the water rushing in the culverts along the highway. Even with the wipers full on, I was having a hard time, bending over the dashboard just to try and see.

As Noah grew more agitated, so did I. And pissed too. Not at Noah, although his editorial comments as we went on were getting me crazier than I was when we left the farm, and I was pretty goofy then. I was just pissed at the whole bizarre situation.

Noah pointed out each stalled vehicle along the highway. He also recorded one by one those in ditches or wrecked. There were lots of them.

"I sure hope we don't get wrecked like them there. Stew you think we're all right?"

"I think we're fine," I lied. I was leaning over the steering wheel, my face about three inches from the windshield by then because some sort of fog had rolled in to worsen the situation.

I grunted.

"It'd be terrible if we crash, wouldn't it Stew? Look at that one. I bet someone got killed over in that one. Bet there's blood everywhere. It'll be awful if we got killed. I'll bet everyone'd cry."

"Don't worry, we're in control." I drove, but my Tonto kept on.

"Good golly look at that wreck!"

I finally decided to try kidding to calm him down—telling him that if he cited one more wrecked VE-HI-CLE, just one, I would stop OUR VE-HI-CLE on the muddy side of the road and give him the opportunity to walk home, without a VE-HI-CLE.

He grinned that deep, dimpled, loving grin and told me that he knew, "You're just funnin' me—ain't you?"

I was, or at least I thought I was.

We drove on, with Noah wondering aloud if we were going in the "right direction."

This would have been funny, maybe, to anyone but me, who, like my sister, was born with absolutely no gene for recognizing North, East, South, or West. In just a few seconds he'd succeeded in getting me wondering along with him. After all, I knew that I was the guy famous in our family for leaving Chicago destined for Oxford, Ohio, and traveling at breakneck speed to discover after three hours a sign that read "Welcome to Chicago, City of the Big Shoulders." That time forty-three years ago I had my fresh bride with me, who I am sure was wondering for the first time, as she had most recently tonight, what she'd gotten herself into.

I pushed forward into the rainy night.

A CANDY MACHINE AND AIRPORT COFFEE

THE SITUATION WITH NOAH'S DIABETES WORSENED just as we approached the airport. He was not feeling well. In our rush to get out of the house, we'd both forgotten to bring food. We parked the car, got into the ticket lobby, and found a place to sit. I told him to relax, close his eyes, and breathe while I went to look for something for him to eat.

I found a vending machine that had cookies and candy. So far so good. I had no coins, but luckily there was a dollar changing machine and I had a few singles. I got the machine to take my least wrinkled bill, and true to the way the night was shaping up, I got back no change. After trying to ingest it several times, with my prayers of encouragement, with my smoothing out of Washington's wrinkled face, the machine ate another dollar. I gave it another buck. This was no time to quibble. My last single disappeared, and I was getting desperate. I was picturing Noah lying on the airport floor, his tongue dangling from his mouth like Bagel's after too long a run. Bitsy had been reluctant to let him go in the first place. She would kill me if something happened to her baby, and rightfully so.

Out of the corner of my eye, I saw an African-looking lady in a brightly colored dress and an elaborate headdress. She was very black, almost midnight blue of complexion, peculiarly out of place here, quietly sitting awaiting one of the flights. I don't know why, but I rushed over to her out of the few people around, somehow knowing she'd be the most helpful, and explained our situation. She listened to half my explanation, gave me three quarters, and told me not to worry about getting them back to her.

"Please, attend to your friend."

In about any other circumstance I would be bombarding her with questions, but not now. I rushed to the machine, bought a Clark bar, and ran back to Noah. My vision of him wasn't too far off. By now he was pale and shaky. I almost had to put the candy bar in his hand and close his fingers over it.

"Stew, I d,d,ddon't really like this kind of candy."

I did not believe what I was hearing. But despite my dismay, I looked at him and saw trust in his eye. I'm Stew and I can help take care of things.

"Noah this is no time, I mean no time, to play the reluctant gourmet. Please just eat it."

"A what?"

"Never mind, I'll explain later. Just eat it. Please." He did and in a few minutes he was feeling better and his color had started to return. And thank goodness he had stopped trembling.

Now I was the one shaking and, for the first time this evening, laughing. The few people in the airport discreetly turned their heads to see what was so hilariously funny. Noah asked if I was feeling shaky too. The African lady had disappeared. Was she for real?

"Step right up folks and see before you a very odd couple. Two scared PhDs. One who is an expert in Posthole Digging and the other a doctor of philosophy who is about as inept at postholes as his mountain man younger brother is at Shakespeareana; yet they are nonetheless, this night, genuinely worried about each other.

One was terrified that his little brother was in real danger of suffering a diabetic seizure, and the other was worried that his ol' man friend's marriage was splitting and that his beloved Jan was acting as crazy as a mare in heat. Neither situation made any sense.

And all three of them—Jan, Stu, and Noah—in this collective scene were doing about as well as they could do. Talk about frailty thy name is—human.

Back at the airport, I knew that my peculiar behavior was startling to the few people bold enough to turn fully toward me. Could I explain to anyone here, even to that wonderfully sympathetic and now vanished African woman, that I was laughing at myself to keep from crying, as I realized my fears and frustrations and sudden sense that the world was even more goofy than even I was used to thinking it was? Bubbe Choma used to say, "Man tracht und Gott lacht."—Man plans and God laughs—a sentiment I was sure my new Christian friends would not endorse. I did.

My thoughts returned to Jan. Who was this harridan, this bubbling cauldron of vitriol, and, by the by, what was I going to do while trying to live with her? Truth to tell, I was laughing because I was terrified. Had Mother Nature watched and tapped into my deepest fear and created a sick Jan, and then, having cured that, had modern medicine created a sicker Jan— a Frankensteinian-Monster-Medean-Lady Macbeth of the Mountains— powered by a seemingly unlimited tankful of inventive fervor? Was all this behavior really only the result of that magic medical potion, and would it eventually wear off, assuming we could tolerate each other long enough for that to happen? Or? The alternative was too terrifying for me to give it voice. My mattress-burning mother-in-law lurked in the background, warning me. "I lived with his manic depression for twenty-five years and now you will, too." Was it possible? Had the doctor's cure tumbled us into a far worse disease lurking just under Jan's emotional skin all these years, just waiting to make its appearance? I witnessed my father-in-law's torment. I could not abide thinking this could be happening to my Jan.

My companion, Noah, the guy who was supposed to keep me fresh and awake, now told me that he was very sleepy and needed coffee. At last here was something I could handle. Or so I thought.

There was a coffee machine—somewhere. But this was not O'Hare or Orlando International, with food courts every hundred feet. Here, we needed to search. But that wasn't really the heart of the problem. After all, it was a relatively small airport. Indeed, in short order we found several vending machines that dispensed drinks, and they were state of the art, to my amazement. And that was precisely the problem. Noah could not yet read well. He was just getting the hang of short and long vowels and rhyming words; the modern coffee vending machine, with all its conveniences, must be encountered and defeated, and he could not do it alone.

Coffee with sugar, coffee without sugar; coffee with cream, coffee without cream; coffee with cream and sugar, black, decaffeinated, with, without; tea; hot chocolate. With whipped cream, without. Latte? Cinnamon, with and without cream and sugar; Espresso…

What a country! We run the risk of dying from thirst or old age before we can finish calculating the beverage choices and add-ons theoretically available for our convenience. And I ran the risk of insulting my friend by just rattling off the list without encouraging him to try and read the menu. Noah must have black coffee. So I helped interpret. It was a slow process. He wanted to be sure I'd got it right, because he'd learned from long experience that a small mistake can have large consequences. So he was persistent. And contrary to my nature and the stressful house exit, rain-swept ride, and visions of life with Franky-girl, I exercised patience. This was actually pretty cool. We made a reading lesson out of it, and for the moment it took me away from more frightening thoughts.

Having finished the lesson and dispatched the linguistic monster we were ready to purchase. And thank goodness, Noah had come prepared. He had the right change, while my pockets were, naturally, empty.

Now all was well. Noah put in his three quarters (coffee here was still less than a dollar), the cup dropped, the light came on and the inviting, multi-captioned, beckoning, neon-lit machine delivered—an empty coffee cup. It had taken his coins and silently grinned in our faces.

"Jesus," I muttered, but I figured that this was all of a piece with the evening. Chalk it up to a fate that appeared increasingly real.

Noah, to put it mildly, was not happy with my response. "Stew, shame on you." He was right. But for the moment he let it go by. He shifted his gaze from me to the coffee cup. The machine had swindled him and Noah was not one to lose his money gracefully. He may not have been the best counter, but he knew when he'd paid for something and got nothing in return. Now he was most definitely "snappy."

My calm buddy first gave the machine a little coaxing shake, then a rocking (and that thing was plenty heavy), and when no liquid appeared, he whacked the side of the machine with a blow that in all likelihood would turn Paul Bunyan green with envy. When there was still no response, he slammed it again. I tried to calm him. It was only 75 cents, I reasoned. What's 75 cents even to an academic pensioner like me? I forgot that when you make your money mowing fields, driving fence posts, sowing tobacco, and pushing around cattle, losing hard-earned money is not and should not be taken lightly.

Then just as I wrapped my arms around Noah, putting myself between him and the coffee machine, pushing my rock-solid friend back, hoping I could stop him before his growing anger brought the local gendarmes and got us in big trouble, I watched a change come over him. That old dimpled, beatific smile crossed his face and I swear I thought that he'd realized the error of his ways, that his anger was uncharitable and that he had reconnected with deeper values. And I half seriously thought that I might start to subscribe to some religion. If it could effect a change so quickly, I might be barking up the wrong spiritual trees after all.

My near conversion was short-lived. It was not that Noah had been moved to turn the spiritual other cheek; it was that the machine has delivered. It apparently had a delay as part of its mechanism, I guessed, to keep its caffeine-seeking patrons from burning their anxious little hands. And now the steaming black coffee, no cream, no sugar, little taste, was flowing freely and gurgling into his cup, and thank God, that smile stayed. I realized that as perturbed as he was by Jan's and my fight, I was equally disturbed by his anger. The truth is that I was calmed by my friend's general equanimity and shocked when he occasionally lost it. I just did not expect it. And I'll bet that's the way he affected everyone. He is gifted that way. Anyhow, Noah was relieved and sure that he'd struck a blow for cheated coffee drinkers everywhere.

I wasn't about to spoil his illusion; instead, I congratulated him. He grinned sheepishly and told me, "You know, Stew, I was just about ready t' say a bad word. Not as bad as yours, but bad. It was on the tip of my tongue."

I was about dying of curiosity, because in all the months I'd known him, I'd never heard him say anything more scurrilous than "dang." Could it be that in these last few moments I really had discovered a sliver of a darker side in this lovely person?

"What word?"

He blushed.

"Come on tell me. I promise. I won't tell anyone."

"Well," he whispered, "I was just about to say "Shiiiit!"

We were both chagrined, he because of his embarrassment at his near impropriety, I because of how innocent his response seemed next to my usual blasphemies.

He sipped, telling me, "You know, this here coffee ain't bad at all, but they sure have their nerve," he pronounced it "nerb," a variation I found charming, "charging such high prices," and offered me a taste. He was right. For airport coffee it wasn't so bad at all. He was also right that seventy-five cents is still a lot. For the moment we were both content.

A LONG NIGHT

We settled back to wait for Joe's plane. And we waited. And waited. At first, the arrival board told me that the plane was to be a half hour late. Then forty-five minutes. Then an hour late because of weather conditions. Then it was delayed anywhere from two to five hours, depending on which rumor you wanted to believe. And to top it off, the posting on the board for Joe's plane had magically disappeared. When we got to three hours and counting, we were exhausted, having eaten all the machine food we could stand. And we found that in an airport this size everybody you might ask for updated information has gone home except for one old lone security guard with an outsized stomach, who was snoozing on and off on a lounge chair. On the table next to him was a giant cup of coffee and what looked like a freshly baked equally large honey bun. In his waking moments, he took bites.

I nudged him and asked how I could check on the real delay in my son's flight. "Use the phone next to you." It was hard to understand him, what with the accent and the honey bun he was chewing. I turned and looked. I looked hard.

When I really look hard, I squint, and for some reason, I close one eye. It's a silly habit I picked up in college. When I was tired, but still determined to study, I'd convince myself that tight squinting made me look more intensely at the material I was studying. It never worked, but I still do it. Now I was squinting as if the phone station was just on the verge of materializing. There was no phone.

I asked again. "Behind you." I looked once more. No phone. I thought if I asked again and he gave me that same honey-bun–filled mouth and uninterested answer, given my anxieties I would surely do something nuts. I could see the local headlines:

ELDERLY RETIRED YANKEE PROFESSOR ASSAULTS
EVEN MORE ELDERLY (POTBELLIED) SECURITY GUARD

"Early yesterday morning at the Tri-City National Airport, the security guard at Continental Airlines was beaten and nearly killed when he was leapt upon by a man awaiting a delayed flight. From his hospital bed, the guard reported that the assailant attempted to shove what was left of his dessert right down his throat. 'I tell you, things are changing around these parts and not for the better neither.'"

"According to the victim, it took four ladies, who were also waiting for a plane, to pull the assailant away. They say he was screaming something about being a human being too and having an inalienable right to a civil answer."

"One of the ladies, Julinda Grace Joiner of Johnson City, reported that he was yelling something about the right to a fair trial by his peers. And not just a lynching by his wife."

"Mrs. Joiner says he nearly frightened her to death with his shouting. In a later interview, she admitted that it was all kind of exciting, so much that she and the other three ladies began to applaud with their free hands and were moved to tears. In all her born days she'd never seen a thing like it."

This, of course never happened. After a third "Behind you," I did actually locate the Emergency Directions line for Continental behind a faux-Greek pillar and dialed the designated "Help" number. It didn't help. Squint as hard as I might, I could not hear the operator's voice well enough to understand a single word she spoke. I swear she sounded as if she were speaking another language from down deep in a cave. I tried again. No better. This time she sounded as if she was gargling.

I'd had enough. I would comply with the unhelping hand of the universe to say, "I give. I'll just sit here with Noah and wait." My wife, when she is rational, has a philosophy that dumbfounds me. "Everything happens for a reason," she says. I'm no more convinced by her than by Lorne. "Good will come out of bad," she says. "Angels do watch over us." When she says this, I look at her as I look at Lorne with awe and wonder. And I wish I could be them. And a teeny-weeny part of me hopes they are right.

We'd find the right meds for Jan. Joe would get here—eventually. I'd avoided a loony confrontation with the Honeybun Man and there had been no scandal.

Noah and I settled down and waited. They'd get here when they got here.

Noah looked at me as if to ask whether there really was a plane coming. His mom had never been on one and never expected to get on one. When asked why, she returned the question with "Why would anybody trust a stranger thousands of feet in the air flying them in a tube. How do you know everything works?" Pretty darn good question. I looked at Noah and saw not only the question but trust in his eyes. I'm Stew and can make things good.

Finally, we were hunkered down in comfortable chairs waiting for Joe and Matan's plane to arrive. It would be anywhere from one to four hours late, depending on which rumor you wanted to believe. The virtue of this little airport was that it was little. From the time a passenger deplaned to the time he picked up his luggage and had climbed into his car ran about five minutes. Its vice was also that it was little. There were few guards and fewer people who stuck around after ten p.m. to explain where the hell anything was, including the planes.

So, after so much anticipation I was more than a little perturbed by the Arrivals Board listing only three flights coming in this evening: Tucson to Greensboro connecting to Tri-City—late; L.A. to Greensboro connecting to Tri-City—late; Cincinnati via Greensborough—late. There was no mention anymore—none—of Newark, New Jersey.

My angst, in keeping with the current atmosphere of home sweet home, was running high. Could it be that I was here on the wrong night? Was I at the wrong airport? Shit, had I got the wrong airline gor in ganzen (totally)? I was starting more and more to revert to the language of perpetual worry, Yiddish.

Back at home, I'd even started to indoctrinate Noah with the language. He liked it. He now said "oy"—it came out "owey"—when life did him a wrong. The chickens developed pests, owey. One died, owey. His sister-in-law asked him to do still one more job, owey. The insulin pump went on the blink, owey and a huge Appalachian, oweeee for good measure just because he loved the sound!

No, it wasn't possible. Manic Jan checked centuple times. I talked with Joe twice to confirm. But something was definitely amiss. And at this hour, there was no human being anywhere in the Continental area to answer a question; not a living soul. Well, that wasn't quite true. Honey Bun was still here, snoring, but I'd burnt my bridges with him.

Around 11:30 p.m. I was awake. Another plane arrived and two people deplaned and came up the stairs. One was a soldier still in camouflage, wearing those big desert boots. He looked to be in his late teens. Either his girlfriend or wife, younger yet, saw him and changed from appearing exhausted to relieved. She ran to greet him before he'd cleared the last step. They hugged and kissed and kissed, teetering, looking more than a little like that famous photo of the sailor and the girl in Times Square after VE Day when everyone around was celebrating. But that photo seemed to always express total relief and exuberance; it seemed to shout "It's over! We did it." This present embrace felt more—desperate. There were no crowds greeting him. No showers of confetti. "We're together again, now! You're safe!" Their meeting was actually against FAA law, since she had run across the "ONLY PASSENGERS BEYOND THIS POINT" sign to get to him. But Honey Bun was asleep and probably would have been unable to stop her even if he had wanted to. They left wrapped in one another's arms.

An older woman with a cane was the second one up the stairs. A young man, probably a grandson, greeted her, took her free hand, kissed her, and they left. Now a sleeping Noah and I were the only people left in the waiting area.

At 2:30 a.m. Joe's plane, unannounced, finally arrived. I knew because a bleary-eyed Noah shook me awake, "Stew, another plane just landed. It must be Joe, right?"

Up the stairs came our youngest son carrying his little boy, who was fast asleep. Joe looked exhausted, but he was trying to put on an "it wasn't so bad" smile. Over his shoulder was slung a stuffed diaper bag. With his free hand he was pulling a folded stroller. He's six-foot-four, so he had to bend a little for me to kiss his forehead. I kissed Matan's cheek.

Noah was holding back a bit. Joe, exhausted as he was, would always make the extra effort. He's very like his Mom.

"You must be Noah. My Dad's told me lots about you." They couldn't shake hands until Noah took the stroller from him.

It took only minutes to retrieve Joe's additional luggage (enough luggage, I was thinking, for that soldier's entire brigade), but when you traveled long distances with this little guy you needed to be ready to provide many activities. You needed to bring lots of poetry books and music, DVDs, and changes of clothes. At three-and-a-half, he was fascinated by poetry and could tell you which Elton John track was on which CD, but he would not or could not tell you when he was ready to go to the bathroom. He was a gorgeous little human puzzle. So, what else is new?

It had finally stopped raining, and the ride home was easy. The stars were out. Joe told us that the same storm we had was with them the entire flight. It had spread all the way to New Jersey where they were delayed almost three hours sitting on the tarmac. He'd run out of the reserve food he'd brought for Matan. And most of the books were packed in the luggage. A frustrated Matan cried himself to sleep. After they finally took off and were close to Tennessee, the crew discovered that an instrument required for landing in mountainous terrain was not working, so they had to go back to Newark for repairs.

Still, they were both finally here, and beautiful. We dropped off Noah. Bitsy was there waiting up for him. Jan was waiting too. Seeing her baby with his baby calmed her. She smothered him with kisses. I think—I think—she was happy to see me, too.

The next few nights were difficult for Joe and Jan. He was not used to seeing his mom so agitated, up at all hours of the night, cleaning, moving furniture, and baking a few 3 a.m. pies to boot. And during the day, shouting orders at me and paying too little attention to him and her beloved grandson. At one point when she was preparing to bake again at two in the morning, we were all wakened by the rattling of pots down in the kitchen. Joe asked her why she was baking at this hour and told her that he thought something was really wrong. Her response was a curt "What's it to you, bub? Mind your own business." Then she stopped everything she was doing. She put down a mixing bowl. She was shocked by the hurt on his face, abruptly, desperately, hugged him, apologized, and excused herself.

Joe decided to leave earlier than planned. He told Jan he was worried about her, that he thought we both needed help. They hugged and kissed and cried before he and a bewildered little Matan left.

I took them to the airport and when I got back, for the first time in weeks, the house was quiet. Jan was sitting on the living room couch. I awaited another angry, frustrated response. Instead, she just said, "Stu, we'd better call Marian." Marian is our friend—a psychiatrist.

Where I couldn't, Joe, her youngest, had gotten through to her.

THE CURE CAN BE WORSE THAN THE DISEASE

WE CALLED MARIAN. SHE INSTRUCTED US to come home to Florida, which we did, and after two weeks of talking and experimenting with treatments, we settled on Lithium as the right drug. Jan's mother came along to check on her condo.

I had been wrong. The television reports were not pumping up the storm coverage to win ratings. Trees were down everywhere. Shirley's second-story ceiling had collapsed and fallen into her living room. She was devastated but relieved as well that her daughter could be on the way to recovery. Marian confirmed what I had suspected early on. Prednisone can be a monster for the wrong patient. The cure, it turned out, can be as bad, or often worse, than the disease. It can be especially explosive for someone with bipolar disorder in the immediate family.

In a couple of days, as if by magic, the drug started to work. Jan was less manic, and we were on our way back to the mountains, both feeling grateful that our lives seemed to be returning to normal. When I told Jan of her and my antics, she recalled some, but, amazingly, most she absolutely denied. My description of an episode at a furniture store during which she had berated the owner and tutored him on how to run his business as she flitted around the store, moving sofas and chairs for better display, she laughed off and told me I was inventing. She absolutely denied the bagel-art gallery idea, even when I showed her the detailed drawings she had made in its anticipation. She admitted to occasionally being angry at me, but not to the tirades and extreme language.

While we were gone, Lorne and Noah had volunteered to tend the garden. This was, of course, in addition to working in their own three gardens, each of which was triple the size of ours. After we returned, we saw little of Noah but much evidence of the work he'd done on our behalf. The lawn was cut and fallen fruit picked up, and he'd even weeded the garden and weed-eaten the entire property. He'd built a little protective house over the lock on the studio door like the one on the gate, and he'd hung "No Trespassing" signs that he'd printed himself on odd pieces of wood about everywhere any tree or post space was available. He'd even placed signs deep in the woods where no one could ever see them. But Noah, himself, did not appear.

After some coaxing, Bitsy told Jan that he'd been even more badly shaken by hearing our fight than we thought, particularly by seeing Jan so angry, believing that he was in some way partially responsible.

I called him, thanked him for looking after the house and garden while we were gone, and invited him to go with me for lunch, my treat, at the Bridgewater Grocery. We sat down at Steve's near the river, eating barbecue and slaw and drinking diet Nehi. Noah needed reassuring—and he wasn't the only one—that Jan was going to be all right. Looking at him, I wondered why the kindest people are always so willing to blame themselves for the catastrophes of the world, while real bastards don't see or care, and in fact even relish the havoc they cause.

By the time we finished lunch, Noah felt better about Jan and me and himself. In passing, he told me that while we were in Florida, he'd been worried not only about us but about his daddy, because he'd been to the doctor again. They didn't tell us because they didn't want to give us more trouble.

Jan and I went down to visit with Lorne and Bitsy the following morning, primarily because he was once again laid up, this time after knee surgery, a detail Noah had left out. At 63, even without the knee, he was a mass of pains and replaced or repaired parts, the result of various falls suffered during his 18-hour-a-day life as a country carpenter and mountain farmer.

The worst injury for Lorne had occurred years before when he fell from the second story of a house he was framing. He said he was distracted because it was tobacco harvesting season and he was thinking about all he had to do when he came home from the carpentry job. Somehow he mis-stepped and fell off the second-story scaffold, landing on his back. That time he was in a body cast for months and had been in pain ever since. The situation was made worse by another terrible fall out of the loft of his tobacco barn, where he suffered a "broken back," a general mountain term used up here to describe a variety of back injuries—slipped or ruptured or crushed vertebrae, fractures, compressed bones—that left him in constant pain and flat on his back for nearly two years. Without Noah they could not have kept going.

Such injuries were common up here, given the exhausting and danger-ous work people were required to do to make a living and keep a life they genuinely cherished in the place they genuinely loved. This life's work al-lowed no fakery, no celebrity photo ops. People didn't pretend to do work here; they worked.

Lorne was in constant pain, and now he'd had the addition of a dete-riorating knee that locked up on him at unpredictable moments, causing him to increase the methadone to which he knew he'd become addicted. Finally, last week he had agreed to surgery. For a man used to constant hard work his whole life, with always some task on the farm waiting for his at-tention to insure the well-being of his family, the prospect of sitting in his living room chair in front of the TV watching news or some dopey sitcom was just unacceptable.

The surgery now appeared to have been unsuccessful. The pain was worse. He could not sleep at night. He only got some relief when he was sitting in that danged chair. Inexplicably, now the pain in the front of his knee had subsided, but a new and worse pain had started, this time run-ning down the side of his leg from the knee and radiating into the calf.

When we arrived, there he was, plunked in the chair, foot up on the hassock, unshaved, plastic tobacco juice cup in hand into which from time to time he spat, listlessly. There was no verve; no enjoyment; no pride in it.

When we first moved up here and met the neighbors, this chewing and spitting felt really repugnant. We wondered how anyone could chew like this, knowing what everyone knows about the connection between tobacco and illness. Even the labels on the tins reluctantly printed the FDA warnings. "Just how stupid and backward can people be?" we wondered.

A few months later, I was still amazed by the habit. Now though, the repulsion had changed. I didn't see dopes doing dumb things. Instead, I worried for them as I would if any of my sons chain-smoked. Further, I thought I understood the reason, and it wasn't as a judging outsider might expect, out of ignorance. These folks were smart. Or because of folk habit, "Well, my daddy did it and I guess I do it because he did." In fact, I'd never heard this explanation. I think it's because people in these mountains used their bodies so hard and in the past used them even harder.

Jan and I listened enrapt as they told of their parents only forty years ago planting acres of vegetable seeds, wheat, alfalfa, rye, corn, and tobacco without gas-powered machines. You plowed with horses or mules or oxen. And you doctored them yourself. And you shod them. They told of tending the garden and picking off the bugs by hand. And then they told of the family effort at harvest, working six days a week, from dawn to dusk, followed by their mother's canning fruits and vegetables again from dawn to dusk on an outdoor wood cook stove, the remnant of which still stood down by his daddy's house.

They talked about living through the winter in an unheated clapboard cabin and foraging for stove wood up the mountain during subzero temperatures and in the spring busting this clay earth with a simple iron plow. Misstep too close to a scythe and you could easily lose your scalp. Noah had a scar above his eye that he got from getting too close to Mark's scythe one morning as they were cutting bush.

People in these mountains still get hurt often and severely, with the injuries lasting a lifetime. The pains are residual and cumulative and it was only very recently that medical attention and the money to afford it were much available. And so I think that chewing tobacco was and is a cheap, consistent narcotic, especially here where the strict Baptist admonitions against the evils of drink and the sins of disobedience to God's law were announced on wooden signs throughout the mountains.

"Be sober, be vigilant. The devil seeks to devour."

But nowhere will you see a sign that warns against the sinner's taking a chaw.

For the devout, like my friend Lorne, drinking was simply a demonic habit. You didn't do it even to kill pain. It promised to destroy a man and then his family. There were confirming examples, like people in one's own family living in shacks or rundown trailers next to burned-out cars, the result of a crazy night or a drunken quarrel or desperation for drug money, just off the side of the road, barely surviving from hand to mouth and all because of drink or drugs or both.

But chewing was an aged tradition and probably an essential one, given the pain of this place.

Lorne seemed a little embarrassed when we came in, but as always, he was gentle and welcoming. He didn't get up, simply because it was too painful. It was already a week since the operation, and he had been back to see the doctor, who reexamined the knee and told him the problem was inflammation. The diagnosis troubled us because we figured that the doctor was guessing, "Hmmm, hurts, something's wrong; must be "inflammation." His solution at this point was a shot of cortisone.

Lorne thought there was something else in there that needed fixing. I was even more skeptical, hoping that he hadn't developed an infection. Jan and I urged him to go back again and suggested that maybe the doc should call in a second opinion—an opinion from outside his practice. Jan ventured a little further. "And if he refuses," she said quietly, "I'd take it as a sure sign that I needed one."

He and Bitsy nodded that slow "yes" we'd learned was a real solid agreement. At this point neither of them was any more convinced about the vague diagnosis than we were.

I hoped he would take our advice, although in his situation I think it must have been hard to think clearly. Then again he had lived a lot harder life than I had and put up with more personal pain and still worked on: a full shift at carpentry, home repairs, care of forty head of cattle, and gardens (more like a small farm) and the planting and harvesting of ten acres of tobacco. And he did all this no matter how he felt. Bitsy worked right beside him. He looked back at those days as wistfully as I do at my first years as a beleaguered graduate student at Northwestern.

Lorne told us that the worst part of his current situation was not being able to get up and do what he knew needed doing and what he wanted to be doing around the place. Simply put, he loved his life. He loved work. And now for each job he did, he paid the price in pain.

In private, Jan wondered to me how Lorne kept from getting depressed. I think he *was* depressed, but he was of such a kind and tough disposition that even in depression he maintained resilience. And yes, even a twinkle in his eye, especially in front of the grandchildren. But he admitted to me in private that it was hard. He explained that he was shaving only twice a week lately—Wednesday and Sunday—the sacred days of church. And he was watching too much daytime TV.

Noah sat quietly, watching his father, whom he still called "Daddy," as do all the male children in these parts, no matter how old. The patriarch–son relationship is strong in these mountains. You relied on your father to give advice that had been tried and proven again and again, often at much personal expense. To do less was to run the risk of a costly, repeated, and unnecessary error, and there were enough new ones without repeating the old.

Daddies don't last as long as you need them.

To an outsider, Noah would probably seem to be doing nothing, thinking nothing, just staring, but even in the little time I'd known him, I had learned that the quiet stare was him thinking hard, trying to sort out a problem—something like my little grandson, Matan, who was born with a brilliant mind but with an assortment of bewildering physical problems that are mostly related to hypotonia, a lack of tightness in his muscle mass, as well as a serious lack of depth and space perception and poor eyesight.

Some of Matan's problems manifested themselves in the following way. You would ask him to do what seemed to you a simple physical task for a child of his age: "Take off your shirt, Matan." He would pause for what seemed an excruciatingly long time and then slowly would begin to manipulate and maneuver: move the left arm slowly and sideways, then up, then finally down and out of the sleeve, feeling it catch and then after more manipulation, slide through. In the long pauses, which earlier we thought might be indifference to the mundane or a show of defiance, we have learned that he is trying to figure out what for him is a confusing spatial problem. We assure ourselves that with work and practice Matan will overcome most of his physical problems. And there is little doubt that he will always be good in school if he can learn to concentrate.

So it must be similar for Noah, who can maneuver a four-wheeler up a narrow, dangerously uneven mountain path or drive a tractor, or run a chain saw, but who needs long staring time to work out the solution to a mental problem, particularly one that he knows has deep meaning and long-lasting implications for him.

As Noah watched his daddy adjusting his body, trying to get comfortable in his recliner, all of us talking about pain and unsatisfactory doctor visits, I wondered what was going through his mind. From one of our previous conversations, I thought I knew.

"What will happen to me if Daddy gets sicker?" Noah once asked me after one of his long quiet studies. I did not know what to answer but assured him that his brother would take care of him. Noah, my strong friend who did all the work around the farm the last time his Daddy was laid up, shook his head. He was not consoled by my answer.

"I don't want to live like that. I won't live like that."

I was not sure what he meant, but clearly he did.

"And I won't live in one of them places either. I'll put a shotgun to my head before I do that!" I told Noah that there would always be people who love him. We love him; to stop fretting.

I knew Lorne was worried about Noah's silence too, because as he glanced at his youngest son, he turned the conversation to world events.

Because his pain would not let him sleep, Lorne was out of bed early and watching CNN. As usual, the news was filled with the world's disasters; this day it was reports of a new famine in Africa. Hundreds of thousands of children were dying, due to the combination of drought, the locusts that devastated what was left of the crops, and a government that abused its own people. It was the usual story with the relief efforts: too little and too late, too badly planned. And rampant corruption. The conditions created the Wasteland, and the innocent suffered.

The pictures of the bloated and listless children, ten-year-olds looking like two, with their swollen bellies, pale skins, yellowish hair, and protruding eyes, visibly shook my friend. After only a few minutes, he said he needed to switch off the TV.

Now, having thought about it, he wanted to talk about the catastrophe over there as much to unburden himself, I think, as to distract his son. Their pain was far worse than his own, he began. We agreed as usual that the world was in a terrible mess and that this event was particularly horrific.

"What can you do?" Jan asked without expecting an answer, "except to send money to UNICEF, Doctors Without Borders, and other aid agencies?"

Jan and I had been making monthly contributions to Doctors Without Borders, a tiny way to make a difference or assuage our guilt about having been born lucky, in freedom and relative prosperity, growing up in the later years of the twentieth century. We belonged to an exclusive club and we knew it.

Lorne's strategy had worked. Noah came out of his reverie and joined the conversation. "What's them?" Noah wanted to know. We explained. Doctors Without Borders were volunteer doctors from everywhere in the world who went where there were sick and poor people. They brought medicine, got fresh water into their villages, and tried to help them get better.

Lorne filled in, "Them's real good folks, not like most of them here who're only into it for the money and such." He paused. "But, good as they try, it won't do much good, none at all."

"Well," we said, "it's an honest and humane effort and more sincere than our government's."

He agreed, but I thought we might be getting into dangerous territory here. Maybe even Bush country. But that's not where he was going. His personal vote for President Bush was about being a lifelong Republican and about Bush's support for Israel, nothing else.

I was confused and as I looked at Lorne and waited for his explanation, I caught a glimpse of Bitsy, whose lovely face had tightened just perceptibly. When she smiled her smile was beautiful; she lit up the room. She was not smiling now.

Now the crow's-feet around her eyes were just a little tighter, the weathered wrinkles seemed deeper, her hands folded in her lap like a child's. "Disturbed" is the word I thought of for her expression now, but that wasn't quite right either. More like reconciled or resigned, like the expression you saw on those nineteeth-century portraits of Indian squaws who looked so stoic.

"It won't help because what's happening is all in the Bible. Just like the Lord and the Jews. Them people are suffering because they haven't taken Jesus into their hearts. And as sad as it is, that's all there is to it."

Jan was looking at me and was, as I was, speechless. What do you say to a new friend whom you've grown to love and to respect in so many ways but who you think was what I called faith-crazy? But it wasn't even faith-craziness, really. Lorne believed deeply. There is a Plan. There are no mistakes, no accidents. In a way, I envied his certainty. I, on the other ten hands, had a few doubts. Was there such a neat Plan, or did nasty things just happen to you? "Gott lacht." God laughs. Get a shot of medicine to cure your pain and, as a result, whack out your nervous system for an unpredictable chunk of time.

If God was responsible for the suffering of the unconverted poor, what was the explanation for why Lorne's beautiful son was a wonderful person but not so quick thinking, or for why my gorgeous grandson had to work so hard at the simplest physical tasks? Were they the unconverted poor, too? And what if there were no Plan? With my friend I did not go there.

I looked at Bitsy as Lorne explained the African children's suffering. She was watching her son with love and sweetness and an understanding only a mother can have—and that tightened face. I wondered what she was thinking.

Ol' Man on a Mountain

MOUNTAIN
MISHAPS

"YOU HAVE NOT BEEN WRITING; BLEEDING, yes; bruising, emphatically."
Jan passed me a new bag of frozen peas. "Writing, no!"

I hated to admit she was right again, but she was. The country life and
my devotion, my dedication to proving that I was as much a mountain
man, as much a real man, as Viking Steve, had taken precedence over re-
cording our experiences.

I'd gotten into trouble simply because I was trying to prove I was more
than a mechanically challenged kid raised in Chicago in an apartment
above our bakery, amidst brick three-flats serviced by large, muscular
blond janitors named Erik and Fred and occasionally Jake, whose job it
was to shovel the coal and stoke the furnaces and cut the few pitiful blades
of grass that had the temerity to try and grow in the buildings' backyards.

No, no, a little confidence, a sprinkling of adventure, a patient tutor,
and I was determined to do it all now: to plow and plant and cultivate,
to cut down large trees and lay rock paths made of our genuine mountain stone personally hauled down our very own ankle-twisting, uneven,
treacherously beautiful mountain slope. I resolved to tone my sixty-three-
going-on-sixty-four-year-old slightly potbellied gangly body into Appalachian sinew. In my fantasy of renewal, I even almost convinced myself that
I could grow a brush-like crew cut like Noah's to bedizen my forty-year-old
bald head. My attempts, which Jan chronicled weekly by telephone to our
family, did not go unnoticed.

My older sister called from her condo in Chicago to plead with me.
"Remember to have someone with you at all times, watching you. You're

not used to that kind of work; you were not raised to it! Baking bagels and babkas and strudel in your youth does not qualify you as a lumberjack!"

"Tell him he's still just the kid from Albany Park," my brother-in-law chortled in the background, hunched over his computer.

The truth was they were both right. But the greater truth was that I was no longer satisfied with these restrictions. I would, like my Chinese college friend Hong, who majored in physics and set every academic record but collapsed at six push-ups, then at ten, and finally, after an entire semester of calisthenics, succeeded at thirty, press on. I would succeed. A few mishaps might discourage a less courageous, dedicated, radically defiant, or disturbed person but not this kid.

My list of mountain mutilations along my journey toward self-sufficiency and true manhood went something like this.

The first big event happened mid-summer on the day my sister and her spouse were to arrive for their first review of our land. At the time, I was busy slicing open my right hand just above the thumb, almost severing the tendon, as I hunched in the woods trying to fix a tiny leak in our gravity-fed waterline.

I've got to blame someone, so I blame Noah for this debacle. Earlier that morning, I had seen a teeny pinhole leak, a mere trickling spray, as I walked along our wooded path that paralleled the line. An hour later Noah had come up the drive, and when I mentioned my discovery, he'd warned me.

"You better fix it quick. It'll get way bigger and you don't want to run out of water when your kin are here."

I explained I did not know how. He was unconcerned because he did.

"Just cut away the leaking part and shove in them little plastic connecters. Then just clamp them tight. And it's all fixed."

He'd seen his Daddy and uncle do it "hundreds" of times. "Won't take but a few minutes." All we needed were some plastic connectors and four water clamps. We also needed a tool to cut the hose where the leak was located. Noah couldn't find the kind of tool his uncle used, but he assured me that a sharp hand-saw would do fine. We also needed a sharp shovel so we could first dig out and expose the hose. I had several.

So we were in business. The ground was wet from the leak, and so digging down and exposing the little leak was easy. Cutting the hosepipe was another matter. The saw blade was at too awkward an angle and too dull to cut accurately. But it was sharp enough to make a jagged half-cut, enough of a cut so that our hole around the hose filled with muddy water until we could no longer even see the new larger leak we'd created. Desperately chopping around in the mush, I managed to make a much bigger hole somewhere else in the hose and the water pressure coming down the mountain enlarged on my work and kept blowing off the plastic thingama-jigs I'd barely slipped in and the clamps I'd managed to slide on.

By this time Noah was starting to panic. "I just don't understand it. It always worked before when Daddy and Monroe done it."

We tried what amounted to more frantic chopping. That effort got us a flood. I yelled at him to get some other cutting tool, to get something, to get his Dad.

"He ain't at home. He's gonna kill me." He was white with panic.

Trying to disguise my own panic, I calmly instructed him. "Go back to the garage. There's a filleting knife on the shelf near the garage door. I just sharpened it. Maybe we can use that."

He left on the run.

A filleting knife, it turned out, was not even remotely the tool of choice for this job, and someone less "flummoxed" would not have tried it. After only a few knife jabs, I stood ankle deep in the rush of an icy flood that was mixing with my own warm blood.

Noah had beaten another retreat to try and find someone, his brother maybe, to help us. I had by now finally sawed the hose in two and jammed in the connectors, tightening the clamps enough to reduce the gusher to a formidable geyser. The connections were not going to hold even in their tenuous state.

"Stu, Lorry and Howard are here. Stop what you're doing honey and come greet them."

Yes, my sweet sister, Lorry, five years my senior, who has spent much of her life worrying about everyone else, including me, and as a result is hyper-frenetic and anxiety ridden, picked this moment to roll up the driveway after a long tiring drive from Chicago to see her little brother's latest folly. And, dear reader, you do remember she had warned me to be careful?

In tow was the previously mentioned chortling Howard, aka Dr. Howard Gerber, Professor of Electrical Engineering, my brother-in-law, who was raised in the same Chicago neighborhood as I. Son of a kosher butcher, he had scratched his way free of the frightful lessons of killing and eviscerating chickens, earned one of the most difficult of PhDs, and now thought in immaculate mathematical formulas and risk-free investments. No more chicken blood for him. In fact, no more red meat. Health was his business, cereal and trail mix his cuisine of choice.

Howard was the only man I'd ever met who, upon entering my living room for the first time, asked its dimensions. When I answered that I did not know, he whipped out a retractable metal tape measure from some hidden crevice on his person and deftly solved the problem I did not know I had—to the centimeter. Both he and my adored sister were what you might call "cautious" individuals.

But, though an electrical engineer, Howard still lived under our old neighborhood's unwritten rules of technical taboos. He viewed changing a light bulb as a task worth serious, meticulous study and preparation. He also was possessed of a sincere and deep-seated distrust of the outdoors. He avoided most activities that involved fresh air, sunshine, and every kind of insect life, as if such avoidance were ordained in Exodus, all chapters, every verse. Do not get me wrong. He was a fine person and caring. He had some legitimate reasons for his outdoor aversions. He was of fair complexion; Apollo was his enemy.

There were other factors that encouraged his predispositions. Howard had two children who were physicians, one an international expert in infectious diseases and the other an internist. On the occasions that we'd met, both impressed me as being intensely aware of all the possible illnesses one can contract, including those caused by breathing normally, not to mention the ones caused by the sun, moon, and stars.

When together, Howard and his kids involved themselves in debate over the relative tonalities of their liquids. When they traveled, Howard and my sister toted a suitcase filled with vitamin pills. Breakfast was a marathon of swallowing gigantic bowls of oatmeal, laden with walnuts and berries, followed by twenty or thirty vitamin supplements. Jan and I had watched in amazement as they downed their stash.

The neck-protecting wraparound long-billed cap he wore in all but the cloudiest winter months that made him look like Daffy Duck was startling to those unused to seeing such a chapeau on a grown man. He didn't care. I actually think he enjoyed the stares. Despite his personal idiosyncrasies, he was a loving, tender-hearted guy.

But he was CAUTIOUS. And, I suspect that he saw not himself, but me as something of an amusing eccentric. If I was the loose cannon, Howard regarded himself as the proficient sailor trying to lash me aboard my foundering ship.

When my sister heard my cursing echoing through the trees, Jan told me later, she urged Howard to the rescue, and, to his credit though he blanched several shades lighter than his usual pallor, he overruled his fear of deer ticks and Lyme disease, spritzed himself with one of the "bug juice" bottles he'd loaded into the glove compartment for the expedition, and tiptoeing on his clean white sneakers bounded into the woods.

He answered my sister's command.

Upon seeing the blood-soaked evidence of my failure, the dangling thumb on my right hand, he thought for a moment, came down off his tiptoes (I gather he ran that way to save what he could of those shoes), and then, seriously assessing the situation as the scientist he was, suggested that I could still accomplish the precise cutting and proper mending of the water hose by riding down to the hardware store and purchasing more precisely calibrated connectors and by using a saber saw to finish the cut.

A saber saw? Did this scientist not realize that the distance between a power source and my bloody swamp was roughly 400 feet? "Dear brother-in-law, Professor of Electrical Engineering, reformed chicken flicker," I thought, "I will need an extension cord roughly the length of Massachusetts to reach the leak, not to mention that I may not want to continue operations, seeing as how I seem to be bleeding to death." While wrapping and compressing my mangled hand in a few kitchen towels supplied by Jan (I'd also punched a couple of sizable holes in my right palm trying to use a mud-slicked screwdriver to tighten the clamps), I not-so-calmly suggested what he could do with the saber-saw idea.

Reluctantly, he agreed to resubmit the idea later, I suppose in fear that I might be tempted at the moment to try to cut something else, namely his achromatic gullet, and even suggested that I might be right in screaming that what I wanted was, if I wanted anything, a portable, battery-powered jigsaw, but since none was available, that I might drop the knife I was still clutching, abandon trying to fix the line altogether, and instead take a trip, not to the hardware store but to the emergency room.

That suggestion sounded reasonable to all. So a trip to the ER it was, with my dear sister trying hard not to grow completely hysterical, Howard making medical suggestions, Jan resigned to still another accident, and me hemorrhaging. The ER staff wondered aloud before they stitched me up whether the curtained alcove they put me in should be embroidered with a dedication to me. I'd made a few trips here before.

So began my sister's first visit to the mountains. The rest of her stay was not nearly as pleasant.

With my hand stitched and bandaged, it was impossible to show her that I really could garden. Walks into our woods became a Woody Allen routine with Howard wondering aloud alternately what a virulent tick bite felt like and singing Yiddish lullabies at the top of his voice, louder when my sister asked him not to, possibly to keep up his own sinking spirits as we traversed a messy cow path here and deer trail there. Each time I would wave my bandaged limb to point out a beautiful vista, or Jan would praise a local flower and my sister would agree to its beauty, he would wonder at how hot it was and at the abundance of gnats along the path.

"A tree's a tree," he would grumble. Or "Why travel? It's the same shmutz (dirt) everywhere."

By the time one of these rambles ended, it became evident that a smidgen of luck was on all our sides given that no one was armed.

Noah did return late in the afternoon of the slicing with Lorne, who came dressed in wading boots and equipped with what I later learned was a PVC cutter. In a few minutes he'd repaired the line and told me that sometimes it "wasn't a good idea" to trust everything Noah said about repairs. This was a lesson I've since learned to take to heart.

But only partially. The greater truth I learned that first year was that it was often a first-rate idea to listen to him.

For example, I sit here writing in humiliation and pain, several bags of frozen peas on my bruised behind, as a consequence of not heeding Noah's warning to "leave the mowing t' me." Earlier in the week he'd told us that his Dad's mower was broken and it would be a week or longer until it could be repaired. With the heavy rains we'd been having, our lawn and lower field were very overgrown. They needed to be cut and soon; otherwise, it would be near impossible.

Long grass and the busted mower provided the opportunity that I'd been waiting for. I longed for a small herd of goats. But the majority outvoted me—for the time being—and concluded that we needed, instead, our own, riding mower—now.

Jan, Noah, and I began our shopping expedition at John Deere Inc., manufacturer of the Rolls Royce of mowers, the Hope Diamond of precision motorized cutters. Priced in the thousands, the deluxe models were gorgeous. I wanted one, sure, but not to the exclusion of eating or being able to pay for long-term health insurance, which, since taking up residence here and experiencing a few mishaps, I'd concluded was a requirement.

So, we lowered our sights and were off to Lowe's Home Improvement and into the second level of mower world. Here we discovered smaller Lincoln-like mowers. In only the $1,500 range, these were a comedown, but Jan felt even these were too expensive.

Among the bladed herd, we saw one anemic model that was dirt cheap, four hundred bucks, and guaranteed by Noah and a consulting phone call to Lorne to break down every couple of weeks.

I wanted to purchase the Lincolnesque version and be done with it, but Noah and Jan convinced me that we needed to be more cautious, to follow in the footsteps of Uncle Will, who had bought a middle-of-the-road machine, the Murray, 42-inch cut with 15 horse power, that had taken care of his needs and had worked like a good old mule for years.

So I ogled less, agreed more, and we finalized our purchase on a K-Mart Murray, Chevy quality, candy-apple red, nine-hundred-dollar machine that came with a dandy warranty.

We tied Murray into Noah's trailer with enough rope to execute every dishonest politician, banker, and CEO in the land. Noah was going to be darned sure we didn't lose his new vehicle rolling out of the trailer on the way home before he had a chance to try it out. He did as soon as we got it home and untethered it, and as soon as he tried it, Noah fell in love with the machine, managing to cut the grass with precision in half the time it had taken with his Dad's old mower. When he finished, he drove it up the hill next to the Pool Room (the name had stuck, even though it was finally cleaned and almost ready to become my study), and using water from the nearby pump, washed our new machine clean of every speck of grass. It shone like my father's prized Oldsmobile on a Sunday afternoon.

"If'n you don't take the time to wash her, Stew, she'll be gone in a year." This was the way he treated everything, trying to do his best to protect what he valued. It was the way he treated us.

Each time Noah returned from mowing, easily maneuvering Murray back into its designated parking space between two upright pipes in the garage, I wondered: Why not me at the controls? I could, at least, try it out in the more open areas of the lawn. He'd shown me the fundamentals: clutching, starting, warming up, putting her into gear and reverse, adjusting her speeds, lowering and raising her deck, shifting into reverse. Hey, if I couldn't have my goats, at the very least, it was my turn for some fun with Murray; it couldn't be that hard. After all I'd been driving a car for fifty years. I was almost competent with the weed whacker. And damn it, I had paid for it!

So, six weeks to the day after purchase, after Noah had cut the lawn thrice with me watching closely and from secreted vantage points, I quietly descended one promise-filled morning into the garage and approached the saddle. To be sure I wouldn't make a mistake when I started her and plunge through a wall, I put her into gear without starting the motor and pushed her out onto the driveway. I hadn't realized just how heavy this beauty was. I felt a little ping in my pectoral muscles; nothing a little Ben Gay wouldn't fix.

I saddled up without even Bagel knowing it. Noah wasn't scheduled to arrive to help me repair a back fence for an hour. And Jan was walking up on the mountain.

It was just me and beautiful Murray.

Starting was easy. Twist the key and she purred into life. I eased her (Murray in scarlet red couldn't possibly be male) into gear and drove slowly down to the first lawn, the closest, just in front of our house, where the majority of our fruit trees were planted in a row along a five-foot bank and intermittently down the middle.

My plan was to take it easy, staying far away from the bank's drop off, away from any tricky hills, just rolling along on flat, smooth, even expanses. I would eliminate some of Noah's work for him. And I was doing splendidly, creeping along, backing up to cut little patches missed with my first sweep, increasing speed ever so gradually as my confidence grew. With each additional maneuver, I got better.

I was moving now, a little faster and more assured, venturing into areas that required slightly more sophisticated skills. If I could get within a foot or two of the largest apple tree trunk, which was just up a slight grade, finishing off this border around the tree with the weed whacker would take me half my usual time. Noah never got close enough with Murray to suit me.

Shifting the frozen pea bags now from my rib cage to my lower back, I can see as clear as my bluing hand before my blackened eye that trying to duck under the low-hanging limbs of an old apple tree, while directing a vehicle in a liberal circle, even as relatively slow and timidly controlled a circle as mine, required far greater flexibility and skills than I possessed.

My story—and I still swear to it—is that the limb reached out and grabbed me by my cherished Northwestern University Swimming tee shirt, the one I wore to all semi-physical events to impress bystanders with my still being a little athletic, hooked me just under the neckband with one prong, while at the same time punching me just above the eye with another. The more I struggled, the more the limb twisted me into my shirt.

Imagine a sea bass, equipped with vocal cords, capable of screaming, and skewered on the end of a treble hook and you've got the picture. After the moment of its being snagged, imagine that same sea bass bent backwards, pitifully squirming and squealing, certain that its life was about to end, not in the depths of a sea but somehow, inexplicably, on a gently sloping North Carolina lawn.

"Found this morning by his incredulous (and despondent) wife under the largest and most productive of his beloved apple trees, the deceased was diagnosed by the coroner as having a neatly snapped neck, the unsuspecting victim of an aggressive tree gone suddenly berserk."

I saved myself only by a desperate decision to let go of the wheel and allow my body to dangle and slide backwards off the saddle until, I hoped, my weight would rip my beloved shirt and let me loose. It worked. I hit on my backside and both funny bones, although there was certainly nothing funny about it. "Excruciating" was more like it. Dazed, I watched through one good eye as Murray continued to chug forward, still slicing grass as she rolled. Luckily, Murray had sharper reflexes than I, slowing down almost as soon as I was airborne. I learned later by reading the Owner's Manual (was I supposed to have read that first?) that she possessed an automatic pressurized cutoff "kill" switch designed into her seat, fixed there, most likely, to save herself from pilots like me. She stopped moments before she, too, was airborne over the grassy knoll.

I lay there, propped on reverberant elbows, sucking in a little air at a time, amazed that I was alive. I also knew by the way I was breathing that the little ping in my chest muscles had spread into a far larger pain around my ribs and that I had probably ripped something important like a kidney or spleen, liver, or heart valve.

Just then Noah tootled up the driveway on the Ranger with a greeting.

"What do you think you're doing down there, Ol' Man?"

"What's it look like?" I wheezed.

"Close as I can tell, you're taking my job and trying to kill your own self?"

"Close enough," I managed.

Gently, at an amble, and in his usual good humor, he got off the Ranger and, sliding his hands under my armpits, helped me—more like lifted me—up. I had to hug my ribs with both hands just to inhale.

"Stew, you're not lookin' too good. Whyn't you just go on up to the house and rest? Let me finish up my job."

First, I protested. Then, I agreed to go, but only after he promised never to tell Jan what he'd seen. Not one word.

"Well, I sure don't see how you're gonna keep her from knowing, what with the way you're limpin' and snortin' an' holdin' on to yourself."

"You—let—me—figure it—out. Promise?"

"Well, Ol' Man, have it your own way so long as you go." As I leaned on him, he asked another question. And I sincerely confess that the query squeezed what little breath I had left out of me.

"Why didn't you just mush on the brake?"

Mush on the brake? Mush on the brake! It never occurred to me.

His vow of silence was too much for him. As soon as he got me to the couch, Mr. Innocence gleefully revealed all to Jan. Later that day, he told his Dad. He told Will, Isaac, Will's son. He told his Mom. He made a special trip to tell Shelly Sue. He told the old guys on the porch.

"Finding that ol' man flat on his back; listening to him death rattlin'; seein' that tore up shirt; watchin' the mower teeterin', just about to smash to smithers, why he would've had to buy his self a brand new one. And Jan," dramatic pause, "he never even mushed on the brake!"

To this day Noah loves talking about my "flying" off the mower. Lorne said he couldn't recall anyone else ever doing that. Bitsy would nod her head in agreement and say that if I kept it up I could officially become Lorne's non-identical twin brother. She believed Lorne to be the second most accident-prone man in the county. I leave it to you to identify the winner of first place.

FLOORED

AFTER TWO WEEKS OF RECOVERY, I was able to resume shlepping (dragging) the last garbage away from the Pool Room. Then with Jan's and Noah's help and Noah's side coaching of my paint job ("Stew, you missed a place right there," pointing out the three square inches where the roller hadn't reached), we finished cleaning and painting its interior.

Finally, I was ready to put in a floor, our last step in remodeling. I got prices for knotty pine that seemed reasonable to me and asked Lorne if he'd help with the installation.

"Let's take a ride, never can tell what we'll find. Seems to me like them prices are way too high. Plenty of little mills off the road if you're patient." So off we went in his pickup deep into the countriest version of country. Off a back road in Tennessee, we saw a small sign advertising a lumber yard, which turned out to be a two-building affair owned by a couple of brothers.

It was easy to find the office. It was the smaller of the buildings, and when we explained what we needed one of the brother-partners quoted us a price for tongue and groove pine that was a third cheaper than anything I'd found in town. Lorne nodded approval, and the boss directed us to the larger building, as if there was another choice, where we could load up the truck, come back, and pay.

"Be sure you tell the tall boy to load you twenty or so more boards." he said. "Some of them is bound to be ruined, smashed as they are in the pile. You'll find enough good ones in them twenty to make up the difference." Out in the bigger building, the taller worker was easy to spot. He looked almost adult, maybe eighteen, and turned out to be the only one of the three helpers who spoke any English.

They all went to work snaking boards out of the pile for us. To expedite what could be a long job, we threw in to help them. I explained about the extra boards, but they already knew. As we worked, I talked with them in my broken Spanish to pass the time.

We finished loading and asked for some heavy twine or rope to tie on the load. There was none. If you wanted that kind of amenity, you apparently brought your own. The price didn't include perks.

"You speak that lingo pretty good," Lorne laughed. "Good I took you along."

Back at the office, I paid and we were on our way. Lorne drove extra slowly, particularly on turns, and although we felt the load shift a little, we were fine, that is until we came up the steep slope of our drive. Then, to the last board foot, the load slid off the truck bed.

Lorne and I got out into a scattered, jumbled, line of knotty pine. And reloaded. It was the second time that day we'd handled the wood and this time without the muscular aid of those young men. He drove on and I walked behind the truck putting all my inconsiderable might behind the load to hold it on.

Then, because the door to the Pool Room was separated from the extended drive by a barbed-wire fence, we handled the wood, one board at a time, again, with me on one side, lifting every single one off the truck, and he on the other side, receiving through the wire.

Lorne was not happy, but it wasn't because of the extra work. He pointed at the mountain sky behind the Pool Room. A big black cloud was forming. "We're gonna get rain. If the clouds are there, over that mountain, count on it. And if this wood gets wet, it's ruined." So for the fourth time that day, we handled the wood and carried it inside.

"Them Mexican boys make you appreciate them now, don't they? Smile all the way through with no complaining. I'd hire them any time." I'd heard very different ideas expressed about Mexican workers around here. Most opinions ranged from sending them all back to where they belonged to retrieving our troops from Iraq and Afghanistan and posting them all on the Texas border. As far as I could tell, the immigrant workers were doing jobs nobody else would take. They were loading wood, laying asphalt, hauling.

One young man we'd met working in a plant nursery on a Sunday and who worked for us several Saturdays clearing weeds and planting told us that he'd been working at tarring roads for three years so he could send money back to Mexico where his mother and three sisters still lived in a rural village. He was eighteen. He had a social security number, paid into the system, but was not legally a resident and so filed no taxes and never got the social security back. As long as he could stay healthy and unhurt, he would be fine, he said. But should anything happen to him, he would be in trouble since he had no health insurance and was afraid to visit an emergency room. In the neighborhood where he lived, people relied for medicine on an old woman who'd been an herbalist in Mexico.

The nursery worker lived in an apartment with five other young men and when we called him one Friday to see if he could help us, the usual lively salsa music that ordinarily greeted us followed by a recorded message was gone. The number had been disconnected. He'd disappeared.

It was dark by the time Lorne and I finished unloading, and we agreed to take a day off before we started in—or rather, before he started the work with me as his helper. When he agreed to help, doing the main part of the job was always his plan. He just didn't want to insult me by suggesting that I'd probably mess it up. I would not have been insulted.

Lorne was a master, and he was lightning fast. He cut the boards to length and placed them without measuring. And they were perfect. The guys at the lumber yard were right. We did need the extras to make up for smashed pieces and knots that we couldn't cut away without spoiling the pattern Lorne was creating.

Initially, my job was just moving stuff out of the way. But by midday we were working together and I was nailing under his direction. Not much was memorable in the process aside from getting the four-times-handled load in and my discovering that I could do some simple carpentry under his instruction, except one event. It marked a turning point in what was becoming our friendship.

Lorne arrived early. He was sporting new work boots and was eager to show them to me since he knew I was really getting into the equipage stuff.

"Stew, how do you like these?" he asked.

What could I say? I was envious and told him so. He turned them this way and that so I could see every angle. He even took one off to show me how it was fully lined in leather. I already knew that good boots were expensive. Good ones could run upwards of a hundred and fifty dollars. These were beautiful.

"How much you think I give for them?"

"No idea, but they look expensive."

"They was asking one-thirty but I didn't give but one-seventeen. No tax neither. I Jewed 'em down."

Old bells went off in my head. Very old bells; rusty, but still solid metal underneath. I was angry, offended, hurt, and disappointed as hell all at the same time. What to do: I could keep my mouth shut or say something. I chose the latter.

"Lorne, have you got any idea how offensive what you said is?"

He was confused. "What? Ain't no reason to pay taxes when you don't need to. What do you think the government's gonna do with that money?"

"Not taxes. You just said that Jews were all connivers, money grubbers. You just insulted a whole bunch of people—including me and Jan."

"I did?"

"You betcha! You did! You bet those boots you did." I lost it. No, not really. I merely figured that our friendship had to be based on openness, and if it ended here and now, it ended. "How would you like it if I said 'I Christianed' somebody not up, but down. 'I Baptisted down some poor fool?'"

He thought a moment. This was no small matter and we both knew it. Our collective fat was in the fire. "You know, Stew, I guess you're right. Just never thought nothing of it. Just the way we was raised I guess. My daddy used to tell us we were going down to the old Jew store. That's where we could get the best stuff, cheapest too. Daddy would say, 'A Jew could stand on a mountain in the middle of a desert and still make money.'"

He looked right into my eyes. "I'm surely sorry."

I was too. The truth is I knew in that moment that he didn't mean anything malicious. He was not that type of person. To a great degree, we are the summary of our raising. But it's not our limit. If we are called to consciousness and are willing to become conscious, we can say we're sorry. We can stretch. We can open.

As a kid, I heard many relatives and neighborhood people use the word "shvartzes" (blacks) to refer to African Americans. Although the word literally means "black," it had come to carry all sorts of connotations that could vary with the person saying it. To some it meant not only black but also dumb, slovenly, without common sense, sexually promiscuous, and possibly lots more, depending on the speaker. For the most part, I believe that those who said it were decent people who would have furiously and sincerely denied that they meant any of those ugly associations. But I am sure that for others, the term carried the full freight of prejudice.

My mother and father, feeling that the word had become pejorative, would not allow it in our house, but even to them, in subtle ways, the "shvartzes" were somehow "less." My mother, for example, referred to her cleaning lady, Lottie, a woman she regarded as a good friend, a woman older than she, as "my girl" or "my Lottie." Yet Mom took pride in insisting that Lottie stop working and eat lunch with us at our table. She thought it terrible that other members of our family, cousins and aunts, expected Lottie to eat separately. And Mom never thought a thing about the contradictions between her speech and her behavior. Neither did we. Later, when she was in her seventies, Mom wondered aloud how she could have ever been so insensitive to a woman she admired. The answer was probably, "it's just the way we were raised" or the way our immigrant culture was raised.

Lorne and I said not a word more about the incident. We were both contrite. That was enough. When the job was done and we shook hands to say goodbye, we were closer friends. Later in the fall, he and Bitsy took us for a ride out to see Bitsy's mom's house. On a rise close by, he stopped and pointed down at a pretty little farm in the valley.

"Look down there," he said. "You know who lives there? Black folks. Been there as long as my family. Some of the best people you could ever want to meet. Daddy and them used to help each other come harvest time. They can flat out farm!" He went on, "Never too late." We both knew what he meant.

Back in the Pool Room and after nailing the boards in place, all that remained was filling the worst knots with wood filler and spreading polyurethane. I wanted to do this all alone. Lorne gave me simple instructions. "Get you the best brush you can. Brush it on, don't try and roll it. If you do, you're gonna get bubbles. And start in a far corner and work out. You don't wanna be stuck in a corner and bawling like a calf for Jan. Most of all, work slow and work careful."

He should have added one more step: open all the windows first.

I started slowly, filling in each missing knot and the few bad cracks with wood putty. Then I stained the entire floor, from inside corner to door. And let it dry thoroughly overnight. With the small exception of using the wrong filler, one that refused to take stain and having to chisel it all out and start again, my work was pristine.

Then I began with the poly. I worked in small increments, three board lengths at a time, crawling along, stopping frequently to stand, step back, and admire my work, more and more frequently, since without realizing it I was getting plastered on fumes. The higher I got, the surer I was that I was, at the very least, a neat Jackson Pollack. And since the only audience I had was me, I needed to stare at the work up close and personal, bent from the waist, nose a foot from the floor.

It was on one of my more frequent admiration pauses that I stepped backwards onto the section of floor I'd forgotten I had coated, twice, and felt myself going, going, not airborne as in accidents past, but into slow-mo skating, arms extended in an attempt to rebalance the moving floor while my feet were operating independent of one another, finally coming together in an unsynchronized forward slide up and out from under my body to deliver me with a sonic boom. My wrist hurt. Had I had broken it? Surprised, but still under the pleasant influence of fumes, I lay there trying to calculate how that floor had shifted. Then, I checked for further injuries. I could wiggle my wrist, so maybe it was just a severe sprain.

Finally, after a lull when I guess I must have sobered up a little and started to feel really uncomfortable, wanting an audience of more than just myself and needing a little sympathy, I bellowed for help, punctuated by stronger and stronger epithets—the ones that were sure to draw attention—hoping these words would alert my wife, who was across the field, or on the bedroom deck, or inside the house.

She did not appear. Where was she when I needed her?

A few more shouts produced the same nonappearance, so I collected my really pained body, dragging it and my bruised ego into the house. There in the living room on the new denim couch sat my devoted mate of forty-one years. She had heard the thunderous bang of my fall and had assumed correctly that I'd fallen again, but so tired was she of warning me to hire people who were experienced and competent to do the big jobs around our manor, that Madame Empathy had concluded that I was either one, all right; or two, critically injured and flat on my back. In the latter instance, she figured I would continue to lie there and so she could retrieve the body and, if appropriate, call the county medical examiner later, after she'd finished cleaning the house for the fourth time that day or completed the current chapter of Book of the Dead she was reading as a way of renewing her exhausted spirit. In the first instance, she'd concluded that I was probably okay and would continue to be the thorn in her side. No need to hurry toward that either.

On a deeper level, I think she concluded that if I could survive my earlier swan dive—and here I am serious in the use of that word—on the tile of our upstairs bathroom (about which more later), I would survive a minor skating accident on a wet polyurethane floor.

And, of course, as with all things semi-catastrophic, she was predominantly right. In any event, I could cut her some slack. After all, the swan dive took place during the previously mentioned hurricane months, when after the poison ivy patch found her she was maniacally careening about the property collecting shopping bags filled with small stones that she planned to use in resurfacing our fireplace wall, or she was scrubbing boulders with a toothbrush and soap, an activity she envisioned as a memorial to all our female ancestors, starting with Bubbe Choma.

My bathroom fall occurred only a few weeks after I had emerged, bubbling, from being submerged deep in our marble Jacuzzi after realizing that I could not voluntarily drown myself. I stepped out onto the second step ledge that is raised two feet above the bathroom's floor, and—yes, dear reader—slipped the really big slip, the swan dive slip, off into the air, taking my biggest flight thus far and landing with all the toes of my left foot bent completely under that foot which, in turn, was bent under my left leg which, in turn, itself was under my behind, with all my muscular 175 pounds leveraged full down on all those poor contorted appendages.

Miraculously, my knee—my lifelong trick knee—did not dislocate, but oh did I feel the pain in my ankle, my toes, my arch, and my heel. Several high volume curses, including the usual, but concluding with an "Oh my God" (strange how I get religion when in pain), followed. Five minutes later, Jan's half-mad face appeared above my naked body. Staring down, her hand extended in an instinctive offer of help, she looked, at the very least, put upon, if not, downright nuts. After all, she had been occupied downstairs destroying another part of the bathroom. In one hand, she still held the hammer.

I needed the empty hand, wanted it, even if she'd been treating me like a cur, but I also feared taking it, partly because I was convinced she would lift me only high enough to then drop me again.

Discretion and a compromising physical position that even someone as immodest as I found intolerable, overcame me. Too, I was chagrined at the idea of my mother-in-law charging onto the scene. This would be the proverbial last straw. So I grabbed on, covered my private parts in a futile effort to retain some dignity, and maneuvered myself up onto my still-operable right foot, hoping and hopping for the best.

Ms. Compassion dropped me onto the bed, went downstairs, and reappeared a few minutes later with a bag of Birdseye frozen peas to apply to the hematomuscular area.

In an hour, the foot had swollen to double its normal size and was beginning to turn a fetching shade of magenta. By midnight, it was deep purple, highlighted with an astounding array of reds and blues. A marvel of engineering, it would still move. The body is an amazing machine.

Our collective conclusion—mother-in-law, errant son by marriage, and sweetheart turned self-proclaimed bitch goddess—was that I had torn every ligament in my foot but hadn't broken anything. I deemed it another Appalachian miracle. I mean, by its looks the foot needed amputation, perhaps a tiny exaggeration but not much of one.

But let's say its salvation was a miracle. If so, granted by whom? By now I'm sure the reader has concluded that unlike our neighbors', my own faith quotient ran a tad towards the thin end, vacillating (when present) from Yahweh to Isis to the fates to… an unpredictable Mother Nature.

So what was the explanation for my series of disasters? Were all these accidents due to some kind of genetic ineptitude, or was there indeed a Someone with a plan, orchestrating these mishaps, elbowing to tell me something?

What if there was a Force? I would be in deeper trouble than if I were immersed in the sumptuous piles of poop we gleaned up on our mountain paths. And at that moment of exquisite pain, shallow reflection, medicated reverie, and timorousness, I swear I heard a Voice, a reverberant, operatic voice in all ITS capital letters, speaking to me, and I swear it had a Yiddish accent. And in the background, I'm certain I heard a klezmeric clarinet: "Cast thyself out." Waa, Waa. "These aged mountains are no place for the Judaic, even the fallen Judaic likes of thee." Waa. It sang. It wailed. It chanted cantorially. It whispered. It even implored through the hemlocks (which I had spent the last week spraying because of the new invasive blight—to no avail, by the way).

Then, when my reply was a sputtering series of "oys" but no definitive acclamation, It seemed to get really perturbed and took off the ram-skin gloves.

"Hey! Do you see olive trees? Date palms maybe? A glessella (small glass) wine from vineyards flowing free? The folks up here don't even take schnapps (a short whiskey) now and then."

As you might conclude I was, for once in my garrulous life, speechless. If Jan had been present in the room, I know she, too, would have been in awe. But she'd left and was downstairs. I could hear her hammering away at what remained of the bathroom vanity.

The chastisement continued. "I don't care if you ate Tollhouse rolls in the 1809 room of a hoity-toity hotel, with the starched white tablecloths. And it doesn't matter to Me if you, my boy, thought you were the best student of English Renaissance literature, which I am personally not so sure of either, and passed your written exams faster and better than all the blondies at Northwestern, that big-shot university, with all the fancy-schmancy professors. What was the matter with being a real doctor?" (By the way, my Bubbe had asked the same question after she'd questioned me about how many years I would have to spend in school and what I'd be earning afterwards.)

Now I was getting irritated. It was one thing to make light of my academic achievements; that was an acceptable target. But those cute little egg-washed tollhouse rolls and the linen tablecloths? And our mountains? I began to protest—after all, that is a large part of our tradition—but this time I was struck dumb by a lightning bolt that fried the pillow just above my head.

"Good! Don't talk! Shut your big mouth, always challenging, and listen for a change. Do you see a synagogue? Even a shul?" (Rough translation: the modest center for study, prayer, and, most of all, continuing debate in a small village long ago in Europe and then transferred to the cities of America as a tradition of questioning—around the same time Bubbe came over.)

"Go down to Shelly Sue's store over on Sugar Mountain. Look around. Give a good kook" (simple translation: a little look). "Can you buy even a Kosher dill pickle? A bottle horseradish? A piece gefilte fish? A box matzos? And I'm talking plain here, not the fancy egg and onion or the delicious 'everything.'"

The Voice grew louder and even more sarcastic, as only a fed-up Yahweh on the outskirts of Maple Run could be. "Baptized you can get here, sure. But circumcised? Forget it. Barbed wire is not bris-friendly" (bris: the ritual circumcision all Jewish boys undergo at 8 days of age). "Period. End of the line. Genug (enough)! I, Lord of Hosts, have spoken."

Enough already! "Why? Why? Why? Do you hear Me? Hear me? He ..?"

But I wouldn't shut up, at least in my mind. "I'm already circumcised, thank you very much. Kosher pickles? Horseradish? Come on! We'll grow it. And You've got to admit the people here are beautiful. Didn't you always say that being a Jew was trying to do good, and that trying to heal the world was the most important thing? We've put it on our doorposts and in our hearts. Let's be friends."

Thereon followed a Jahovian silence. And then. "Okay, boychik" (kiddo), "you've made your point. And you're right; it's lovely here. I love when you people give me a good debate. And you know what, I like your chutzpah" (gall); "reminds Me of the good old days with Job. Be happy. L'chaim!"

The Voice and Its accompanying music receded to be replaced by the soothing sounds of Mark and Melanie's cows mooing in the field just above the studio, only to be overpowered by the warning drone inside of the ever-on TV reporting Florida's newest disaster. And the news was re-repeated by Early Shirley in her bathrobe and supersize hair rollers as she watched, bleary eyed and worried, all day and most of the night—turning up the volume and re-echoing the news to Jan each time she entered the room.

My crippled foot and the excoriating warnings from the Voice, even the lightning bolt, struck me as negligible compared to the TV's five-minute toxic interval reports of wind velocity, rain volume, roof losses, pet drownings, imminent floodings, zoos exploding, and various other terrors that monopolized each and every channel and permeated Early's consciousness. They had her! They damn well had the whole country. Yes, the weather was horrible, but if this wasn't also the highest media art and most glorious moment of our frighten-them-out-of their-wits culture, I was no judge of dramatic art.

As I lay propped up in bed, moaning, my throbbing foot elevated, tenderly placed by me atop three puffy pillows, rotating my soggy peas, listening to my mother-in-law moaning oy veys punctuated by my own, searching in vain for the scorch mark on my pillow, it suddenly struck me that something was missing in the whole ghastly catastrophic picture. Why, if the Apocalypse was so close at hand, hadn't the Lord of Hosts even given it a teeny-weeny mention along with His objections to the local pickle shortage? My answer: either the Voice was so preoccupied with us—and this I found a tad hard to believe—or the TV reporters, swaying in the winds, were getting swept away by their own enthusiastic rhetoric.

Or maybe, just maybe, the Voice wasn't out there at all or was merely a function of all those splendid little pink and white pain pills I was swallowing by the handful. I nodded off into narcotic dreamland as my poor mother-in-law continued to terrify herself.

Whatever the reality, we were staying put. Voice or no voice, pickles or no pickles. Hurricane or no. The mezuzah was hung.

FENCES

Halfway down our driveway there was an old locust split-rail fence where our most productive grape arbor grew. The fence, like the arbor, had probably been in place close to thirty years, and although locust wood is reputed, according to local folklore, to "last forever" or almost that long, ours was in a state of falling-down senility with about half of its rails rotted through and collapsed on the ground. But even in decay, the fence was beautiful. However, because of the fence's decrepitude, vines searching for support and finding none nearby had somehow reached up and coiled themselves into and through the highest tree branches, making many of the grapes nearly impossible to reach, let alone harvest.

Looking at our fallen fence posts, my first thought was to tramp up the mountain into our woods, find a dead locust tree, chainsaw it into eight-foot log lengths, and then split them. If Daniel Boone or Paul Bunyan or Lorne's Daddy could do it without power tools, surely I could try with the assortment of tools we'd already bought.

Noah said he'd be happy to help. He knew how to do it all, he said, "and we could drag them logs out by chaining them to the Ranger."

"Do it all" should have been a clue.

The next morning sitting on their front porch while I waited for Noah to pull on his work boots, listening to the grand plan, Lorne looked me dead in the eye. "That's a whole lot of work." He repeated, for emphasis, "a whole lot" and spat a gob of tobacco over the porch rail. "It's awful hot. Hot already and it's gonna get hotter." His blue-eyed stare spoke more than words. "As hot as it is and as tired as you'll be, a feller might just lose a couple of fingers, too."

Now, my wife's constant cautions were one thing. I was used to them. But coming from Lorne, my friend who rarely offered advice unless asked, this skepticism was something else. In his few words—and especially in his stare—here was a dire warning. But the most ominous sign—and I'm not being facetious here—was the size of the tobacco gob. I'd learned in our months here that the strength of his response, comic or serious, could be measured in the volume as well as the frequency of his expectorant. And this morning's was a pip.

Shakespeare spoke in paraphrase of my Appalachian buddy. "That way madness lies." Lorne's word-packed stare and the Bard's wisdom sent a clear if unaccustomed message to my mountain exuberance: be rational for a change; for once in your life, be rational. Invoke "saichel" (use your God-given common sense).

So, taking care not to offend Noah who, booted, was already tightening the chain and revving up his saw, I explained that we had a new plan. I would locate a place to buy the rails and we'd spend our time on the actual job of repair. It would not be as much adventure for him or me. Merely finding and transporting the already-cut rails would just have to serve as sufficient amusement and adventure for us all, including the staff of the ER.

And so I began my quest to seek out a source, starting on the phone. The response from the larger lumberyards was generally the same. Each courteously explained that they carried fencing: wood, chain link, and wrought iron, but none of the old roughhewn stuff.

"Most people around these parts are switchin' over to mill-planed boards. It's easier, and by the time you're done it's a whole lot cheaper."

One guy told me that there was an old yard over in Johnson City that might have some. When I phoned there was no answer and so in my determination I grabbed Noah and we rode over.

Here the owner, a crotchety old bird, was less politic.

"What d'ya wanna mess with that for? Anyone who got one made it hisself. Old timey people." Disgust soaked his words. "Don't wanna move forward with Progress."

"Well, I still want one. Maybe you can tell me if there's any place local I can find some?"

"Sure stubborn ain't you? Sure you ain't from around here?" He knew the answer to that one. "Get up on the mountain. Hire a couple of Mexicans to haul it out if you can find some. Cause I'll guarantee none of the locals is gonna do it."

So, it looked as if we were stuck. On the drive back, I tried to relieve my disappointment through self-inflicted punishment by taking a short-cut across the mountain. I was desperate. In all probability, we'd get lost. That would show them! And we did. Maneuvering around tight turns, we saw carefully tended gardens and small farms dotted with old bathtubs now innovatively in service as watering troughs. Frequent sightings of old refrigerators and stoves tossed into ravines and rusting old cars minus their hoods and abandoned motors, stripped of any useful parts, lying around in side yards—these were way less picturesque.

From our first days in these mountains, the local habit of throwing stuff you didn't want just about anywhere you did not personally have to see it drove us crazy. We could not reconcile the reverence most people had for their gardens or their houses with what seemed to be total disregard for the rest of their environment.

I'd seen Noah load his Ranger with broken pieces of tile or chunks of concrete and dump them into a crystal spring without a thought about it while at the same time rhapsodizing about how beautiful the mountains looked. His seemed to be a typical disconnect here, and even though I'd taught aesthetics from time to time before we moved here, I never realized in a practical way how people might exhibit a strong sense of beauty in one direction and absolutely none in another. It seemed a matter of their vision. They just didn't seem to see how tossing stuff into a handy gully blighted the place they so revered. Or enough of them didn't so that the accumulation was horrid to an outsider's eye.

Or maybe it was a combination of attitudes and the result as much of the overwhelming individualism so prevalent here that insisted a man had the right to do whatever he wanted on and to his own property? Or maybe it was just having so much land. Was it that simple? Having too much meant they didn't hold in reverence all they had? I'd not figured it out. But I knew it still bothered Jan and me. And for Steve, an artist whose paintings were love affairs with the mysticism of Nature, this disregard caused near apoplexy. He saw an open junkyard along the road and turned purple with rage. Did scarcity of anything we needed bring a higher respect for what we did have? I'd heard that Americans in general wasted enough food to feed all the hungry people in our country and more.

As we rounded still another curve, this one sharp enough to interrupt Noah's telling me that, "if it was him, he'd just tear down that old fence and make him a whole new one out of modern slats" I saw it. Just below and ahead of us was an old shotgun farmhouse, rose garden, and pasture, along which was the most beautiful crookedy fence I'd ever seen. And next to the barn, there was a big pile of what looked to be extra crosspieces.

"Look, Noah, our prayers have…" A quizzical look stopped me mid-sentence. "Well, our deepest wishes have been answered." We were past the farm so I pulled into a gravel road, backed out, and reversed direction.

Noah was still bothered. "You know who lives here?" He was several shades paler than his usual suntanned blond complexion. I'd seen that blanched hue before too.

"No."

"Well, neither—do—I." He spaced the words for emphasis. And then he slid a bit lower in his seat. "You're gonna get us shot. That's what! Folks don't take t' strangers just driving on up."

"Don't be such a mountain man fraidy cat. Just go on up to the door, knock hard, and introduce yourself. I'll bet you a barbecue lunch at Bridge-water they know you."

"I ain't goin' nowhere." He scrunched down about as low as he could get into his seat and pulled down the brim of his John Deere cap so that it covered his eyes. His mind was made up.

I had learned that when Noah decided, the issue was closed. The many times I'd asked him not to scalp the grass with the mower, he'd given me the same stare I was receiving now and made the clear argument. "It'll grow back." This response meant he wanted as long a time between mow-ings as he could manage. End of discussion. I might be the one paying, but he was the one doing. So at this juncture, if I had any chance of getting the fencing, cold introductions were up to me.

The door was nearly as roughhewn as the fence, slivery, constructed of thick old oak planking. It was built to last; hell, it was made to withstand a siege. As I knocked, I wondered if anyone could even hear me through the thing. But apparently someone could. Maybe there were two somethings from the volume of the barking and growling. Bagel barks a deep throated bark. If you didn't know him, he'd scare you. But this was different. This was the mastiff sound that terrifies you when you turn the corner on a country road and spot a stockade and hear lunging and howling behind it and are sure the hounds of the Baskervilles are readying to leap over and tear you apart. I was beginning to think that this wasn't such a hot idea after all and, as much as I hated to admit it, that maybe Noah had a point. Too late.

A voice too much like the timbre of the hound's boomed, "I'm coming, hold your water." The door opened, and filling the doorway was a man as large, no, as thick, as I have ever seen and that includes those wrestling-show guys on TV where one behemoth lifts the opponent over his head, over the ropes, and flings all three-hundred pounds of him into the audience. No, he was more the girth of a champion sumo wrestler. Dressed in filthy overalls and heavy boots, with knife in hand, he looked at me from clear blue eyes that were set off by a thick, tangled blond beard that started at the top of cheeks and ended below the chest pockets of his overalls. Without turning his head, he reached behind him and with one hand, effortlessly picked up by its collar what looked to be some sort of giant wolf and flipped it back into the room with a "shut up and set." It did.

I'm six-feet-two-inches tall and not used to the sensation of being looked down upon, but that's exactly the way I was feeling—probably because the guy was just so overwhelmingly big, easily double my soaking-wet fighting weight of 175.

"Sorry to disturb you," I began, my words coming with markedly less fluidity than usual. His face changed during my midsentence and he began a sort of wheezing laugh. Now I was sure I was in the presence of a mountain spirit.

"It ain't a problem," he said as he closed the knife he was holding and slid it through the bottom of his beard into the bib pocket. "Been sharpening her. Fixing t' go fishing later after it cools down some. Something I can do for you?"

"Well, to be honest, we were driving by and saw your fence and that pile of railings. I wondered if you might be interested in selling a few?"

"You're not from around these parts?"

"No." I explained our recent move to Maple Run and my crazy desire to mend and keep our old fence. And how most of the folks around here thought me a little daft.

"Well, I guess it ain't crazy if you want to do it and it don't hurt nobody. Anyhow, it's nobody's business is it? I like them old-timey fences too. I'm right sorry to be unneighborly, it ain't my way, but I split those for my own self. Need t' run the fence all the way back and around. Guess I'm crazy too then. Probably have to cut more, too. So I just don't have none to spare. Otherwise, you'd sure be welcome to it." He was embarrassed, even "flummoxed" that he couldn't help me out.

He was looking over my shoulder and out the door. "Your friend there looks like he's getting ready t' disappear through your vehicle's floor."

I turned to see the last vestige of Noah's cap sink like a summer sun below the window. "He's a little shy," was all I could manage.

"Yeah. Lots of folks turn shy when they see me... Say, is that turtle a local boy?"

"He's a Simmons, Lorne's younger son."

"I know Lorne. Knew his twin brother too. Went to high school with the two of them. Teachers couldn't tell those boys apart. We had some fun with them."

"Those Simmons boys worked plenty hard," he resumed. "Real good people. Say, wait a second. I think I do know where you might get some crookedy. Well, yes, I believe I do. There's an old feller down in White Tail Falls, just on the other side of Sloan Mountain. Used t' have lots of wood, but I heard his wife died and he give up the business. Most likely, he's probably still livin' thereabouts and who knows but he might still have some. Problem is I ain't sure, and I hate to send you and your bobbetty friend there on a wild goose chase. And his place is real easy t' miss lessen you know where you're going. Can't get there from here." In local lingo this meant it's awfully hard to find unless you know the way.

He must have realized we were still standing in the doorway. "Where's my manners? Come in for a minute an' I'll draw you up a map." He saw my reluctance to enter the wolf's den. "Oh, don't mind him. He won't do nothing t' bother you now that he knows you're a friend. If he does I'll just have to break his neck and yank out them vocal cords." He winked and put his arm around me, pulling me in where I got a good look at the dog—an even better match in size to his master than I'd originally thought—relaxed now, clearly not abused or in fear of a neck snapping but intent on wrapping his enormous tongue around my face without moving from his spot beside an old raggedy chair.

Joshua, that's what the giant's name turned out to be, drew the map on a piece of cardboard. He sketched out a road over the mountain that he labeled as changing from blacktop to gravel to dirt and back to blacktop; barn landmarks and two lightning-struck trees, a wood creek bridge to cross until reaching the outskirts of White Tail Falls.

"Joshua, you've just given a map to a guy who once drove from Chicago to Ohio, arriving after three hours of hard driving at a sign that read Welcome to Chicago."

That brought a guffaw and a one-armed hug that I am happy to say came short of crushing vertebrae. "Oh, you'll be all right," he said, "just fine," leading me out and extending his fireproof hand in new friendship. "Just take her easy. It's been a real pleasure to meet you. You come back real soon you hear and maybe we'll all go fishing together: you, me, that Simmons boy, and him," he said, nodding toward the loving Fang. "God bless. And when you build your fence, you be awful careful with that chainsaw."

The ride back felt like triumph. There were no guarantees, but Joshua seemed pretty confident that we would find our prize in White Tail Falls. As a bonus, I'd made kissing friends with what was probably the largest canine in Pelion County. The worm had turned, with one small exception. Noah, now sitting upright next to me was adamant about not going on to White Tail Falls.

"Had just about enough for one day," he said, with what passed for indignation. "Drop me off to home. When you come back with the fence, I'll be here ready t' help."

So it was Jan and I who followed Joshua's map over the mountain and actually located the place on the first try: Wainwright Fence Yard printed in bright orange letters with three delicious, deep piles of the real thing, genuine split locust rails sitting right there in the front yard.

A few hundred yards down the road was a collection of small antique shops that Jan had spotted and where she wanted to get out, so much so that almost before I stopped the truck she was closing the door, kissing me goodbye, wishing me good luck, and taking off for fun of her own. It was one thing to ride over the mountain and act as my navigator in order to prevent our sudden demise in flight off the pavement and over the mountain's edge, another to endure the next part of my mountain nuttiness.

Wainwright's Fencing was located between 'WAINWRIGHT REALTY' and "Old Red Wainwright, the Auctioneer," each of the signs scripted in the appropriate letters, color, and style. The word Fencing was printed in letters shaped like slats; Auctioneer was more or less a scrawl in drippy red barn paint and Realty was professional in neat looking black block letters. Whoever Red Wainwright was, he was obviously one heck of an entrepreneur.

I pulled into the yard between the stacks, looked around for an attendant, and then called out: "Hello in the house," just like I'd heard in segments of the old Davy Crockett series. As soon as I'd done it, I felt really silly. No answer. Nobody around. Maybe Joshua was right. Mr. Wainwright had decided to call it quits and just left the remaining inventory, but with all these signs of energy and enterprise still around and looking pretty fresh, I doubted it.

Set back maybe one-hundred yards from the wood yard was a clapboard farmhouse that looked abandoned: unpainted, some roof shingles missing, the plants around it untended. But there was a small lit lamp in the front window and a door around the side, which when I got close enough to see it, was ajar. I knocked and, after no reply, knocked again louder and got a high pitched, "Door's open. Come on in."

Inside, in shadowy light stood an old man beside an even older desk piled high with papers and a stack of leather-bound books. As my eyes adjusted, I saw that I was in a large room that looked as if it served as living-dining-bedroom-kitchen. The walls were uninsulated, chinked here with clay, there with cement, crowded eye-level to ceiling with deer heads, enormous champion-size antlers, and what must have been a fifteen-pound bass. Racks of expensive-looking rifles and a couple of shotguns hanging next to the fish all looked unused and were covered with dust. Above the twin-size bed placed in the exact center of the room, next to a gas cook-stove piled high with dishes and a few not-so-recently-used cast-iron pots vintage 1940 or so, hung a carved and lacquered wooden sign, "Jesus Is Lord Of This Home."

If I had to go out on a limb, I'd say this was Mr. Wainwright.

Dressed in worn, starched overalls and rail thin, he was bent over like a well-worn bow. Not knowing me, he reached out his hand in welcome. The top digits of his fingers were at odd angles, gnarled with arthritis or perhaps bent from breaks acquired over a long life of hard work. We shook and he smiled. It was a good ten count before he let go of my hand.

I am ordinarily not at a loss for words—after all, I've spent most of my professional life talking to students, actors, teachers, and customers of my wife's business—but at this moment in these mountains I was again verbally stunned and could not take my eyes from his face. Every one of his teeth was gold. Each and every one. Mr. Wainwright's mouth was unlike anything I'd ever seen outside of the old Hollywood pirate movies, and even in those there was no mouth so unabashedly resplendent.

He held up his hand, a mountain traffic cop. "Don't pay these teeth no never mind. Enough to surprise anyone new. A little bit like coming on twin cows at the bottom of a barrel, don't you think? Truth is I love to see people's faces, and then I can tell the story. Had 'em done years ago by old Doc Curly. He was our dentist, least ways I think he was a dentist. Never saw his diploma, but he did us good work. Took care of most folks here about. Time I was first auctioneering and a man traded me some old gold coins for a 1946 John Deere tractor. Bright green, no computers, no gadgets, put in gas, turn it on, and it ran. Fix it in a minute if you had the part; earned its keep."

"Anyhow, I was having terrible trouble with my teeth about that time. Talk about pain. I'm not much for drinking but I remember one night the pain was so bad I went down to Elmer Fratten's still and practically begged him for a whole jug and drank it right there. Pains started in the army and I guess I could've had it taken care of there, but I just wanted to get out after the war then, t' get home to my new bride I'd not seen in three years."

"Lots of folks back then around here had teeth troubles and most just yanked 'em out and that was that. My daughter—she's a teacher in Jacksonville now, graduate of Appalachian State, proud of that child—told me my teeth were because of poor nutrition for pregnant women around here when my mother was young. If she says it, you can be sure it's true. Anyhow, I figured I had that gold and I could do better. So, I went to Curly and asked him if he could keep one, melt down the rest and fashion me some first quality teeth. And he did. Haven't had a bit of trouble since"— he gave me his 24-carat grin—"lessen you consider it trouble when I meet somebody new and it startles them. Do you?"

The great talker, me, lecturer to thousands, had a clever comeback, "Do I what?"

"Consider it trouble?"

"Uh-uh."

"Well, son, that's fine."

I know it seems as if every time we took a new curve in these mountains we met still another fascinating person. The amazing truth is we did. Shakespeare's "What a piece of work is man, infinite in his variety," takes on daily reverberation here, or maybe it's just because we're so attentive to everything and everyone, but Jan and I think the sense of a world new every day is not going to wear off no matter how long we're lucky enough to stay.

With his teeth, Mr. Wainwright had developed his liking for other gold, too. On his twisted left-hand ring finger he wore a quarter-sized golden nugget the face of which was plated as a cross that looked as if it was made of small diamonds. On his little finger, half of which was missing, he sported a star sapphire or a very fine imitation of one, and on his right thumb an emerald. Between his mouth and his busted hands the old fellow was wearing a small fortune.

Stunned, and trying unsuccessfully not to stare, I stammered out an explanation for my uninvited appearance at his door.

"No need, son. I know just how hard it is to find good fencing nowadays. One of the reasons I'm still malingering hereabouts. Sure don't need the money no more. But I figure so long as I got the stock and there's a few customers, might as well keep the doors cracked. Don't really know how much longer though. Can't do the work by myself any more. Carrie, my missus, died last month after 58 years of marriage; that woman could do the work any man could do, most times do it better than any two."

He ran a finger over the top book. They were bibles.

"And it looks like nobody wants to work no more—least not, nobody white. Don't know what they do instead. Drink or pop pills most likely, or take the government's money. The gov-ern-ment—don't get me going on that bunch." He sighed, "Yes sir, me and Carrie could turn out the work like nobody's business."

"Now Mexicans'll work. Work hard. I've got nothing about them people. Trying t' make a living just like everyone else. But they want too much money—I end up making two dollars a man by the end of the day. Can't make a living that way. Can't really blame them. I know it's hard work. Done it my own self all my life, for over fifty years—right up on that mountain right there." He pointed out the window.

"For real fencing, yellow locust is the onliest kind you want and the only kind I'll take in. This here is the best," he said, touching a small piece of the wood on his desk, "the best, and don't let nobody tell you different. Some folks, them's that still got it, use Red. Terrible stuff, thorns yea long," he said, holding up a thumb and a bloody index finger two inches apart, "tear you up! Took in a few yards yesterday just to help a feller out and look what they done t' me. Gonna burn it up later. Awful foolish of me, but that poor feller had worked so hard and looked like he had a need. And them that grows in the swamps is no good at all; won't last even a few years."

I don't know whether he was just making conversation or this was his sales pitch, but he had me educated as well as convinced. I imagined him in his auctioneer heyday. He must have been phenomenal, and despite my normal skepticism I had the sense that Mr. Wainwright was the genuine article: talkative, yes; charismatic, absolutely; but I'd bet my mule, if I owned one (and I intended to eventually), that he was honest day in and day out.

"How many you think you need young feller?" Oh, how I loved being called young. "I got 'em all, 5-, 7-, and 10-foot long. Six dollars for the short ones, eight for the bigger ones. Take you just as many as you want, seven and tens the same. Take 'em all!"

We were walking out into the yard. I snaked out a 10-footer from near the top of the pile. The slat was easily 6-inches thick and must have weighed a good 70 or 80 pounds. No wonder these things lasted so long.

The wood was dense; one side still had its bark. And I figured we needed twelve or so more to do the job! As with all my farm projects this was shaping up to be way bigger than originally planned. As I lifted I wondered if maybe it was hernia time for me.

Mr. Wainwright stood there, watching me picking a couple of long splinters out of my palm. "Son, why n't you take a little break." Break? I had barely even started. "Let me get you a pair of gloves. These things'll give you some real mean slithers."

"No thanks, really, I'm fine." I didn't want him thinking I was one of those Yankee ski slopers.

But he was already heading back to the house. "Won't be but a second. You just take a breath. Just relax yourself a while."

I'd barely begun to load one rail and he was already concerned about my health? He returned at a slow wobbly trot carrying a pair of leather gauntlet work gloves, handed them over and, with the mountain stare and wink I'd come to appreciate, insisted, "Put 'em on son. No sense letting pride ruin your hands. No one else around to see and I sure won't be telling a soul. Believe in the Good Book don't you? 'Pride goeth before the fall.'" I was getting to like this old guy with the James Bond villain teeth. I pulled on the gloves, which, by the way, were a perfect fit.

Then he did something so charming, so disarming, I was speechless again. Being nonplused was getting to be a habit up here. He reached out and lifted up one of the too-long straps of my brand-new overalls, the one that kept sliding off my shoulder, and patted it in place, like a concerned parent for a child who had just learned to tie his laces and was in danger of tripping and falling on his face. And then he adjusted the strap so that the damned thing fit snug. Neither he nor, more surprisingly, I felt any embarrassment.

"Need t' watch yourself when you're workin' this stuff. That's all."

While I hefted a second 10-footer into the truck bed and felt a distinct strain in my groin, I made another executive decision: the rest would be 7-footers. More pieces at less weight per unit equals possible avoidance of the surgeon's knife. He reached over to help me with it. I stopped him. I was learning mountain courtesy.

"Mr. Wainwright, I hope I'm not showing any disrespect, but I noticed you limping when you came back from the house and I guess it's probably not the best idea for you to do heavy lifting."

"Right you are, son. Right as rain. I forget, just so used t' working. Makes me a little crazy just sittin' in the house doing a lot of nothing. Sometimes I find myself just walking around the yard, searching for something to do."

I moved to the other pile and he moved right along with me.

"How long you been up here?" he asked.

"Just about five months. We still live down in Florida during the winter."

"Where 'bouts?"

"Near Orlando. Place called Winter Park, about 25 miles north of Disney."

"Uh-huh, been there. Nice place. Me and my wife took that boat ride goes through all your lakes. Been to Disney, too, when my grandson was little. Don't really like it, though most people seem to. Too many people for me and too many lines. Hot dog costs nearly as much as a store-bought turkey. My one girl, my only child, lives down in Florida now. Oh, I believe I mentioned that. Did I? Grandson and son-in-law too. Grand's about to start college. I've been blessed, thank the Lord."

I had five in now and I was puffing, leaning on the tailgate.

"I seen your bumper stickers. Front and back. That yellow one's something. 'Criminals in the White House,'" he traced each word in the air as if reading it, but with the tailgate down I knew he could no longer see it. "The other one ain't far behind neither, 'Republican or Democrat: Vote for Change.'"

I figured it was time to load the rest and get the hell out of Dodge. Gloves or not, strap adjustments or not, this was deep Bush country and my Judaic anxieties were telling me I was about to be ground up for a political heresy lunch, mashed between those sparkling choppers.

"Y' know, son, I voted for the President."

I gingerly removed his gloves. "Most of the people I know voted for him." I handed him the gloves.

"I know my whole church voted for him." He shook his head and my guess was that he was still thinking of those unpatriotic stickers. He paused, holding the delivered gloves. Questioning. Was this a confirmation of modern politically divided America, with him lamenting, shaking his head in frustration that an American could be so unpatriotic, so debased? Was he thinking that he'd now have to go back into the house, take down one of his many hunting rifles, dust it off, and blow the head off of this bald antlerless young 'un he'd sort of begun to like?

He handed back the gloves. "But I sure wouldn't vote for him again. None of them. Not a one. Not for local dogcatcher. Promises. This war is wrong in every way. We're sending young people over there to fight who don't know nothin', nothin'. It's criminal and I sure am sorry I have to agree with them bumper stickers. But I surely do. National Guard! Kids! Babies! Got no idea; send them off to get blown up. Bless their souls."

He was shaking his head in disappointment not at me, but at himself, at being so bamboozled. "I was a machine gunner in the second war. Eighty-nine pounds of weapon on my back. Two assistants to carry my ammunition. I knew how to kill a man. I was trained, really trained. Could take that weapon apart and put it back together again in the dark."

His eyes were closed. Remembering? What? I think he was back there somewhere in Germany or Italy, crawling under barbed wire, powering over trenches, falling, setting up, loading, and shooting the Nazi enemies, absolutely certain of who he was and what he was fighting for. With a President he believed in and an entire nation there, sacrificing beside him.

"They trained us and they trained us to kill a man with our bare hands, and believe me, I did it. Yes sir, I did it. I'm not proud of it, but I did it and I knew who I was killing and I knew why." He opened his eyes, refocused. "I just don't know what this country's about no more. Do you?"

He didn't wait for my answer and I'm not sure what I would have said if he had. Probably that I didn't either, but that I still believed in the idea of our Republic and that I was as angry as he was about all the lies and the awful war and the Republicans and yes, about the mealy-mouthed Democrats playing the handler angles instead of speaking truth right out and calling the liars, liars.

"Time was when people cared about one another and when you could sort of trust the government. Not all, but some. Send a boy to war, he was trained, prepared. Now, they're all crooks, just care about their rich friends, about lining their pockets. They send kids off and they got to make their own armor. Criminals."

I was finished loading: eleven rails: nine at $6, two at $8. He had them listed on a little square of paper.

"That'll be seventy dollars son. Sure you got enough?"

"Yes, Mr. Wainwright, I've more than enough to cover it."

"No, not money, son, wood. Enough wood. Take some more. You can always bring 'em back, y' know."

I assured him I had plenty.

"Well then, good luck son, and... God Bless you."

He was teary, this old, gnarled, tough-as-yellow-locust American vet. "Oh and here, put this on the back of the truck." He handed me a scrap of dirty red cloth. "Don't want you getting in a wreck on the way home."

"Say, am I okay you think? Should I tie them in? These won't slide off on the ride over the mountain?"

He laughed. "Son you've got a ton of wood in that truck. It ain't goin' nowhere. Wouldn't let you go if I thought it would move."

I shook his hand.

"Would've helped you load you know, but I done had two strokes and the doctor told me t' take it more easy. That and had me some heart failure a few months back and things ain't nearly as easy t' do as they used t' be. I'm not much good no more. If I take it any easier I'm thinking I'll root."

I climbed in and started the truck. Jan was probably already picturing me flipped over somewhere lying in a ravine. My new friend stood near the cab, with still more to say.

"You know my grandson, the one who just graduated high school, the one who's just about to start college? Did I mention my wife?" He trailed off. "I reckon I did. Blessed."

I turned off the ignition.

"He told his daddy he was gonna volunteer for the Navy instead of going right to college. Well, my girl told me I should have heard my son-in-law! About went right through the roof. My daughter said she was surprised they didn't hear him all the way to Raleigh. Told that boy that he'd volunteer over his dead body. His daddy was in Viet Nam serving as an Army Ranger. Hero. Silver Star, Purple Heart, Silver Cross. I never met a man who loved his country more."

Then he tossed me the last curve.

"Well, maybe you and me, son." He shook his head once more as if agreeing with himself, reaching through the window and offering me his hand.

"Sure is a strange time, ain't it?"

"Sure is."

"Well, God bless."

"And you," I returned, meaning it. Then I started the truck and left to pick up Jan.

TRUST

NOAH WAS AS GOOD AS HIS word. He was waiting on the driveway in his Ranger when Jan and I got home. And he was ready, armed with his dad's sledgehammers, iron wedges, a tree saw, the chain saw, heavy-duty galvanized nails, and my brand-new battery-powered hand-held one-hundred-and-fifty-dollar power drill.

We could begin.

We laid the new slats into place along the old fence. Then we removed the rotted pieces and proceeded at Noah's direction to lift and place the first seven footers, with me holding one end trying to balance it on my knee and pushing like hell to hold it flush against the existing upright post. Noah tried to drill a starting hole through both the slat and then the post so that we could drive a first nail through and secure the two.

The result was Noah pushing that drill with his full body weight, the drill worrying like it was going to burn up, and the hole he'd made smoking, after only a quarter inch or so of penetration. Only five inches more to go and we would be through the first hole of the first slat. At this rate, our operation on one slat would take about half a day and a fortune in drills, if it happened at all.

I told Noah, "There is no way we're going to do this. The cross-piece is far too thick, the wood too dense and thick." And because the slat was so heavy, the whole operation was way too awkward. I would definitely acquire my hernia even if by some miracle Noah managed to get through. The new cross-piece itself would look monstrously out of proportion to the other older pieces still in place. Nonetheless, despite my periodic monosyllabic groans and protests and his sweating like an attendant in a Turkish bath and the drill's wailing, that boy persevered.

"Stop! In the name of heaven stop, Noah. We're going to burn up the drill!"

He was red as a ripe tomato from his dad's garden. He was dripping, and looking more desperate by the second. Like most of us or, at least, like me, Noah, finding himself inadequate to the task at hand, went into panic mode. If at first you're not succeeding, go into overdrive. But here clearly overdrive was another accident waiting to happen.

"Noah, I think we've got to split these babies and then we've got to lay the piece flat on a log or something and drill straight down first, before we even try to lift it into place. What about it?" He was staring down at the power drill as if it would speak and provide better answers.

"You said you knew how, right?"

"Well, I think so. Seen Daddy do it. Seen Uncle Monroe." He was trembling, but not from exertion or diabetes. I think he was guessing I was mad at him, or that he was worried that he'd messed up. He looked ready to cry. He looked like he was on the verge of saying a bad word. Another small failure in a life filled with little failures is no small matter, and I was afraid that I'd set him up for a beaut. I remembered Steve as a little boy saying morosely, "I messed up again." It tore my heart out.

"What's the worse thing that can happen, buddy? We ruin some wood and call your Dad to give us a hand. If those two could do it, so can we."

"I don't know. You paid a lot of money on that wood. Daddy said it'd probably be over a hundred dollar."

"Noah we told each other we could do this, and we are going to go ahead and try. If we fail," wrong damned word, "maybe can't do it with the first piece, we'll go down and ask your Dad and we'll have only ruined just a little wood. No big deal." He was examining the drill bit. The point was gone. "Come on! What's the first thing we've got to do before we get the holes? I've got plenty more drill bits. You're an artist with that sledge. I've seen you sink a stake without ever missing."

"Well, I reckon we might try t' split some of them rails and make 'em skinnier."

"If that's what you think, that's what we do." He nodded, placing a wedge horizontally at the end of a thick slat and using all the strength he could muster, lifting the hammer high over his head and preparing to drive it into the wedge.

But at the top of his arc he just stopped, gently lowered the hammer and rested the sledge on the ground. "It ain't gonna work this way; can't get no bite. That wedge'll just jump out. Ain't no use."

He thought for a long moment, analyzing our problem. "When I seen my uncle and Daddy do it, one of them holds and the other hits. We need us a holder." He looked at me. "You reckon you can do that for us, Ol' Man—till we get her started?"

Now my big brotherly, caretaking, Knute Rockne routine was coming home.

"Maybe we can squeeze a rock against it or something," I offered, knowing I didn't know what the hell I was talking about but damned sure I didn't want to be holding a wedge as he swung down on me with fifteen pounds of steel.

"Won't work. Just hold her still, real still, and don't wiggle on me. You told me your own self I'm mighty good with this here hammer."

What could I do? Either I had confidence in him or I didn't.

I knelt, took hold of the slat with one hand, placed the wedge with the other, holding it as far away from its striking surface as I could, got my body and head as far removed as was humanly possible without being a contortionist—and closed my eyes.

"Now remember, Ol' Man, don't you wiggle."

I think I learned more about friendship, fate, and fatalism in that moment than in all the high-powered philosophy classes I ever took. To say no to his request was to tell him one more time that someone did not trust he could do the job. That all the talk about how he could do it was just hot air when it came down to reality. And I wasn't going to do that. And it was true that I had seen him use that sledge with absolute accuracy.

"Okay, I'm as ready as I'll ever be." I closed my eyes. "Now remember, friend. Bury that wedge in the wood, not in me. This ol' man wants to get a little older with both arms in place."

I didn't see it coming, but I sure felt the vibrations in my arm as Noah brought the hammer down square on the wedge head and drove its blade into the poplar.

"Now that's a hit. Yes sir, that did her good."

I don't think anyone has ever been as grateful to stand up and move his fingers as I was at that moment.

All of his might made only a small fault line, a tiny crack in the grain, sinking the wedge in perhaps two inches. But it was a start, and the look of accomplishment on Noah's face was worth the few years of fear I passed in the couple of seconds it took him to drop the hammer.

"Okay, Ol' Man. Let's get on with it. We got a lot more to do today before the sun sets."

"Yes sir, boss."

The process from then on was pretty simple. My boss took a slightly bigger and heavier second wedge and set it next to the first in the original crack, at any angle we could manage. Then I steadied the wedge while he hit away. Music to our ears was the sound of the wood ripping and splitting lengthwise along the grain. Enough repeats of the process and we had two long and thinner slats. And you would have thought that we'd just won the lottery.

"Look at that Noah. Beautiful isn't it?"

"Right pretty, if I do say so."

As we worked splitting and then using the drill and nails to build, we both gained confidence. We were mountain men in the old tradition, working with simple tools and a trust in one another. It felt great. In two days we had a fine looking strong fence that would support those grape vines for a long time to come.

Repaired poplar fence and grapes.

Ol' Man on a Mountain

HORNSWOGGLED?

"STU, HONEY, THERE'S A FUNNY SMELL out there."

Her voice was that of my old Jan, but the message was trouble. She'd gone out to check on the blueberries but came back in with empty hands, wrinkling that beautiful, sun-tanned model's nose instead. No mention of berries.

"Like what?"

"Like, stinky. Worse. It's down and out nasty."

"Like?"

"Like fertilizer gone bad. Just come outside and smell it yourself. It smells terrible."

Recently, in our farm saga, I have learned to dismiss nothing Jan says about smells.

I did disregard my Cassandra two weeks before when she warned me not to dump the thirty pounds of leftover catfish food (I'd bought fifty in my enthusiasm and thirty had turned maggotty), into the gully beside the house.

"It's organic," I had argued. "It's good for the earth."

"Have it your way!"

So I had it my way, dumped it, and three days later began a smell. A few more days and we were in a stench, one whiff of which practically crossed our eyes. The stench of thirty pounds of rotting catfish food defies description. Incredibly, she said nothing as we detoured in a wide arc for two weeks. But you and I both know what she was thinking. And she was right.

So, on this gorgeous morning, I immediately went out to investigate and, if possible, lay her concerns to rest. Coffee cup in hand, nose in the air, I sniffed too. Fertilizer it couldn't be; I hadn't fertilized in a month. And her description was an understated euphemism. Either the garden had developed a case of earth-fracting flatulence or I was inhaling raw sewage.

For a short moment, I was in what the pop psychologists call denial, like that moment of truth when you are assuring the plumber that he's made an awful mistake about your plumbing as he is calculating his future bill. It can't cost that much! You think, no way! There had to be some reasonable explanation for this stink and the squishy bilge underfoot other than the one my brain kept pressing upon me.

Perhaps, as in a bad science fiction film, a new variety of vegetation had produced its nauseating floribunda overnight, one that makes itself known only on a single morning for a few hours, and only in reflexive response to the aromatic beauty of Paul Newman coffee brewing inside the remodeled kitchen, finding its aromatic path maliciously stimulating some kind of otherwise benign plant's growth. Then, mysteriously, after the world is nose pinned and on the verge of asphyxiation, the monster suddenly disappears, like some mephitic century plant. The air clears. The birds sing again. The mutant plant must rebuild strength over the following hundred years in preparation for its next occurrence. And by that time, scientists have figured out a way to stop it, perhaps by something as unusual as a new variety of coffee. Or maybe by that time people have stopped drinking and eating, or their olfactory systems have been eliminated by evolution. Something. Any explanation was better than...

Then the plumbing and century plant fantasies evaporated while the stink forced my nose to talk with my rational self. I strove head on into an alluvial swamp. The muck between my toes was undeniable. My beautiful nurtured grass smelled like Cora Jean's billy goat's urine-soaked beard. Worse!

It being Sunday, I put off calling Lorne with news of our latest catastrophe until 8:30. As I briefed him with the details, his response was an Noahian pause, and though I couldn't see through the phone, I sensed it was many shades darker.

"I'll be up there just as soon as I put some clothes on. And Stew maybe you and Jan want to stay up on the porch and not wander about in the yard?"

He's a fast dresser. Ten minutes later he was at the door in high rubber boots and old coveralls. One sniff was all it took.

"Stew you got a problem." So, we were in a horror movie after all. "Your septic's busted. It's overflowing and flushin' up."

I looked back over my shoulder at Jan, who was staring out through the new picture window in the kitchen. With arms bent a little out from her waist and hands open at ninety degree angles from her wrists, her gesture was unmistakable. "So? How bad?" read her gesture.

I tried to pretend she wasn't there. When you've no answers, we've learned from our politicians the best strategy is to ignore the questions. And to ignore the questioner. But I was no politician and my wife was never to be ignored. It made her really mad.

"So I fix it?"

"Sure, if you can. But first you got to pump it out."

"And…?"

"And then you got t' dig down t' the field and pipes t' see just how bad they are."

Jan's signing was larger now, tracing letters on the window: Cassandra in frustration.

"And?"

"And then you can see if it's fixable."

"And?"

"And if it ain't, and from the look of things, I hate t' say it, but I'd guess it ain't, you gotta replace it. Probably the whole system."

"And it's a big job?" Was I smart?

"A real big job."

Lorne paced out what he figured was the length and width of the field. Jan watched his footwork, I am sure coming to the conclusion that such meticulous footwork boded no good. Then as he paced, she ceased her sign language and with her model's nose and perfectly formed lips pressed to the window, she slid, ever so slowly, to the floor until she was the mimetic picture of Madam Butterfly in her last moments. She was splendid!

I said, "Lorne, your brother said it was practically new. That it had never caused a problem. He said we wouldn't need to pump it for years." I thought, Lied to by a deacon?

Lorne was collecting a little puddle—if that's what you call the pooling of human guano—by stirring the mush with the toe of his boot. "He musta knowed this tank was in such terrible shape."

"I don't want to think that," I said, but I was thinking just that and more. Hornswoggled by a country quacksalver! By a sharp-sighted pigeon poacher!

"Don't see how he could've not. Shameful is what it is."

I wanted to get past what we were both thinking. "Lorne, it's going to be really hot today."

"They're giving ninety degrees."

"Can I get someone to come up here to work today? Now?"

"Sunday? T'ain't likely. Not on such short notice."

I went into the house to deliver the news and hope the queen wouldn't kill the messenger. Jan was packing and I'm sure silently reprimanding herself for being so naïve. In a crisis, I tend to blame others; she blames herself and only then adds me into the mix.

"City slickers. Are we the twosome?"

She looked at me, I at her, and then we both burst out laughing.

"Was that door-slide Butterfly or Theda Bara? Whatever, you were impressive."

Instead of an answer, she offered a high five. "Is this a deal or what?"

"I'll tell Lorne we're getting out of Dodge until the weekend's over and we can start to get this sorted out. Sure glad we agreed to live here 'as is'!"

Another high five.

I walked out to tell Lorne our plans

He was way ahead of me. "Now, wait just a minute. Just a second. Let's not get our noses so bent out of shape just yet."

"Our?"

"It don't really matter why this happened. But we gotta fix it."

"We?" We both owned the problem?

"I been thinkin' about it while you was in there trying to make it nice with Jan. By the way, she's a pretty good little actress ain't she?"

"Good, not great, but I'll give you good."

"I went to school with this boy who works for Five County Septic. He might have his truck home. We ain't talked for a while, but I recall sometimes he goes straight there and parks it over the weekend, dependin' on where he ends up on Friday's last job. I'm gonna call that boy. See if maybe he'll come up. Doubt it, but he's a real good boy. It don't cost us nothin' t' try."

Jan and I sat in the innermost bedroom only moderately hopeful for an early intervention by Lorne's old classmate. But we both figured the chances were slim to nothing. After all, we were nothing to him, and as Lorne said, he hadn't seen him for a while.

The probability was that we'd need to find and hire somebody else next week. We had no idea what something like this could cost. But judging from Lorne's initial assessment, this fracture in our guaranteed-and-won't-cause-you-a-bit-of-trouble septic system was about to absorb lots and lots of money.

Steve might know a reliable company. Lorne probably wouldn't. He and his family did things like this on their own backs. If Steve came through, we might get someone by the end of the week. In the meantime, the day and stench were both heating up.

"Lach a bissel!" (laugh a little)

"Jan, my dear," I ventured, pinching my nose and sidling over on the bed to steal a kiss, "have you left something on the stove? There is, if I may suggest, a peculiar odor in the house, reminiscent of your burnt turnips. Or, my love, have you incinerated our grits again?"

"One more like that and I'll incinerate *your* grits."

Around 11 o'clock the house began to tremble. Bagel began barking, even howling, which he never does, even in a terrible thunderstorm. Evidently, the season's final catastrophe was upon us. And I wasn't a bit surprised.

This area had never suffered an earthquake, not since those eons gone by in the murky past when these now ancient mountains rose out of the sea, at least not that anyone wrote about, but our, no, MY presence on the land, in defiance of the Voice's commands, might just be commandeering a cataclysmic change.

Just when I'd really begun to think that we were safe, that we'd defied all the odds, that the Voice and our kids were as wrong as my buying and operating a weed eater, it was upon us. We were about to sink into a capacious fissure, down, down, down, into an infinite version of our septic sludge. We were bound for the quagmire of middle earth.

"So there! Defy your kids, defy Me," whispered the Voice "and you will sufferrrrr."

I was snatching together toothbrushes, pajamas, extra rolls of toilet paper, for obvious reasons given my thoughts about our present problem and our next otherworldly destination, when Jan, annoyed by my panic, told me to go downstairs and see who was coming up the driveway and making such an awful racket.

I put down the toilet paper rolls and complied.

The cataclysm looked a lot like a ten wheeler. Its guide, whose face I could see just over the top of the steering wheel, was grinning. And next to him was sitting an exultant Lorne. The truck pulled up and out popped a sharp-faced little guy, dressed in what looked like a shiny rubber banana-colored jumpsuit. He stuck out his hand.

"You must be Stew. And the lady in the door with the surprised look on her pretty face must be Jan. I'm Ken. This worthless feller here still a sitting in the truck y'all know, I reckon. He might be worthless, but he surely knows how to put out a S.O.S. Even without my answerin' machine, I could of heard him clear down in Fenton. Sorry I didn't get here faster, but my wife and me was out shopping."

I started to explain.

"Whoa Nellie, you don't need to tell me no more about it; could smell it all the way at the bottom of your driveway." He turned toward me, but spoke as much to Lorne as to me. "Who'd you buy this place from anyway? Some folks look better goin' then comin'. Don't you think?"

Lorne spat out the window and got out of the truck.

"We can get acquainted later. First off, let's see what we can do to help you." The lovely sound of "we" again.

He yanked a heavy-looking hose from some compartment under the truck and he and Lorne pulled it into the swamp where Ken found a hookup to drain whatever was still sloshing around in the septic tank. He returned to the truck and threw some equally mysterious lever, activating a vacuum system.

A vacuum cleaner never sounded so good before. This one sounded to me like the Chicago Symphony on a great night. While the pump sucked, the two old friends caught up on things. Ken was remarried. "This time I got me a good one." They talked about growing up here, about their fondest memories, swimming in the river, shooting at breakneck speeds down the snowy hills using linoleum remnants as their sleds.

"Talk about fast! You couldn't steer and you couldn't stop till you hit the bottom. And fun!"

Forty-five minutes later, the fractured tank was drained and Ken was preparing to leave. "That should take care of the problem till y'all decide what you're goin' to do."

What do you do for someone who's been so kind and helpful on a moment's notice? Especially on his Sabbath! We offered lunch, soda, blueberries… something, to do a little more than just saying "thank you."

He politely refused. "Don't believe I can take anything now, but I thank you."

I asked if I could write him a check.

"Don't believe you can. Not now. I'll think on it for a time, and mail you some sort of bill after a while. Bet by then you'll have it all figured out with the help of this here no-good feller." He waved. "See you, Lorne. You tell Bitsy 'hi' for me."

He navigated a three-point turn in our narrow driveway and left. Most of the worst stench, safely contained in his truck, left too. So did my fantasy about the Voice's wrath. The final disaster wasn't sucking at our mucky heels after all.

I am nothing less than a drama queen. My conservative father, who loved me dearly, saw my imagination as a great relief if a little too often in overdrive. He'd look at me after some episode of overreaction and with a mix of admiration and curiosity either bang me on my head or ruffle my hair, saying, "Son, you need a keeper."

My mother, like her mother, Bubbe Choma, was less restrained in her response.

"A meshuggene." Can there be any city American reading this that does not know the meaning of this word—a crazy person? Up here, though, until our arrival it was a different story. Nobody knew it. Today, I've even got Noah using it perfectly.

"Stew, you sure are a mesh-u-ga-na!"

I explained that to my Bubbe (my grandma) and to me and Jan, this word, like when he called me ol' man, was loaded with fun and admiration. Calling someone a nut case in the right way, in the right language, with the right feelings, was the highest form of praise.

"Stew, you definitely are a mesh-u-ga-na!" He now uses it interchangeably with ol' man.

Anyhow, we were in the middle of no earthquake, no Golems, no discernible deity's conscientious revenge that I could detect. Instead, there was a kind man going far out of his way to help a friend of a friend. The immediate crisis was over. We could probably sleep at home tonight without army surplus gas masks.

Let's face it, as much as we'd prefer to imagine that our sins, even imagined sins, or misdemeanors are worthy of detailed oversight from above, the truth is that we are much more worthy of a Greek god's guffaw. Bubbe would say again, "Mann tracht und Gott lacht." Personally, I don't think there is much heavenly reaction one way or another. As you know, our neighbors say that there are no mistakes. Everything is in the Plan. Jan goes along. Boy, on this big one—the Plan—do we ever disagree. But in our friendship, how we open ourselves to one another and how we interact— we'd agree on that for sure. Maybe God is collective kindness?

"So, now what?" I asked Lorne

"Well, now I'm gonna go on up to Mark's and get his tractor, rig it with the backhoe, come back and dig out this mess. I'll throw on some shovels too." This was my friend with the terrible knee and back troubles talking. This was my friend who most certainly would be needing surgery again this year.

"Lorne, you know we appreciate all your help, but we can't let you do that. You've done enough already. All we (now it's my 'we') need now is for you to hurt yourself worse. Jan and I would never forgive ourselves. We'll wait and find a good company to do it."

His eyes narrowed. "Can I tell you something? I wouldn't volunteer if I thought I would hurt myself too bad. Probably can't do a thing I ain't done already. And if you go and hire an outsider, it'll end up costing you a fortune. An' they'll want t' pull permits, and that'll mean all kinds of inspectors, one thing and another. What you don't need now is a bunch of inspectors who don't know nothing running around here making you a bigger mess. Nope. I'll do it, and Mark will help me, and so will Noah."

Like Noah, once Lorne set his mind on something, there was no changing it. I had seen him work on fixing the roller mechanism on a garage door for hours and hours until he had corrected it. I had wandered around the hills and lakes of Tennessee with him, searching for a particular trailer camp, driving into and out of one after the other, asking directions, getting lost for hours, until finally he found it.

"Stop trying because there ain't no way you're gonna change my mind. And besides, I'm ashamed t' admit it really ain't all for you and Jan. I'm pretty sure that my brother and that wife of his had t' think something like this could happen. How couldn't he? I'm embarrassed. You just don't do people this way."

I finally agreed, but with one stipulation: he'd stay put, up on the tractor. I'd stay below working with the shovel. He was skeptical even as he gave in. "Stew, no disrespect intended, but you don't look much like a shovel man t' me."

On almost all mountain matters Lorne was almost always right. So, too, I had learned that he was first rate at sizing people up. But on this one he was dead wrong. He couldn't possibly know it, but the one tool that I *did* know how to handle—long before we arrived here—was a shovel.

THE RENAISSANCE ICON

FOR THREE SUMMERS IN MY MUCH younger days I worked as a laborer and ditchdigger. The first summer was right after Dad suffered his first big financial crisis. For the first time in his new career as a furniture salesman he'd sold a boxcar of furniture. He was elated and felt relaunched, but then the company he represented went under and his commissions evaporated. A month later he suffered a near-fatal heart attack just as I was about to enter college.

Several months later, when Dad felt sufficiently strong enough to work again, typical of his tenacity, he got two new lines of furniture and a second job on the weekends selling "electronic" (i.e., super modern) houses, working for his cousin who was a developer in Skokie, one of the northern suburbs of Chicago where Jews had just begun to migrate from the north-side neighborhoods.

And using his leverage as a salesman and a relative, my father landed me, his 6' 2" 155-pound son, a laborer's job with the cousin's cleanup and landscaping crew. Dad was working seven days a week after suffering a heart attack. As skinny as I was, I took the job. It was a find. It paid that princely $6.50 an hour. None of my friends had anything like it.

It's not as if I was a stranger to work. From the time I was eleven I had taken on lots and lots of little jobs at my mother's insistence, including helping Dad. But those jobs were all pretty benign. My "employers" were kind. I worked for Mr. Spatz, the kosher butcher who had the shop next to my father's bakery and who insisted I take breaks to go and play basketball. I worked at stocking shelves for Mr. Adler and his sons at their drapery shop. I worked for Cousin Gershon, a saintly baker who studied Kant and Schopenhauer in the toilet while eating his lunch and who would call to tell my mother that I should not come to work on many August days because it was too hot near the ovens. As I remember it, the most stressful part of that job was finishing the leftover chocolate frosting in the cupcake pans. In short, everyone took care of me.

But now I had a new type of job with a different kind of boss and more difficult work companions. But even before dealing with those issues, I had another challenge: my physique. A generous person would call me wiry; someone less prone to euphemism might use the words gaunt or puny or gawky, or "a bag of skin and bones." But the largest problem was not physical stature; it was emotional stature. My previous life had not prepared me to meet and deal with my new fellow workers.

Let's call them the simian trio. Vince, the crew boss from Mississippi, had never met a curse word he didn't embrace—the filthier and more scabrous the better. Next in command was his son-in-law Zebulon, a rock-hard brute, sullen and, I suspect, sadistic, whose main virtue was the ability to outcurse Vince. Completing the triumvirate was Harry, Zebulon's kid brother, a guy about my age, who after numerous violent episodes in more than a few high schools had been finally and irrevocably expelled in his sophomore year and had subsequently been taken under his brother's raven wing to work on the crew. It was Harry, bless what passed for his smutty soul, who turned out to be both my nemesis and my teacher by leading me to discover the truest multiple possibilities designed into a shovel.

Harry fancied himself a ladies' man. When he had spare time, and there was a lot of it since the principal occupation of all three was filching that commodity—and whatever else they could grab without being nabbed—from their supposedly too-rich Jewish boss, Harry stood before the mirror of any bathroom in any one of the unfinished homes and admired himself. Stripped of his shirt, he'd arrange a few blond hairs on his chest, flex his muscles, and then work his way up to his head where he'd repeatedly run his comb through his pomaded blond, duck-assed hair with Zen-like concentration. He'd smile at himself. This was the most perplexing of all his maneuvers, since Harry had a mismatched set of the most rotten teeth I had ever seen. Harry, for some reason, was as proud as a black-beaked rooster. Somehow, to him, his rotten teeth were a sign of manhood. And his ideas of manhood scared me witless.

When Harry and his brother weren't viciously fist-fighting and cursing one another and, in turn, being vilified by Vince as "lazy fuckers" (as far as I could tell, a fair evaluation), they amused themselves by laughing at my oozing palms, my sunburn blisters, and most side-splitting of all, my sensitivity to their minority baiting. Whatever the race or ethnic group, they labeled it with a derogatory obscenity. In fact labels were their specialty. When they learned that I was a distant cousin to the boss and so a Jew—and only a summer laborer at that—they tripled their amusement.

Like some perverse Renaissance icon, Harry's outer shell was an accurate reflection of a vicious inner self. He bubbled vitriol. Lunchtime conversation was a nightmare. To this day I don't know whether it was designed purely for the purpose of torturing me or it was just run-of-the-mill shoptalk. But I have no trouble remembering it. He would first set the stage by reminding his brother of a particular work site, a house they had worked on, for example. Then he would report on an incident that supposedly had taken place there, involving a shapely female resident and himself in which the woman would have exposed herself and enticed him into having sex with her. He would follow the description of the sex with some derisive racial epithets and end the exposition with a taunt in my direction, soliciting my opinion on his future moves with the female partner. All this punctuated by the coarsest and most vulgar language I could ever have imagined—beyond my imagination, actually.

The dialogue was followed by leers, elbow jabs, and a brotherly congeniality otherwise not seen between these two. I'd like to say I said something, did something devastating, but the truth is I was so shocked, appalled, angry, scared, and most of all, previously innocent of such hateful ugliness, I just got up and walked away.

I registered these assaults as attacks on my mother, sister, and aunts. I went home at night physically nauseated, determined not to go back again. At home, I was inconsolable. Even when I ashamedly (and only partially) told my parents what was bothering me, I got a less than sympathetic answer. My mother's response was that I'd better grow a thicker skin if I planned to live in this world. "It's full of these people... get used to it."

At work, I determined that I wouldn't put up with listening to any more. I tried telling them to shut up. They laughed as if I couldn't take a good joke. I started eating lunch alone, or with some of the plumbers who kept separate from the monkey boys. But I could not avoid them or their mouths on Vince's clock.

At home, I remained miserable. The first week I was not only too physically exhausted to eat, but too emotionally exhausted to think about much other than that I had to go back and face the next day. I swore I'd not go back.

My mother, who rarely raised her voice, was adamant. "Oh yes, you can and will. You need the money. Are you crazy? Your father's working seven days a week. Who else is going to pay you $6.50 an hour?"

Bubbe told her she was too hard. "So what's so gefehrlach (terrible) if he stops? Les ihm. (let him.).

"No, Ma, no, that's all! No! He's too sensitive." My mother at 28 had suffered what they used to call a nervous breakdown. She sat in a darkened room for three years and the only visitors she allowed were her mother and two sisters. At the beginning of the fourth year she finally emerged from that room. Jan says she came out scarred and never really healed.

Thereafter, my mother saw herself as tough as nails. And she determined that whatever had hurt her so deeply would never get to her again. Her son would develop an elephant hide.

Dad sat silent. For one, he had to protect himself from too much emotion. He was still in the early stages of recovering from the heart attack. Too, I think he was embarrassed that I really did need the money, even if the college I was to attend was state run and inexpensive. I think tuition was one hundred and twenty-five dollars a year. But there was the expense of carfare, books, and clothes, too.

So, I stuck it out, more afraid of disappointing my parents and being a soft lout than losing the income. I actually dreamt of suicide, picturing myself leaping off the roof of our apartment building, splashing onto the concrete courtyard. My mother saw all my moping around histrionics as foolishness. Thin skin. "Sticks and stones can break your bones…"

That poem is nonsense. Names can hurt. Words can shred you.

After a month of digging ditches, though my hands were pretty tough, my insides were much the same. I'd consciously decided against my mother's commands to "thicken." The price was too much to pay. By then I'd decided that if I couldn't avoid them, it would be better to see the bastards, feel their ugliness, confront it, and tell them it was, in their lingo, shit.

One morning Harry and I were in a trench and as usual, he started in again:

"Did I ever tell you about the time I...?"

"Not interested."

Despite my refusal to encourage his storytelling, he then proceeded to launch into a revolting sexual fantasy, heavily invoking rape, violent sex, and anti-Semitic vitriol. He was preparing his old story with new, juicy details.

Something happened to me in that moment. Did I snap? No, I don't think so. In fact, I remember the moment as soothing. I turned to face him, holding my shovel in front of his grinning face and knowing in that moment that I was just one Neanderthal word, one second, away from a violence of which I never before supposed I was capable.

"Harry," I began, just above a whisper, spacing my words, "I want you to listen closely. This is important. If I ever hear you say another word about Jewish women, about niggers, or spics, or wops, about Jewish people, about any women, if you ever even speak to me again, I swear I will take this shovel and split open your skull. I will put a permanent part through your greasy hair right down into your filthy brain. I will kill you if I can."

He stopped grinning.

In that instant, I knew I was frightened about what might happen next, not about what he would do, but about what I might do, about what I longed to do. Then I saw the sarcastic grin and the color on his face drain away, replaced by fear. This wasn't a high school fistfight. He was looking into the face of a murderer. And he was a coward.

"You're crazy, you know that? You mean it, don't you?"

"I am as serious as my father's life. Believe it. And you won't know when it's coming, you malicious bastard."

He threw down his shovel and clambered out. And I just watched him go. I turned, started digging again, and even though it was wet and cool in the ditch, for the first time that summer the shovel felt pleasantly warm and right in my hands. I was comfortable in my skin for the first time in three ugly, long months.

From "declaration day" on, Vince assigned me the dirtiest, most isolated jobs he could find. His masterpiece was basement inspection. In 1956, the toiletry custom in the building trade was for the skilled workers, carpenters, plumbers, electricians to use the corners of basements in the unfinished homes where they were working as latrines. The refinement of a Port-A-Potty was not yet in vogue. My new high-level assignment was to travel from basement to basement, scrape up the leavings, take them out, and give them proper burials. I became the company's excremental undertaker.

Strange as it sounds to me remembering it even now, 45 years later, as revolting as the job was, just being away from the brothers and "Dad," who now avoided me as a maniac, rendered my worst scrape-ups acceptable. I'd traded one kind of crap for another. The latter was without legs, didn't curse, didn't slash with vicious labels, and so was vastly preferable as a companion.

I lasted through most of the summer's end in my subterranean isolation. If shit needed cleaning, I was your boy. What's the old joke? Your crap is my bread and butter? When asked what I was doing for the summer, I told people I was in environmental construction. As soon as I made tuition and all my year's expenses, I turned in my shovel and quit. When I left to start school, I vowed I would never work or associate with such two-legged pollutants again. The "family" didn't throw me a going-away party.

SAY UNCLE

THE FOLLOWING SUMMER, TEN POUNDS HEAVIER after a semester of weight lifting and a second semester of wrestling in elective classes at the University of Illinois, Chicago, I was searching for a job again. And again, the best pay by far was construction labor. My Uncle Morry found me a place, this time working for his friend who owned an industrial plumbing company. Uncle Morry sold them on me by bragging that I had valuable experience and that I was a college weightlifter! He sold me by suggesting that I closely examine my financials.

My first day on the job I reported to Angie, the crew boss in the construction shack. Angie was a wiry little guy, maybe 60 or so. What immediately got my attention was a smoking and smelly black cigar stuck into a gangster-like face that sported a wide scar that ran down his left cheek from eyebrow to chin. What could it all mean: Angie—Angelo-Italian-scar-tough-guy, cigar-heavy, construction—must be MAFIA! Talk about frying pans and fire! No Harry here, just a gangster under cover. But somehow Angie didn't talk Mafia. And he smiled, not the ugly leer I'd seen all last summer but something entirely different: sweet or perhaps resigned. Something in the situation or me seemed to amuse him.

Angie took me outside to meet Rodger, my new co-worker, another college student earning some money for the summer. We were to be paired up—two guys with not much experience—for the next few weeks. A flatbed truck drove up and parked outside the shack.

"Okay kiddos. Get busy. Unload it." Rodger and I looked at each other. He asked my question.

"The whole truck?"

"No, half of it. Shu', the whole truck. Managia!" (I learned later in the summer that "managia" is the Italian equivalent of a combined "damn" and "oy." Being confronted by a fool's question stimulated Angie's frequent use of the term.)

Rodger and I climbed the truck. Angie watched us, sucking on his cigar. We stood on top of the concrete sewer blocks piled five tiers high. And we did exactly nothing. In a voice too tired, or resigned for so early in the morning, he called us down.

"Boys, come down here," he said, not as an angry command, but more like the request of a tired parent. "You boys never done this before, eh? Mr. Dentist," this was Rodger, who was studying pre-dentistry, "you go up. And then you hand down the blocks one by one to the Professore." Me, obviously. "But first, put this on." He walked him over to an outdoor locker and took out a hard hat. "And don't let me catch you on the job without it." He tossed me another. "Mr. Muscles, Mr. Weightlifter, you too. One of you kids gets hurt, crack you skull, break a toe, my Missus finds out about it, she kill me and you go to jail for murder, eh? My grandchildren no see their papa eh? So, be careful. Angie's first rule: Take you time."

"Professore, you take the blocks and stack them neat, over there. Remember. Nice and neat."

Tidy appeared to be the rule for everybody there. That morning and every following morning, the men, all of whom seemed to be about my grandfather's age, came to work in sparkling white T-shirts or undershirts, head kerchiefs, and freshly laundered jeans.

"First lessons over. Now you start, eh?"

Rodger climbed up slowly and carefully this time and began to struggle with his first ever block of concrete. It was heavier than it looked. And it had sharp corners, unlike the icy beer mugs he was more used to hefting.

"Tony, find some leather gloves, eh?" Tony brought two pairs, labels and staples still in place. He tossed us each a pair. "I want the gloves back tonight, after work. Tomorrow you come with your own. Leather, you capisce?"

We capisced.

"And steel-toe boots, not sneakers! Go to Sears. You no work here without steel toes. This is not the gym. And take you time. Careful. The bosses no pay extra for heat stroke, eh? Now you start. And make sure you drink plenty water."

One of the men was placing a large water cooler in the shade of the truck.

It took us until lunchtime to unload less than half the truck bed. In our first half hour, I learned another lesson: college weightlifting classes do not prepare you for real nonstop weightlifting in full sun.

At first, we couldn't even manage to hand off the blocks without dropping them. We discovered that when concrete blocks drop a few feet they are likely to explode. The accumulating pile was humiliating. Then, bright college students that we were, we figured out a rhythm that worked, as well as a way of holding on as we passed them. We became almost smooth. Unfortunately, as our technique improved, the blocks got progressively heavier. By noon both of us were soaked in sweat and covered in concrete block dust.

We found shade near the blessed water cooler. Collapsed, with legs thrust straight in front of us, we guzzled water and eventually opened our lunch bags: peanut butter and jelly for us both and Oreo cookies, yes both of us, and a banana each. Had our mothers talked, deciding on All-American lunches for All-American boys? Rodger was the first to wheeze sounds something like speech.

"I-don't-think-I can-last."

As the senior, experienced partner, I found myself reassuring him. "We'll last."

After all, I'd coped with Harry and the subterraneans.

"But, I don't think I can eat."

"Ditto."

Comatose would be a fair way to describe the way we both felt and clearly the way we must have looked.

I guess Antony was watching us from a group of the men who were also preparing to have lunch. He was speaking to several of the men and gesturing in our direction. He whistled over to us. Then he walked to our cabana and squatted down. Yes, this rotund ball of an old man, 70 going on 40, actually squatted down after an entire morning of laying brick. I could not have so gingerly bent my knees even if the penalty for not doing so was a solid week of truck unloading or double dating with Harry.

At ease, squatting there, balanced on his haunches, he looked pityingly at us and then at our untouched sandwiches. "You fine. Don't worry. When you go back to work, you soak a handkerchief in water and wrap around you head, like this." He demonstrated on himself. "You keep changing all day." Then he took two freshly ironed kerchiefs out of his pocket, soaked them, and gave one to each of us.

"Boys, why you sit so lonely here? You no like us? You come over; sit with us. You rest. Take a little more cold water." Before we could answer, he gathered both our lunches. He stood straight up, reached down for my hand, paused until I uncramped my legs a little and yanked me to my feet. Then he did the same for Rodger, a movement more like a dead lift than a pull. Seven men, looking to be all past 70, all stoutly powerful, sat together on wooden boxes and upended plastic buckets, under a tree. As we approached they were speaking Italian but switched to English as soon as we stumbled over.

If I said they were preparing to eat, I would be far off the mark. It was more like strategizing to dine. Spread before them on a tablecloth was lunch: assorted smoked meats, cheeses, tomatoes, cucumbers, peppers, green and red onions, little bowls of olives, loaves of Italian breads, grapes, oranges, apples, several bottles of red wine and jugs of water and coffee.

They even had salt and pepper shakers. They opened a space in the circle so we could sit. Antony raised our lunch sandwiches above his head like some odd trophy he'd just won. That got a laugh and some raised eyebrows. One of the men split a loaf of bread, stuffed each half with meats and vegetables and gently put them down on some napkins. He pointed to a tomato juice can filled with water, a piece of soap, and a towel.

"You eat this today. No can work like a man if you no eat like a man. But first have a wash. This is dirty work. Tomorrow you bring a real lunch. No peanut butter. Food! No pop. Water!"

I was sure I couldn't manage a bite. But with this little giant's suggestion you weren't about to protest.

He handed each of us one of his creations. Plastic cups of lemonade appeared from somewhere. One bite and both of us were launched into what would be a daily ritual. If we showed up with a too-meager lunch we would get an inspection and a scolding, then some shared lunch and a warning.

"Tomorrow." Before the present discovery about teamwork in the workplace, these gentle little giants made us part of their team.

And so my first morning on this job ended in a feast, supplied by a group of surrogate self-appointed uncles who spoke broken English but who insisted on a food regimen that would get two semi-shocked kids through the rest of their first day.

As the summer drew on, we came to realize that we were under the tutelage of a soft-hearted but demanding supervisor. By the way, I learned later into the summer that Angie's scar was not the result of a Sicilian knife wound or a Chicago mob fight but of walking into the edge of a truck bed when he was a young laborer in Italy. As he grew older, the scar kept growing too until it stretched the length of his face. The lesson was not lost on him. He looked after every workman, 17 or 70, as if it was his solemn responsibility to keep each one safe. In our case, he watched over us as nephews, as kids not yet old enough to know much of anything, but game enough or prodded enough or hungry enough to try and do the hard work he required of us.

"Don't stand so close to the pit; somebody down there, you loose a rock, that some body gonna get hurt, capisce?" We capisced.

"Sharpen you shovel. Sand or clay, no matter. Make you job easier, not harder. Capisce?"

"Take small bites, more times. You move more dirt; not so tired."

"Watcha watcha!"

On a particularly hot day, I remember him asking Rodger, "Hey, Rodge, you like do this for the rest of you life, like Angie? No? It's too hard, eh? When you go back to you school, no fool around no more, eh?"

Rodger had already come to that conclusion all by himself.

After a few weeks on the job, Rodger and I were taught to mix "mud," their word for the masonry cement used to build manholes and seal together industrial-size concrete sewer pipe. We'd mix it in a wheelbarrow by a hydrant, add water, and then push it over to varying locations where the building was in process. At first, I'd load the barrow over the top, determined to show I was strong enough to do the job. As often as not, I'd hit a bump, tip over the barrow, and spill the entire load.

Angie was admirably calm. Not once did he yell or tell me I had "shit for brains," a common epithet used by my former boss, Vince, paternoster of the unholy trio. But Angie made his point.

"Professore, no prove you muscles. Take half, make more trips. Get there! Pusha! Pusha! Professore."

I listened. I took less. I pushed and I got there more often. And when I got there, more times than I care to remember, Antony or Paulo or Giuseppe would take my concoction on a trowel, push a finger through it, wrinkle a nose, and reject the batch.

"Not so good, Professore. Too much water," or "Not enough sand. You make again, eh? Better."

Then they'd wait as their part of the job stopped until I got back. Occasionally, one would show frustration, slopping the stuff back into the barrow, accompanied by a nasty sounding word in Italian. For the most part, though, I never heard a curse word that summer—at least not any that I could understand. Each man took his cue from Angie. Each made it clear that we still needed to learn.

Ah, but when we started to get the mix consistently right, a little different in texture for the requirement of each workman, we heard praise usually addressed not to one of us, but to Antony or Angie, or one of the other most senior "boys."

"He's got it!" Giuseppe would tap his temple with his index finger. "Hey! I'm a good teacher, eh?"

Those words were as sweet to me as a semester of A's.

Toward the end of summer, I was sent with half the crew to a job on the South Side of Chicago where our company was the sewer subcontractor to the city, building a highway plaza on the new Dan Ryan Expressway. As a matter of course, the city sent a construction engineer to review each subcontractor's work and make adjustments as he deemed necessary. The bigger the job, the sharper the emissary. And this one was huge. Our visiting inspector this afternoon was a youngish guy, probably in his late twenties and five or six years out of engineering school, just long enough to be confident in his work and just foolish enough to be this side of cocksure.

He walked around, seersucker crisp shirt, pen saver, creased chino pants, Cub's hat, clipboard in hand, making notes, notes, notes. He'd filled a pad. He spent an entire morning with us. In a nod to democracy, he called a brief meeting at the field shack with Angie and the rest of us, with even lowly Rodger and me attending. Actually, I'm not sure it was he who invited everyone. In retrospect, I have a sneaking suspicion it was Angie.

The shack was crowded and it was hot even though the air conditioner was going full blast. He explained the reason he was on site so long. One of the city's comptrollers felt that too much material, cement, oakum, and other supplies were being delivered to this site. After looking carefully at our work, he now agreed. Because I was taller than everyone else, I could glance over his shoulder at his clipboard where he'd recorded tight little mathematical calculations and diagrams on the dated page. There were quick sketches of each sub site. He said he was sure we could use less oakum in the joints, less lead-fill pours for the cast-iron piping. We certainly could use less cement to secure the concrete pipes. He could definitely figure different "trajectories" (he glossed for us peasants: "angles for the pipes") and thereby save plenty of pipe, too.

He was authoritative. Under his assertiveness there was a threat. Do exactly what I say or there will be consequences with the big bosses. I remember thinking, "How much adjustment does he want? We'll make it."

It did not cross my mind that someone in a little office somewhere at City Hall was thinking "theft," even though I'd seen it big time the previous summer with the simians. But this summer my friends were meticulously honest. Maybe, I thought, Rodger and I are the culprits; all those spilled or returned barrows full of poorly mixed mud. All those broken blocks. All those dropped and shattered clay pipes. Now because of our blunders, we might be getting our people in trouble and we might be seeing some very angry Italian uncles this week.

I was right—and wrong. There were some very angry Italians, but they were not angry at us. What had just happened here was nothing less than an enormous, professional, and therefore personal attack on their integrity. Even though they were all members of the Union, it was their own sense of the work, not the Union's power, that motivated them.

Antony, self-designated as Rodger's and my on-the-job mentor, just under the watchful Angie, and also the elected union steward, spoke.

"Sonny," he said, "I've been work almost sixty years, from little boy to old man. My work, she still stands up on the Outer Drive, downtown, and in Old Orchard. I no cheat on materials. Someone gets sick, someone gets hurt in ten years, it's my responsible. No yours. We all use what we need. No more, no less. We make good, all the time. I'm no gonna listen to you. You no like, okay, you business. I no like—my business."

He almost sang it; an artisan's aria.

I was astounded. I was filled with admiration. I looked at Angie, who'd not said one word. He stood at the drafting table, straight faced, but the crow's feet at the corner of his eyes told a different story. Either he was furious or working hard not to smile. I think it was the latter. This was potentially big trouble, but I had the feeling he might be relishing it, like one of those salty olives he brought each day at lunch. And I thought, he's been here before.

"Angelo, my friend, maybe you tell this young fella, go someplace else, insult some other people. We wait outside, have water. I'm feel my temperature raising."

In line, following Antony, one by one, we all filed out. A couple minutes later, the engineer, as formerly innocent as I, exited the shack and looking straight ahead, climbed into his official city car and drove off—perhaps a little too quickly.

It looked as if all kinds of people were learning lessons this summer.

Nobody said another word about the incident. Angie told us to all go back to work. We did. That day Antony instructed me to take a little more time to be sure that my shovel was sharp and extra clean when I began mixing. He wanted not a speck of dirt. For the rest of that week no one hesitated to send mud back if it was even a smidgen off the mark. I think some sent it back even if it was perfect. I didn't care. I mixed and remixed. We never saw the young engineer again. Come to think of it, we never saw another inspector all summer long. When Rodge and I left that summer we got warm goodbyes, hopes that we would be back the following summer, and compliments on how strong we'd become. Angie gave each of us a cigar.

A PURTY GOOD
SHOVEL MAN

So I REPEAT, LORNE HAD IT all wrong when he doubted my competence with a shovel. But then how could he know? He made the all-too-easy assumption that because I knew nothing about living on the land, not handling a shovel came as part of my package. I'd learned to use that tool from the best—after working with the worst.

Lorne returned on Mark's tractor and began at a far south sector of the yard. Since he'd built the house by himself from foundation up, including the addition, he knew where the edge of the drain field was located and about how far down we'd have to go.

In a few minutes he'd skinned away our lovely lawn, then slowly and carefully dug down layer by layer as he excavated the clay sludge. The deeper he dug, the stronger the stench became. His plan was to keep layering until he located the drain hoses and the concrete conduits that carried the waste into the holding tanks. At that point, he'd stop and I'd start to dig by hand until we'd exposed the rest of the hoses and feeders, assessing the damage and seeing how badly they were ruptured.

If we only had to cement at a joint or two, if the hoses could be repaired, if the old concrete holding tanks were not a disaster, we'd do some fancy cement work and cover it all up. Right now the idea was to eliminate as many ifs as possible.

"You now, Stew: go at 'er."

I climbed down into the pit he'd excavated and prepared to use skills and muscles I'd neglected for 45 years. But neglecting is not forgetting. Ditchdigging is like biking. Most of my college German I'd forgotten, but cutting and angling efficiently with a square-faced shovel I remembered.

Here I was, "Professore" Emeritus and a novitiate farmer—in the heat of the day, back in a ditch, digging away through sewage, strangely enjoying myself and proud of my performance.

"You know boy, you ain't half bad. I'll just sit up here and watch a good man work."

My inner Angie advised, "Hey, kiddo, take it easy. The boss no pay you for heat stroke. Take it easy. No make it worse and have to do double work. We all know you have muscles."

I slowed my pace, being careful not to strike the hose, taking the clay bit by bit, eventually exposing a piece of a pipe surface, then angling down along what I figured was an imaginary line, exposing more of the outer hose's surface and then its diameter.

"Hey Tony, look at the Professore. He learned good, eh?"

The line was torn in four places. The edge of the first connecting pipe had a football size hole in it. We could replace the line by digging out the whole corner. We could patch the holes with wire and cement. Probably it would last another year, even two, if the rest of the system wasn't much worse.

Lorne started the tractor and went to work again. Now it was easier to find the next corner. I dug. By now I was overshoes in crappy clay, my jeans soaked, my shirt sopping wet. The second hose was worse. The connecting pipe was rubble. I looked up.

"Well, what do you think?"

"First off, you need a hosing terrible bad."

"About the system, wise guy."

"Well, it's your land, your system, your decisions, I reckon. Expert advice is free. Everybody hereabouts knows how t' tell you what t' do with your land."

I climbed out. He climbed down. We met under the shade of the cherry tree.

"Here, take this. He handed me his handkerchief, yes, the polka-dot kind. Pretty much the kind Angie had given us to cool down so many years ago. "Kindly give that back when you're done with it. Washed."

Three days with this septic tank and it seemed a week. What the hell. I wiped.

"Lorne, I hate to patch and cover if it's all gonna be this bad. In a year, I know we'll be doing it again."

"Can't say I disagree, but you never can tell, could last longer."

"But the truth is we've poured a bunch of money into the property already, money we haven't budgeted. Replacing is going to be a financial bear."

"Well, let's look at 'er some more. We come this far."

So we did. He scraped. I dug. Our hole got deeper, muddier, smellier. I was in knee deep. My inner Angie offered advice. "Hey, kiddo! What you thinking? No cheat, eh? Later, this thing leaks, you getta sick, mamma getta sick. What you save? Smart now. You no sorry later."

I stopped, tossed my shovel out of the pit and climbed up. Angie and I had made a decision.

Lorne was chewing. I started to speak, but Lorne was way ahead of me. "Stew I been thinkin' while you been diggin'... I gotta admit, I never would of believed it... I got time this fall. In a little while, Mark and us, we'll have the hay in for the winter. You and Jan are planning to go back to Florida next week to see your kids. Ain't that so?"

It was.

"Why not leave early? Come back a little later. The next couple days use the bathroom at Steve's or down at our place. We get the hay in, an' I'll work up here and dig out the whole mess. Mark and me'll buy a whole new septic field and set her in. Send you pictures all along the way. When you come up for the fall colors, it'll be done. I'll keep all the bills. What it costs me, it'll cost you."

I was dumbstruck. I shouldn't have been. This was the kind of generous man I'd come to know and respect.

"You can't get a better deal 'n that!"

At that moment, if I thought I could bite off a chaw and spit it—without getting deathly ill—or light up a Parodi cigar, I would have. There I stood, shit smeared, a sweaty muddy golem (brainless lump), relieved and as happy as a guy who'd just seen the Light. And in a way I had.

"Deal. And thanks. We'll try and repay your generosity."

He sat there about as fresh and clean as when he'd arrived.

"No need. Ain't doin' it for that—selfish really. Bitsy an' me wanna keep you for neighbors… never do know when I'll need the best shovel man in the county. And that's almost the truth. But Stew," he paused, a grave look crossing his face, "I got a question I been wantin' to ask you all summer, and this appears to be just the right time to ask."

At that moment, I don't think he could have asked any question I wouldn't have answered with a candor almost worthy of Noah. And ask he did, leaning over and resting his elbows on the tractor's steering wheel.

"How do you like the country life so far?"

Perfect! The country coup de grace, by the master of the Appalachian kibbitz.

"Got ya, didn't I?"

"You did, but the answer, my friend, is fine. Just fine."

As he climbed down, a grin on his face, still amused at us both, it struck me that we were the perfect modern mirror of Shakespeare's country-wise farmer and city-slicker newcomer, his Corin to my Touchstone. I tried to hug him.

"Have you gone and got yourself plumb unwrapped? I ain't touchin' you until you've showered—with bleach—and even then I ain't real sure."

We walked back to the house to tell Jan to start packing.

SUMMER'S END

JAN AND I LEFT FOR FLORIDA. It took two weeks for Lorne, Mark, Noah, Melanie, and even Bitsy to dig out the decrepit old system and replace it. The girls helped. We had pictures of the daily progress with everybody standing amidst giant piles of excavated clay and shattered pipes, pointing accusatory fingers at one another and at the mess they've created. At job's end, Mark regraded and reseeded the back lawn. By next year, he told us, it would look better than before.

You're wondering about the garden? Oh my, our garden. We kept a log that we continue to update. On September 15:

Tomatoes: 300+ and still coming on;

Yellow squash, straight and crook-necked: 35;

Zucchini: we stopped counting at 93 (nobody warned us to pick them before they were the size of watermelons);

Watermelon: a big fat zero;

Cantaloupe: ditto, zero;

Corn: a resplendent stand of 50, actually more like 35, since many cob tips were inhabited by voracious little green worms. Still they, the corn not the grubs, were delicious; the best we've ever eaten.

Eggplants: a disappointment sporting lots of leaves and few vegetables.

Onions: more than we could use, and tons of string beans. I think the Hunger Coalition got tired of seeing us.

A few sad scraggly peas.

After only a couple of pickings, every flat surface of the kitchen and dining room was covered with piles of our daily harvest. We'd look at each other in wonder and ask, "Well now that we've got it, what do we do with it all?" Simple answer: some for us, some for Steve and Gretchen, and lots for the Hunger Coalition. The Blue Book, the country bible of preserving, is our next investment. But meanwhile, Bitsy was going to be answering a lot of phone calls.

Although I planted three rows of potatoes in our field far below the house, I slipped up in not visiting them. By the time I remembered to look, the grass and weeds had taken over, and no matter how hard I searched I could not find the plants. Somewhere hiding beneath the surface were Idahos the size of canoes. I promised myself I'd do better the next year.

Our lone plum tree that stood exactly in the middle of the apple trees where Murray the Mower and I had our falling out was, quite simply, miraculous. It produced hundreds and hundreds of the most stunning, the most comely, the most pulchritudinous, shapeliest and most delicious red plums anyone around here has ever seen.

This time I'm not exaggerating. Lorne will testify.

We waited then for October when the apples and pears would come in. Then we'd all really have a time… even Cousin Orville.

Stu and Jan.

EPILOGUE

JAN AND I MOVED TO FLORIDA in 1968. People of our background—urban, Jewish, and spoiled (by being second generation Americans with unlimited prospects as a result of relatively inexpensive, good public educations)—often moved to verdant Florida in the late 1960s as dreamers.

But I cannot imagine that many were in quite our dreamer category.

I recall the day we made the decision to head south without having even the most remote prospects of being able to do so. Jan and I were sitting on our blue-striped, slightly worn, passion-stained Scan couch (wafer thin pillows and inflexible slats), which had been given to us a year before by my father, who by then represented that inexpensive, popular furniture line. We were staring out the window at the third gigantic snowstorm of November. December through April guaranteed more of the same. We longed for the relative warmth of Chicago, family dinners, Moms and Dads.

I was in the second winter of a master's degree at Miami University in Oxford, Ohio, in the Miami Valley, and it looked as if I could be done by summer and we could be on our way to a graduate fellowship at the even more arctic University of Wisconsin in Madison.

Our new baby slept in a makeshift, oddly decorated nursery. This room was the one over which I and my visiting mother-in-law, nervously awaiting the arrival of her first grandchild, had recently battled concerning wall-painting rights.

Jan and I knew the following: we had precious little money and we had a beautiful child neither of us knew how to parent except by intuition and Jan's early practice with her expensive doll collection. We were alternately sure that we were the best match in the universe and a pair of exuberant children in over our heads.

We also intermittently knew that we would not take parental assistance, a subject we disagreed about, with me mostly on the side of manly independence and Jan consistently on the side of eating. And we faced three or four years more of Wisconsin ice and snow and self-imposed student poverty until I had what we considered the Holy Grail, the PhD. Then we would speed off to a real job and genteel life among the intelligentsia. Remember, I told you we were dreamers and, as you've guessed by now, more than a little inexperienced about the world and academic life.

Most important, though, beneath the multi-layered insecurities and fears—mostly mine—we knew we were meant for one another.

So, we sat there, sides touching, holding hands, watching the snow swirl, thinking our separate thoughts, when astonishingly—and to this day forty-three years later, I readily admit to not understanding at all how this happened—we experienced our first real marital mind link. Four decades later, we do "Spock mind melds" at least once a week, not only finishing one another's sentences but anticipating each other's thoughts.

But then, in our Ohio concrete-block, ice-coated gulag, the experience was nothing less than amazing, exhilarating, and mystic. For forty-five minutes we sat having the exact same fantasy: we were sitting on a sunny, white sand beach surrounded by our three sons, two yet unborn, who were building sand castles. We both knew it was early January in the middle of our first year living in the tropics, and we were astounded by the beauty of a turquoise ocean and our sense of relaxed warmth and well-being. We knew that our home was located not far from this place.

Jan and I popped half out of the vision, looked at one another as if through some drugged state, both absolutely convinced that we were still sitting on a palm-fringed beach. The living room was fifty degrees, but we both felt—toasty warm. Together, without saying a word, we breathed in the sea. A few moments later the mist cleared and we both jumped up to check the space heater in our real baby boy's bespattered real room. It was warm. He was fine. We spoke, unnerved, realizing we had just had the same fantasy. And despite our present situation and the prospect of at least three winters more, we understood that our family's life would take the shape of our dream. I swear we hadn't a doubt. I swear we hadn't been smoking anything funny.

Five years, two graduate schools, many Ohio, Wisconsin, and Chicago blizzards, a few more tundra apartments, near bankruptcy, and a variety of jobs later we were equipped with one additional little beach-ready boy, a six-month's-along pregnancy (the third little boy), and a sparkling new PhD, and at last we were heading for a teaching job in the tropics. By what felt like sheer luck or destiny, we were about to realize our Ohio dream.

In 1968, six months before completing the PhD at Northwestern University, we began our rounds of job interviews with prestigious universities and surprisingly plentiful and quick job offers—Wisconsin at Milwaukee, Illinois, Texas A&M, Colorado, even Duke, for goodness sake! Commercial flights. Private university planes. Wining and dining. We were entering the Golden Age of academe, though we didn't know it at the time. We felt like the newly crowned. My friend Lorne would say we were in that "high cotton."

But for us none of it was right. As much as we tried to convince ourselves that professionally we deserved the best, we couldn't dismiss or forget our first mind link. We found something wrong with each situation: too far removed from our parents; too close to our parents; too military an atmosphere; too loose; too large. Name the location and we sought out its flaw. Even Duke with its tweedy jackets, carefully screened students, tea parties, exotic accents, and growing reputation in the academic aristocracy business was too far... North.

Then one day my mother-in-law, yes, my mother-in-law, now recovered from our most recent altercation and her gold decorating spree, saw an ad in the *Chicago Sun Times* announcing a new state school being built in Orlando, Florida.

"Orlando? Where in the hell is that?" my relatives asked. No one knew. We looked it up in my mother's World Atlas.

"How far from Miami? Here it is, in the middle of the state. Somewhere? Nowhere," my mother announced, adding, "And look who found the ad! Your mother in law! Is this some form of planned self destructive revenge? My making you work at that construction job? Something I did to you in childhood?"

Bubbe was a little less sedate in her response. "Bist du meshugah?" Rough translation: "Have you gone stark raving mad?"

Jan and I agreed. All our relatives were right. Turn down sure career op-
portunities to try and go—nowhere? Surely all those years of frigid apartments with roach-plastered floors that moved under our feet and pressure-
cooker graduate schools had damaged our brains. We needed to get a grip.

Get some "saichel!" Accurate translation: the "common sense God gave
you."

Nope.

The new Florida school was ravenous to hire young people from prestigious universities so it could build instant credibility. Finding such exotic
crazies willing to trek into the American hinterlands was not so easy. But
we were not only willing; we were eager.

So all we had to do was present my credentials, explain that we'd already
been offered positions by the above-listed universities, nay, even more
places, and the aged, twice-retired and recycled, wrinkled, middle-parted,
slate-grey–haired, basso-profundo–voiced interviewer, with the quizzical
sort of stunned look in his sun bleary eyes jammed a contract into our
hands.

"Sign right here," he crooned.

Voilà! We were charter faculty!

We learned what the first few years in the new-minted space-age institution might be like when we also learned that the new Vice President of
Academic Affairs, an engineer from Oklahoma, was interested in getting a
few faculty of the "Jewish persuasion, and Aitalian decension," and a few
other "sensions and suasions" as well.

When he wasn't at the University scheming, our academic leader kept
horses which he personally castrated and tarred, a baloney sandwich sitting
on the fence rail beside him as he worked, while humming a ditty from his
beloved Wild West. We found out later that he was reputed to work his
same evil magic on faculty who opposed him.

So we went from the snows of Kilimanjaro to the sun, sands, and
swamps of La La Land, touching down at a two-runway converted air
force base and winding up at a two-building, 1,500-student fledgling university, twenty miles outside the city, staffed by an optimistic, adventure-
some, young—or cynical, very alcoholic, retread—faculty and a tough

bunch of administrators surrounded by oranges, jasmine, palmetto fronds, goliath frogs, pigmy rattlesnakes, and gorgeous clean air.

And to be fair, our almost pastoral idyll lasted for a couple of years—until the Disney conquistadores arrived in 1971, planted their moused banners—and we retreated for summer respite to the hills.

Fast forward to 2004.

With a University enrollment of 45,000, a giant football stadium in the works, an on-campus shopping mall, a student services hospital, and the prospects of a medical school, the tiny sand-in-your-shoes school was a hectic small city. When we arrived in '68 there was no direct paved road from Orlando to the University. It took us a full twelve minutes to drive out, with stops to allow for gopher turtle crossings. Now the drive was forty-five minutes via a six-lane state highway.

So when our friend Steve called us, we were ready. But we had no idea what we were getting ourselves into and definitely no idea that we were on the verge of a life-altering adventure. Who expects to find love late in life? Who expects to forge deep, soul-changing friendships in their seventh decade? We certainly didn't. As you can tell, we've always had a spirit of adventure. Sometimes that worked out well; sometimes not so well. But what we found in a rural community far from our roots taught us that when you're open to experience life in all its countless offerings, you can reap harvests more nourishing than our precious garden of vegetables.

ACKNOWLEDGEMENTS

Many people have been instrumental in my completing Ol' Man on the Mountain. The most important, is Jan—my wife, friend, and co-adventurer of fifty one years. Wow!

Thanks as well to our friends who put up with me, actually asked me to read from the manuscript over and again, and laughed with me along the way.

To Steve, Gretchen, Eleanor, Gerson, Jim, Bev, Gloria, Bernard, and Sabina, Charlie and my sister Lorry, I know what Shakespeare meant when he told us: "We are rich in our friends."

Special accolades go to Karen Lane, my editor, whose critical eye and sensitive intellect kept making the book better and to Anna Truby, photographer and designer whose multiple talents and humility are equally daunting.

And I am indebted to our three sons, Steve, Mike, and Joe whose integrity and kindness mime their Mom's and set the standards for our five fascinating grandchildren, Fisher, Cooper, Kylie, Matan, and Yonit. You guys were really smart when you picked Debbie, Roxana, and Beth as your life partners.

Stu writing his memoir.

GLOSSARY OF YIDDISH TERMS

balegolah: wagon driver; unrefined person

bissel: little

boychik: kiddo

brocha: blessing

bubbe: grandma

challah: egg bread

chutzpah: audacity

gefehrlach : terrible

genug: enough

golem: brainless lump, automaton

gor in ganzen: totally

haftarot biblical selection from the Torah

kibbitzing: offering unsolicited advice

kinahora: jinx; attracting the "Evil Eye"; calling down a curse

lach: laugh

L'chaim!: To Life!

maven: expert; aficionado

mazel tov: good luck; congratulations

mensch: decent, good person

meshuggene: crazy

mezuzah: religious symbol affixed to doorpost of Jewish homes

mitzva: good deed; literally, commandment

nu: so; well

oy vey: woe!

saichel: common sense; "smarts"

shlep: drag

schtick: process; piece

shvartzes: blacks

Shabbat: Sabbath

shma'te: rag

shma'te-dicha: rag-like

shmutz: filth

shtetl: village

shtick: piece of business; act; trait

shul: school; synagogue

tsuris: troubles

zhlob: oaf

ABOUT THE AUTHOR

STUART OMANS' path from total failure as a Chicago high school student (flunking three classes in one semester, something of a record for a middle class, Jewish kid), to Northwestern University PhD., before founding the acclaimed Orlando Shakespeare Theater, must be some kind of testimony to life's infinite possibility. As Professor Emeritus and former Chair of English at the University of Central Florida, he's written extensively on theater, Shakespeare, education, and the arts.

He's won awards and fellowships from The National Endowment for the Humanities, the Folger Shakespeare Library, and the Danforth Foundation, among others.

Along the way his education has been enriched by working as a ditch digger, professional baker (not at the same time), and a salesman of outrageous men's fashions (Zoot suits and pink alligator shoes) at Chicago's famous Smoky Joe's.

He and his artist –wife of fifty-one years are parents of three wonderful sons who have helped produce five fascinating grandchildren.

Stu and Jan live in Winter Park, Florida and the rural mountains of North Carolina.

Ol' Man on a Mountain is his first full length extended memoir.

26461851R00183

Made in the USA
Charleston, SC
08 February 2014